"To be a caregiver is no less than a blessing from God. By His Grace, you have been selected." –Ben Blyton

going home

a caregiver's guide

Ben Blyton

authorHOUSE®

AuthorHouse™
1663 Liberty Drive
Bloomington, IN 47403
www.authorhouse.com
Phone: 1-800-839-8640

First published by AuthorHouse   9/21/2010
ISBN: 978-1-4520-2765-4 (e)
ISBN: 978-1-4520-2764-7 (sc)

Library of Congress Control Number: 2010912885

Printed in the United States of America

This book is printed on acid-free paper.

In this book you will find...

- **Riveting tales of actual caregivers' experiences**

- **What to do first**

- **The Ten Commandments of Caregiving**

- **124 tips for the newbie**

- **A caregiver's most common mistake**

'My patient is dying now'

- **Types of behavior you might encounter**

- **How to handle patients**

- **The latest research from the Sanders Brown Center on Aging**

- **The mother lode of resources**

CONTENTS

SUGGESTIONS AND COMMENTS FROM...

A MEDICAL DOC: "I wish that people would realize the commitment that goes with being a caregiver... some think their patient can just be parked at home while they are off at work."

A MINISTER: "I wish the caregiver knew more about how important taking care of themselves is... the caregiver has to be physically & mentally stronger than the patient or the roles reverse, and that happens occasionally, at which point the caregiver dies first from the strain."

MEDICAL DISCLAIMER:

All references to anything medical represent solely the experiences of the author and pertain to same and should never replace common sense or your doctor's advice or "if somethin' goes wrong, ya didn't 'ear it 'ere mate!."

PRIVACY DISCLAIMER:

All names may or may not have been changed to protect the innocent and no inference or otherwise implication to real or surreal names exists.

DISCLAIMER DISCLAIMER:

Any disclaimer, regardless of how lame, cannot represent less than the actual disclaimant, Q.E.D.

READING INSTRUCTIONS:

Keep book with you at all times. I teach by example. I share 'what works' wisdom and tips that no responsible doc would ever be allowed to share (just joking). As I provide my experiences, I give you your take-away lessons. **If you read, remember, and act upon what I teach you in this book then you will have 'smooth sailing' (well, sort of). What may seem impossible will become possible for you.** For those long bedside watches, I give you the strength of endless quotations from the world's best minds (read them to your patient... or the wall). For those sad days, I give you some of the funniest humor I could find. For those days of grief, I give you assurances from God that you can persevere, and by your stripes, He will know your name.

ACKNOWLEDGEMENTS:

This book is dedicated to all caregivers, that their knowledge goes not unheeded. And to all the families whose suffering and sacrifice were the unforeseen consequences of life itself.

DEDICATIONS:

This work is dedicated to my late sister, Julia, who passed of cancer, and my parents, the eminent Professor and legend in his own time (his words), Dr. & Dr. Gifford Blyton (diagnosed end stage congestive heart failure patient but still doing fine three years later at 102) and the real queen of the ball, his late wife Marion who helped raised me. Marion is truly the gentle lamb, humble, never boastful, unassuming, and Christian (she just doesn't remember who Christ is anymore). She passed at 96. Dad is 102 and will probably outlast the Duracell bunny (and me).

I acknowledge a very talented graphic artist, Mike Kotora, Katie Kotora for proofing, Asa Harrison (graphic designer) for cover layout and Nila Hatfield our respite caregiver and angel. In addition, I acknowledge another angel, Rebecca Miller, caregiver to her late father, whom has been a constant source of encouragement, wisdom and support. Last but not least, the dedication goes to the real underpinning of our caregiving strength, my partner caregiver and loving Ukrainian wife, Lyudmyla.

EXPLANATION OF BOOK COVER SYMBOLISM

The red rose symbolizes the caregiver and his/her love for their patient and reverence for life itself. Rooted in earth, it portrays beauty and purity of the temporal world.

The white dove symbolizes the patient as the departing soul and eternal peace in the afterlife. It points the way to the beauty and purity belonging to the firmament.

SYMBOLISM OF 'THE ROSE' (refer to lyrics for 'The Rose')

To me the symbolism of the red rose represents the struggle with the grieving process wherein caregivers are often afraid to confront their own feelings lest their soul is left to 'bleed.' We keep trying to pretend everything is okay but we fall short of really understanding ... like the 'heart that never learns to dance.' And yet while love is manifested beneath our denials and fears ('the bitter snows'), it is ultimately the free will of our spirit that determines if it will be nurtured, 'like the seed that with... love becomes the rose in the spring.' Our Will changes the experience into something beautiful and sustained forever. It's a choice we make.

MESSAGE FOR THE NEW CAREGIVER

For those who may come through these hallowed halls I welcome you. I feel like I am giving a commencement address on the front lawn of Nassau Hall to the class of Princeton valedictorians or anywhere really.

"Through your rectitude you are bestowed the honors. I am the messenger that brings you good news."

"You have chosen to provide the ultimate service to humanity. You have chosen a commitment of service."

"You will experience the good times, bad times, sad times, happy times, and all the 'times' in between. You will feel the searing pain of rejection, the coldness of separation, and at times the emptiness of your soul. You will feel the warmth of the Father's unfaltering love in the dimmest of your hours."

"Not everyone is given this chance for service that has been placed before you."

"You will suffer every kind of insult imaginable. Your life, your world, your very marriage may be challenged. You remain steadfast to the service that awaits you. **Through your service, you must tame the beasts within yourself. For not is there an ill spoken word that emanates from the caregiver's soul, crying for salvation and healing"** (now that was not me...those words just flowed onto the keyboard startling me for a moment. That is what I mean by divine inspiration and there's more).

"Those who complete their task are the valedictorians. By your stripes ye shall be healed and offered the chance for salvation. By your stripes He knows your name. At the appointed time, He will call you by name."

"That through this inspired work, I give you the sustenance for survival that ye shall not fail. That through this work and your faith, ye shall glorify Him and His work."

Ben Blyton, a messenger

CHAPTER 1
HERE'S WHAT YOU DON'T KNOW....BUT NEED TO KNOW

> Jesus said, "You did not choose me, but I chose you and appointed you to go and bear fruit—fruit that will last."
>
> John 15:16

I have interviewed a great number of caregivers. The undisputed #1 need was—WHAT TO EXPECT!!

Person after person submitted that if someone had just given them an idea of what to expect things might have been so much better.

I agree 100% with that, but the caveat is that knowing information and acting upon information are like night and day.

It does absolutely no good to know if you are not going to act upon the knowledge.

At this precise moment you are heartily agreeing, but come tomorrow there will be one thing true that ain't true now. Tomorrow will start your first day of failing to act decisively on the important first steps.

By this I mean doing things like getting your P.O.A, M.P.O.A., and L.W.—more on these later).

Consider this example: I tell you that a flame is hot. You courteously thank me and then stick your hand into a flame. You have two choices now: You can lament that someone should have told you what to expect, or you can learn from the experience. But it really would have been so much better if you had listened and learned from another person's experience without having to get burned (no pun intended).

The literary contributions to this field are many. There is voluminous information available via the internet and other means that relate to the equipment suppliers, insurance vendors, philosophical venues, interesting stories about 'Aunt Nell' or preserving the 'family unit' in crisis, but you can find this stuff yourself when you have time. There are doctors, lawyers and philosophers pontificating about what you should know (having never been in the trenches themselves of course). What you need (but perhaps don't realize yet) is information, basic information for survival, and right now! This is from people that still are in the trenches, learning, and passing it on to you... cutting edge stuff (like fast diaper changes)[joking].

As you read these real life experiences, hopefully you will come away with three basic things that you must work towards as a caregiver: Don't be afraid to acknowledge and call upon God for help (the converse is don't be the fool that keeps passing up His help because you are waiting for God to do something). The more you acknowledge God's help as being real and not just a series of coincidences, the more you will find His positive effect on your problems multiplying. God is real, and if this scares you then run away. But seriously, I understand that nobody wants to feel unsupported or out of step with their peers. If this is the case, then change peers. Remember, there are just as many believers as non-believers: the choice is yours. Anyway, you will find that your non-believer friends will have less and less in common with you as your caregiver journey progresses. They will gradually drift away... mark my words on that. Don't despair, you will soon learn to make new friends whom are caregivers and whom will understand everything you have to say.

You will soon learn to lean on your God for strength. Soon you will be saying "He ain't heavy Father, he's my brother."

The next thing I hope you receive is the understanding that at some point you are going to have to really understand (as best as possible) where your patient's behavior is coming from. Do not just give it lip service, but sincerely understand so you can forgive and release your pent-up anxiety after just being 'bitch-slapped' because your patient was unhappy about something. I often think of this as being similar to that movie title "How I Learned to Stop Worrying and Love the Bomb." Can you be the Christian that turns the other cheek? I must admit, I am still having trouble with this one, but I am doing much better, and I admit my weaknesses to God (like He's not going to know?). At least I hope I give him a chuckle from time to time.

The third item is to learn that one of the things that must be preserved (as best as possible) is some respect for your patient's dignity. You can't argue with them, and they feel what they feel, although we may be puzzled at their reaction towards us at times. This happens every time I change my mother's diapers. She starts chastising me with "This is just not right, stop it now, let's just let it be." She is feeling her dignity impugned, but there is nothing I can do. I wish I could debate the issue with her, but she doesn't understand the spoken word anymore. I can only keep things as private as possible, finish quickly, and then comfort her back to bed. She really is a sweet munchkin at heart, and every day I am learning to appreciate her more.

This TRILOGY FOR CAREGIVING is what will give you the path and the understanding that all of us need. Dementia and Alzheimer's are just a couple of many natural consequences of aging. Remember, next it will be your or maybe my turn. Hopefully, we will be better prepared to help our caregivers in their job.

WHAT TO EXPECT—A PREFACE

SO YOU WANT TO BE A CAREGIVER?

Here are some of my observations that will be representative of what to expect. These experiences could just as easily have been written about your patient after the fact. Here, you have the chance to understand 'before the fact' from what I will share with you. Many caregivers have it far worse when aggressive mood disorders begin to surface from the patient's psyche. This can be a natural result of the aging process or might be a secondary side effect from medications.

The wonderful part is that through caregiving you are given this rare opportunity to learn more about yourself. The experience will open many opportunities to discover the power of truly believing in your God. *Truly* is the operative word here. Through it you become empowered in different ways. You will be shown your weaknesses and your strengths, and you will have the opportunity to build character out of your strengths.

The downside is learning to deal with new and difficult experiences, having to study about your patient's illness to become as knowledgeable as possible, and learning to make quick decisions with commitment.

The downside is learning to deal with transference and counter transference issues that you have buried deep in your psyche. It means daily confronting all the things that you don't like about yourself but 'transfer' to the patient. This is pretty daunting for even the healthiest of caregivers because we all have our 'stuff,' don't we?

The downside is suddenly confronting emergency situations that you have never been exposed to before. An EMT sees the ambulance environment with real emergencies everyday and his/her BP probably doesn't rise too much, as they do what they have been trained for. But when you have to call 911 because your patient has fallen and is bleeding profusely, your heartbeat is going off the chart. You make the call but feel helpless, you feel anxious, you feel guilt, and you want to shift the blame to someone else for a blameless situation. You want to vindicate yourself less you feel out of control... but you are out of control at the moment. This scene will most likely play for you at some time. Will you learn to see things from a different point of view? Will you learn to be at peace with what nature has wrought?

The downside is suddenly being confronted by your patient in the middle of the night with extreme pain from an impacted colon (acute constipation). As they cry for help, where do you turn?

The upside is that knowing in the near future you too will be making their journey, but with a sense of familiarity. You will have seen the territory before and your fears and uneasiness will hopefully be lessened. You might even be the one to tell your caregiver just what to do in one of your 'crisis' moments. The comfort of wisdom... priceless.

These examples, and many more, will be presented to you on your journey. How you choose to perceive of them will be your blessing. By the grace of God, you are being championed with a new rite of passage. What will you choose?

WHAT TO EXPECT!—WHAT TO EXPECT!—WHAT TO EXPECT!

This is the one, universal complaint that all caregivers have voiced to me. I'm not sure whether it's a good or bad idea for me to try to give you an idea of what to expect. My fear is some good caregivers may opt out and disappear from contact with their patient, drop the patient off at a nursing home, or worse.

On the upside, the caregiver is given a glimpse into what his/her own mortality will be like. If you are like me, the personal mortality issue never hit your radar screen. It's like wearing blinders in the bright sunlight... I only want a peek. I mean, I know that the physical body is living and I will die at some point. What more should I know, right? It will all work out okay, I tell myself. But that's not the truth. Secretly, we want to know what to expect, how it will be. Will I be forgotten? Will I be financially destitute, roaming the streets with my cane, looking through garbage bins behind restaurants for food? These thoughts flow through any normal cranium because we don't know the answers, we don't know the choices. We don't know if we will have any voice, any rights. We fear the unknown. Yes, how we fear the deep, dark unknown. But it doesn't have to be that way.

I can tell you now, that I know my choices, I know what to expect, I have answers. As a result, I am in the process of acting upon my new information so I can be effective, efficient, and energized. Naw... leave off that last word, I lied to ya, I am beyond being energized ☺.

Keep in mind that many people will voice different experiences that caught them off guard, but there is a common denominator in all of this... your commitment and willingness to sacrifice.

MY PERSONAL CANDID EXPERIENCES

How would I describe the experience?

"Sort of like having the life sucked right out of you, arrr matey"!

Why do I do it?

"I do it because it's the right thing to do. It's also about character, commitment toward Christian values, and returning the love and kindness to the people who raised me."

What has been the most difficult change for me?

"Trying to attune my body, mind, and soul to be at peace with the world around me, and see things from a different point of view. You see, everything contradicts my preconceived idea of what caregiving would be like. My sense of values for example: From a religious standpoint, my patient and I represent opposite ends of the spectrum. I believe... he doesn't... it's that simple.

Suddenly, I am living in a relative 'state of deprivation.' I no longer have the stability of the same network of friends; I can no longer travel at will, or have the luxury of undisturbed personal space at home. I am always waiting for the other shoe to drop, the next crisis. Then there is the sheer frustration that confronts you day and night. It comes from a sense of being out of control because nothing seems to happen the way I want it to. I expect my patients to understand whatever I say to them but the truth is they don't. You will discover this also. **Any time we fail to have our expectations met, then we have frustrations.** Frustrations cause stress and anxiety which in turn cause our body to be overloaded with cortisol (the fight of flight stuff). This in turn is bad for our physical health.

I struggle to understand what my parents must be going through from their perspective, but I cannot. Sometimes my patient can almost hear a pin drop... at other times he doesn't seem to register what I am saying as I yell into his ear. I don't understand. He can recall and recite both his and his wife's social security numbers perfectly, but can't seem to remember what I talked to him about ten minutes ago. Usually, it's because he chooses what is important and what is not important to him. This is not a long vs. short term memory thing, I know how that works. It may be that it takes more effort to direct and focus his attention upon what is being said (I say that to be kind ☺).

It would be so nice if a patient could remind their caregivers that they have bad hearing, eyesight, or smell instead of pretending and clumsily faking an answer. That is disrespectful to the caregiver, and makes their role so much more difficult. Patients need to be reassured that we expect them to lose these attributes. I find this still doesn't change them from constantly pretending to hear, see, and understand everything perfectly. As a caregiver, you don't know if they really understood what you told them about washing their hands with soap and water every time they go to the bathroom. The other day my mother was actually eating the soap. Well, technically it was hand crème that just happened to look like yogurt. 'If it looks like a duck...' well, you get the point.

I find it disconcerting when my patient asks my advice, but so easily discards it for advice proffered by a stranger. Other caregivers tell me they experienced the same attitude from their patients. I think the scriptures talk about that. This is often compounded when the patient tries to reward or thank those who helped the least. To me, I find these 'token expressions of interest' substantially frustrating and most ingenuous, but they now have become everyday occurrences for this patient. As a caregiver, I think I know my patients better than any outsider. I have a pretty good technical education from the University of Kentucky and other institutions, thanks in part to the financial support from my patient. I know a lot about the mind. I feel helpless as I watch my patient being given bad advice by anyone, from a stranger to his own healthcare professionals. He doesn't seem to understand that a nurse's opinion is often as valid as a medical doctor's, and sometimes even more so. A degree does not guarantee ya got smarts! Yet he will look down on the ability of a nurse. I remember him replying during a discussion "so she was *just* a nurse?" But then my patient's favorite radio program is by a broadcaster that has

TWO doctoral degrees. Smart is as smart does, right Gump? (He also doesn't believe in global warming... arrgggghhhh!!!! Why am I still alive? ☺ It's my wry sense of humor.)

Try and find humor in your daily life by observing from another point of view. He often doesn't understand that, above all, common sense must prevail regardless of whom we deal with in the healthcare field, and there must be some ownership taken for understanding your own state of health, to the extent that a person is capable. Of course, everyone knows a stranger must be wise, because who knows how much wisdom they might contain, ha... sound familiar? If we speak to a family member, we know they have only a finite wisdom. **In other words expect your advice to be disregarded. In the end, the caregiver is rarely thanked, appreciated, or understood for their role. Thus, caregivers can easily slip into depression and poor health. Don't let this happen to you!**

I also find it disgraceful when a patient promises you anything when they are sick ("save me, save me... I'll do anything you say if you save me") only to show their true colors when you get them back to health. As a kid, we used to call a person like that an "Indian giver" which, according to folklore, translates to "one who gives false gifts." My patient would do that frequently, leaving me to feel like Charlie Brown after Lucy suckers him into trying to kick the ball (I know you remember that ☺).

These are just a sampling of the many different bumps on the roller coaster ride that lies before you. Allow them to massage your own painful areas until you no longer need to hold onto your pain. In other words, when you no longer have pain (mental anguish) then you can look at your patient (and the world) objectively and accept the task before you without resistance from yourself. From atop this mountain of objectivity, you get a glimpse of the glue that holds everything together and that is love.

MEET MY LAST PATIENT

THIS IS THE LAST RODEO FOR MY 102 YEAR OLD PATIENT

(I will briefly share him with you)

MY PATIENT IS AN ATHEIST—'THE GREAT ORATOR'

Such an interesting situation... looking like Einstein with his white hair in disarray, my patient goes out of his way to get embroiled in philosophical discussions that will allow him to repudiate such things as afterlife, the resurrection of Christ, love, and similar issues. Armed with two doctorates and many other awards (which he strategically has placed around the room) he speaks of the difference between the love of a person and the love of an apple... for him it just doesn't fit to speak of love. It can't be measured, and anything you can't measure doesn't exist nor has any credibility he feels. How can anyone be more learned than the great one with all his plaques, trophies, and awards. Upon looking around the room, most people assume defeat and acquiesce on the spot post haste (they just give up right thar and then on tha spot they do).

Remember that "*the one who thinks they know everything... knows nothing*" (-a great mind).

He talks of the women of his past who "loved" him, but he just thought that was silly. He uses the word Hoi Poi in his description of that nonsense. Love is just Hoi Poi he would say. "Women just want a husband." He continues, "I think about this one woman every day." Here he refers to a beautiful woman with beautiful black hair from his past that seemed to love him but neither of them mentioned the word "love" according to him. He says she was ten years older and is dead now, but he still thinks about her every day. Later he volunteered that she was Loretta Skelley whom he said he left behind in Seattle, WA. He says he also thinks about his mother often. He does not mention thinking about his late wife. He continues to tell the volunteer how he is not afraid to die and he understands it... just all cut and dried... no emotion... no regrets. But I see a patient that is deeply afraid of death.

He loves to bring up the discussion he had with the acting minister of our church at that time saying that he wishes for a cremation and that no prayers be involved. To this the minister replies "well, I guess you just won't have anything to say about it." He expresses his contention with a little 'cackle' sort of noise like you might expect to hear from the sly fox who just unfastened the henhouse door.

As their talk was winding up, I slipped downstairs to find a chance to engage the hospice worker on her thoughts. I guess I keep wondering why is it that my patient seeks out the controversial subject of religion and all its investments that seems to require his routine repudiation before he can feel secure for the day. Anyone that walks into the house is fair game... it's just that the game he plays is not fair. It doesn't make any difference how eloquent one waxes there is only one point... one side... his side. If someone else starts making a sensible and opposing dialogue he just quits listening... turns on his radio... abruptly walks away... or changes the subject. I have seen him do all these tricks and yet emerge blameless because after all he is over 100 years old.

My patient has regressed to using gutter expressions routinely. Any basketball game will trigger an outbreak but often he just sits in a chair and repeats his mantra, "no f___, no suck, no fun." Another favorite and simpler mantra is "shit, shit, shit." I do worry when he resolutely proclaims in a loud voice "Well, I'll be God D____ed." I am afraid he just might get his wish soon.

Some types of behaviors will clash with your fundamental beliefs over and over. They will stress you to no end. Know this so you can maintain your core beliefs while being kind to your patient's irrational thoughts and action.

Each trail you endure is a test of your resolute strength. Your endurance strengthens your faith in God. By your stripes, God knows your name.

By now, I have a pretty good idea of what to expect in the months ahead and the alternate paths we might travel. Now I am ready. The sun is shining.

102 YEAR OLD REVEALS HIS SECRET OF LONGEVITY

(ur jeans ain't everything)

Three years ago his heart specialist gave him less than six months to live. I made the decision to cut back on some of his meds and did away with the ones that made him feel the worst (digoxin). Finally, I chose another family doctor (the 'let em' live' type of doc). There are some docs who (rightfully intentioned) understand the futility of trying to keep a dying patient alive. I was the only one in the room that knew whether the patient was just sick or actually in a dying mode. My patient also said "if I keep taking this heart med the doc put me on I think I will die for sure." I also knew he had too much strength to be dying, but I could not convince his first doc of that. I was right.

Choosing the right doc has a lot to do with the outcome. A good outcome is a team result between the caregiver and the doctor.

My 102 year old patient's meds: Notice there is nothing remaining here that pertains directly to heart medication for cardiomyopathy except furosemide (lasix) and that is probably not needed. I powder these five meds together and serve in a spoon covered with applesauce. He left the hospital at 128lbs and six months later stabilized at his present weight of 170 lbs.

1. **81 mg baby aspirin**

2. **Finasteride, 5mg/day - Prostate medication**

3. **Furosemide, 5mg/day or 10mg/day for any pulmonary fluid**

4. **Senna, 8.5mg/day for constipation**

5. **Lisinopril, 20mg/day for blood pressure**

He believes in eating a few almonds every day.

He believes (lately) in a glass of cranberry juice at every meal.

He believes in taking a nap every day (now that is almost full time).

He believes in eating a piece of fruit every day.

He believes in taking a short walk every day.

He believes in eating the same thing for breakfast (now it's one or two frozen waffles for the toaster every day).

He loves humor and quotes the longevity secret of a woman of 106 yrs. When asked her secret of longevity she replied "eat an apple a day and stay away from doctors."

MOVING INTO YOUR PARENTS' HOUSE—WHAT YOU DIDN'T EXPECT!

You will probably miss this one by a mile, ha. The day has finally arrived for you to move into your parents' house for 24/7 support, pretty straightforward and very necessary for sure. The day arrives and you have already calculated that it will take 2.4 days to pack and two, maybe three days to move in (the big stuff, like furniture, you can move most any time when you have a truck). In general you already know where to put your treasures... some in the garage and some here and there. It's clearly a ten day job, but being the practical person you are, you double that to account for Murphy's Law. Twenty days to settle in and make peace with everyone.

What you didn't count on was that you may have only about two weeks once you become situated in your parents' house before you become clinically depressed.

Yes, you read that correctly. It's spelled D-E-P-R-E-S-S-I-O-N. From then on it's a lot of face time with the wall. You have no will power to even attempt to complete what you started. It's no longer a top priority... or even any priority.

For us, we got moved the first week. It was a whirlwind task ending with my putting everything in banana boxes from Kroger's and storing them in my parent's garage. I just dumped them there so I could sort and rearrange them later and everything would be neat as a pin.

Three years later and we are still trying to finish that job. If you are self employed, don't forget that as soon as you close down your office or business (and you should if at all possible) you will need to make what seems like countless address changes on all your mail. Sounds easy but wait till you try. Even when you mail all your utility companies your change of address (COA), they won't seem to do it on the first go around. That means phone time, more mailings, and late fee penalties because of the COA accounting delay. A simple thing like a COA and I am still doing that a month after I moved out of my office. Don't underestimate the moving project because it will bite you. Then there is the phone change. Just a simple porting of your old number to a new location can sometimes become a never ending saga.

Try your best at getting everything pre-moved and in place to the "T." Besides meds, the best tool for fighting depression is to have the feeling of being in control. Being stuck at second base with the move-in job is not a feeling of being in control.

Three years later and my wife and I are still not done sorting through our stuff and finding a place to put it. A huge problem here is having to face the truth about what we treasure so dearly. The truth is most of what we treasure is JUNK. We ruefully tell ourselves we just can't part with this or that. In my field of counseling we have terms for this. Simply put, a caregiver is generally not in a fluid state. The caregiver is bonded to everything from old photo albums to old lawnmowers that can still be fixed. We think we are free but we are not.

A caregiver is trapped within their own web just as soundly as the patient is trapped within theirs. Entrapment by old ideas, notions, and ego can be a caregiver's most powerful nemesis. Until you understand the power it has on you and learn to release it, life will be a struggle.

Once you learn to live with what you need rather than what you want, you will feel like a burden has been lifted off your shoulders. You see, one of the difficulties of this job is that we are reminded constantly of our own mortality... and it scares us. We feel helpless. That side of the equation changes once we learn to empower ourselves and let go of the things we held so sacrosanct. In reality they were just useless tethers to the material world. How often do we find ourselves saying "I could never let go of those hundreds of pictures of Aunt Emma and Uncle Reese" or "I know I can fix that chain saw." Keep a couple pics of Aunt Emma and toss the chain saw. You will begin to feel a wonderful feeling of being in control again.

When the last trumpet sounds, do you think you will be first in line to be called because of your material possessions or because of how you learned to let go and think in terms of true Christian values and service to others?

Of course you must keep everything in perspective and still be a multitasker if you have kids that are staying with you... I know that and He knows that. Do your best, but start cutting the tethers.

MAKES YOU WANT TO KILL SOMETIMES

Ya know, I had heard that expression before but I thought it was more or less just an anomaly... an aberration within the data banks of all the adult caregivers. This is so incredible that now, I, Mr. Easygoing Guy, would ever be caught up in these emotions of rage, anger, and whatever else that wants to scream out. I have tried to examine the underpinnings of these feelings of, let's call them "outrage syndrome" for now.

I can postulate several different hypothetical causes but here are some observations I have made:

THE THREE DON'Ts OF SURVIVAL:

1. **Don't underestimate** *the potential cleverness and manipulative ability of a geriatric patient who does not have dementia.* My patient turns 100 in a few days and my wife and I have almost daily discussions over whether he is extremely clever and manipulative or whether he is showing some kind of natural but seemingly selective dementia at the right times. It reminds me of the scene in *Absence of Malice* when the DA turned to Paul Newman and said "Are you really that smart? Naw, I guess you ain't gonna tell me anyway." *There is some actor in all of us. Who will you be?*

2. **Don't overdo** your helpfulness for your patient. I don't know why but this seems, for my patient, to breed more enablement of his behaviors of manipulation and deceit.

3. **Don't underestimate** how counterproductive visitors and volunteers can be. This is almost universal with anyone that comes to visit my patient. His goals in these final days of life are to maximize himself so he can really become "bigger than life." The usual result is that you, the caregiver, will be minimized to the point of seeming almost incidental and even neglectful to the visitor.

One problem is that often a volunteer will encourage my patient to challenge his adversaries. I listened as the Hospice volunteer said "well that doesn't sound right and you should question... yadda yadda" or "I have never heard of a legal will doing that... I don't think that is right and you should protest..." In this case my patient was confusing his Trust with his Will. They are separate instruments and do separate things but confusion will reign, count on it.

A close friend of the patient's dropped by one day. Neither of the two realized I was still upstairs. Well, it was a field day for my patient. He whined about anything that would bring him a closer hug from his guest I suppose. Finally she told him to confront me on why I am not telling him this or that. I could take it no longer. I went downstairs and set the records straight for both of them. The patient, as usual, had none of his facts straight and the friend was trying to turn my patient against me. The friend was a long time friend of the family and someone I trusted. Someone that was willing to create disharmony because of mistaken beliefs. There is a lesson there, an important one. I think you know what it is.

You will have many days like this as a caregiver. Do the best you can. Be vigilant and use your intercom to allow your ears to hear. But "judge ye not lest ye be condemned" (Matthew 7:1).

Your patient may lie about anything. It's just their manner of talk. They may not intentionally do it, but they do it. Most of the time they just absolutely get their facts totally backwards which they defend viciously as the truth... which still makes it a lie.

It is frustrating to see how he manipulates others with his "woe is me" by-line. Your patient will do this too at some point. I listened as he explained to a Hospice Volunteer about how I, and others, don't tell him anything about his grandson, his bank account, his legal wills, 'ad nauseam.' The truth is we all do tell him, but he chooses to play the role of the victim. Expect this behavior to appear and torment you for a long time (just joking, it's really your chance to turn the other cheek, ha).

Playing the role of the victim is a common behavioral trait of geriatric patients because it addresses a lot of their unanswered needs.

What I don't understand is why trained people like Hospice aides, and the world for that matter, will always believe the oldest person in the room. My dad is 102, he will always be the oldest person in the room. My goose is cooked before the day even starts. But I smile as I ask myself "what will my lesson be today?"

As a caregiver, your voice will not be heard above that of an elder. Savor the humor in this incongruity and don't look back.

Recently my patient was 'entertaining' the new Hospice nurse assigned to him. He starts by telling her that sometimes he "thinks" his nipple feels sore. Yep... you guessed it. In less time than it takes a dog to scratch a flea, my patient has the nurse feeling his nipple. I left to get groceries. Just didn't want to be there in case he tells her another place is sore... yuuuch and double yuuuch!

I think the most important thing a volunteer can do is to be proficient at being neutral. That doesn't happen too often.

WHAT IS THE LIFE LESSON IN CAREGIVING?

What can I expect to learn?

The experience can be the best of times to the worst of times. It's a smooth ride... it's a roller coaster ride... it's a sunny day... it's a rainy day. The way you approach your mission has everything to do with the education you will receive. You are just starting so work on finding the sunshine in every day.

I think one of the things that puts the caregiver into a funk is that at some level our mind is always processing the inevitable truth: soon we too must pass. Are we really ready and if not why not?

The Positive Life Lesson in Caregiving is not any one single thing. It is the experience as a whole. It is the conscious choices we make along the path. It is an ever evolving experience. It is the full awareness that gifts from God have been placed before us and we have a choice.

THE EMT (911) EXPERIENCE

It's a given that at some time during your tenure as a caregiver you will need to make that dreaded 911 call—either for your patient or yourself.

First of all there is nothing to dread about making the call. It is our natural defense mechanism that wants to keep us in denial that anything could be less than perfect lest we feel somehow guilty. As I mentioned earlier in this book I am in the trenches with you. I have been there and done that. Learn from where I have been and my mistakes.

"I knew there was something wrong with me... starting to feel pain in the legs, fluid pressure building up in the thighs, feeling faint, and extreme weakness in my quads (those big muscles on the thigh that help you run, walk, etc). Naturally, I did precisely the wrong thing by taking Aleve to relieve the inflammation. It made sense at the time. The next day my symptoms were much worse. I knew I had to call 911 for help. There was nobody else to drive me the one block to the hospital and my patient was 102 years old and he couldn't see the hospital even if he could drive."

I know this is going to sound silly, but for myself, it was a struggle to make that call. The feeling was as though I failed at my job... I was weak and incapable of finishing this, my sworn duty. I knew that wasn't true, but try and tell that to the male ego.

I made the 911 call. The operator said "what is your emergency." "Well, I'm not really sure I have a real emergency but I *think* I should go to the hospital emergency room." That operator connects me over to the EMT dispatch who asked the same thing. I described my symptoms and requested that they arrive without their siren on if possible. The EMT team was on their way.

Literally holding back something wet in my eyes, I greeted the EMT team with an apologetic "I am sorry to bother you guys, but I really need some help."

Ouch... sometimes it just hurts to be brutally honest with myself and admit that I just have to have help. But this was a necessary experience both for my health and my personal growth. I was definitely in unfamiliar territory.

The EMT's were not able to come up the driveway because of overhanging tree limbs. It was raining hard that day and I knew that every neighbor on the block must be watching and gossiping now. I am sure many of them probably stayed home from work intuitively knowing that something really gossipy was going to happen today. It must of been humorous seeing me stretched out on the gurney thing and the rain gods thinking I must be a thirsty plant and the EMT guys opening the door, adjusting this and that and instructing me where to put my hands before carefully and slowly putting me in the van. Those tree limbs are top on my list.

Now I know that most any woman reading this will be laughing hysterically because to them it's no big deal. Women are so used to the countless women-to-women chats where they bare their souls without flinching. I have learned to accept that women really are smarter. But for men... this is the defiance of the basic laws of being a male most of which are imprinted in our DNA and we are powerless to act and feel differently (I think that's right). We are raised by being told to never cry, never admit it "hurts," and always clean our plate.

Once on the bright red EMT van, they put the IV line in and asked me routine questions about health history. They asked which hospital I would like to be transported to. It was now off to the hospital.

The lesson here: when you need help, get help. The longer you wait, the more someone will suffer. Q.E.D.

HERE IS WHAT YOU SHOULD KNOW ABOUT 911 EMT'S

Every state has their own form of 911 specificities, but generally speaking they all function in the same manner. The following example relates to Kentucky.

The 911 EMTs will be most efficient when you can do or understand the following:

Give a good description of what the problem is. Why is the patient in this condition, do they have Alzheimer's, dementia, allergies, special needs, morbidly obese condition? List their medications. This helps the EMS team determine what types of equipment need to be sent to this address.

Give the correct address and remain there until EMTs arrive. During the emotions playing up to calling 911, it is not uncommon for the caregiver to 'forget' their own address or they may want to run to the pharmacy or run over to the neighbors. If the caregiver is not there, the EMT's may lose valuable response time in assessing the situation.

Have a clear pathway to the patient. Be sure that a stretcher can be brought in.

Insure that EMT's will have access to the house. Try to be specific about where to enter the house (through the side door or front door, etc). It is not uncommon for the caregiver to be absorbed in the situation at hand and forget to unlock the door downstairs for the EMTs.

Insure that family pets are secured away from the patient area. All too often a homeowner forgets to put away their 'pit bull' that has always been so gentle. Animals can sense when their owners are stressed and can react negatively in these situations.

In Kentucky there should be patient DNR (if desired), **LIVING WILL**, and **POWER OF ATTORNEY** (family member whom is usually the caregiver) documents accessible to the EMT and posted in a conspicuous place visible by the entering EMTs.

The EMT's must have the DNR's that are printed off the internet site: LexingtonKY.gov. Go to "Fire and Emergency Services," then to "related documents," and click on "Kentucky do not resuscitate form." This will open a PDF file with the complete form for you to copy and fill out.

The EMT's cannot accept any other DNR document even if drawn up by an attorney or provided by a hospital or any other source. Only the web site document will be recognized. I have printed a sample DNR document at the end of this section.

EMT's will pass along your DNR form to the hospital.

"YOU CALL—WE HAUL"

EMT'S will still deliver your patient to the hospital even if you have no documents (as was the case for me, the caregiver, after forming a blood clot in the femoral vein while caring for my 102 year old patient... go figure ☺).

Who pays for the EMT response?

Usually your insurance company is billed or Medicare, Medicaid, or the individual directly.

What does the EMT run cost?

The Basic Life Support (BLS) currently costs $683. Advanced Life Support (ALS) is $945. Mileage is a flat rate of $11.60 per mile. It is important to check your bill to verify that you were billed correctly by the third party billing. For example, my actual bill was about $790.

The most common problem for the EMT team is a *lack of information on the patient*

Leave all valuables at home

Who chooses the hospital?

If this information is not already on the home data sheet, then a family member, or caregiver in the absence of a family member, can advise.

What if the patient resists going to the hospital?

Anyone with 'power-of-attorney' privileges can decide the matter (another reason to have your POA document ready).

What training have EMT's had?

In Kentucky, all firefighters are trained as EMT's during an eighteen week training course and then put on supervised probation for one year. Paramedic training requires a year of training.

Will the EMT's break the door down to gain entry?

The EMT's will not leave until a resolution is obtained. If the situation is a known emergency then breaking the door down is one option. Caregivers need to be sure access is available and be on site to meet the EMTs.

A SAMPLE DNR DOCUMENT

Kentucky Emergency Medical Services

Do Not Resuscitate (DNR) Order

Person's Full Legal Name _____

Surrogate's Full Legal Name (if applicable) _____

I, the undersigned person or surrogate who has been designated to make health care decisions in accordance with Kentucky Revised Statutes, hereby direct that in the event of my cardiac or respiratory arrest that this DO NOT RESUSCITATE (DNR) ORDER be honored. I understand that DNR means that if my heart stops beating or if I stop breathing, no medical procedure to restart breathing or heart function, more specifically the insertion of a tube into the lungs, or electrical shocking of the heart or cardiopulmonary resuscitation (CPR) will be started by emergency medical services (EMS) personnel.

I understand this decision will not prevent emergency medical services personnel from providing other medical care.

I understand that I may revoke this DNR order at any time by destroying this form, removing the DNR bracelet, or by telling the EMS personnel that I want to be resuscitated. Any attempt to alter or change the content, names, or signatures on the EMS DNR form shall make the DNR form invalid.

I understand that this form, or a standard EMS DNR bracelet must be available and must be shown to EMS personnel as soon as they arrive. If the form or bracelet is not provided, the EMS personnel will follow their normal protocols which could include cardiopulmonary resuscitation (CPR) or other resuscitation procedures.

I understand that should I die, EMS personnel will require this form and/or bracelet for their records.

I give permission for information about this EMS DNR Order to be given to the prehospital emergency medical care personnel, physicians, nurses, or other health care personnel as necessary to implement this directive.

I hereby state that this 'Do Not Resuscitate (DNR) Order' is my authentic wish not be resuscitated.

_____

Person/Legal Surrogate Signature Date

Commonwealth of Kentucky County of _____

Subscribed and sworn to before me by_____
to be his/her own free act and deed, this _____ day of _____,
20_____.

_____, Notary Public

My commission expires: _____

In lieu of having this Form notarized, it may be witnessed by two persons not related to the individual noted above.

WITNESSED BY:

1. _____

2. _____

This EMS Do Not Resuscitate Form was approved by the Kentucky Board of Medical Licensure at their March 1995 meeting.

Complete the portion below, cut out, fold, and insert in DNR bracelet

I certify that an EMS Do Not Resuscitate (DNR) form has been executed.

Person's Name (print or type) _____

Person's or Legal Surrogate's Signature _____

KENTUCKY EMERGENCY MEDICAL SERVICES DO NOT RESUSCITATE (DNR) ORDER INSTRUCTIONS

PURPOSE

This standardized EMS DNR Order has been developed and approved by the Kentucky Board of Medical Licensure, in consultation with the Cabinet for Human Resources. It is in compliance with KRS Chapter 311 as amended by Senate Bill 311 passed by the 1994 General Assembly, which directs the Kentucky Board of Medical Licensure to develop a standard form to authorize EMS providers to honor advance directives to withhold or terminate care.

For covered persons in cardiac or respiratory arrest, resuscitative measures to be withheld include external chest compressions, intubation, defibrillation, administration of cardiac medications and artificial respiration.

The EMS DNR Order does not affect the provision of other emergency medical care, including oxygen administration, suctioning, control of bleeding, administration of analgesics and comfort care.

APPLICABILITY

This EMS DNR Order applies only to resuscitation attempts by health care providers in the prehospital setting (i.e. certified EMT-First Responders, Emergency Medical Technicians, and Paramedics) in patients' homes, in a long-term care facility, during transport to or from a health care facility, or in other locations outside acute care hospitals.

INSTRUCTIONS

Any adult person may execute an EMS DNR Order. The person for whom the Order is executed shall sign and date the Order and may either have the Order notarized by a Kentucky Notary Public or have their signature witnessed by two persons not related to them. The executor of the Order must also place their printed or typed name in the designated area and their signature on the EMS DNR Order bracelet insert found at the bottom of the EMS DNR Order form.

The bracelet insert shall be detached and placed in a hospital type bracelet and placed on the wrist or ankle of the executor of the Order.

If the person for whom the EMS DNR Order is contemplated is unable to give informed consent, or is a minor, the person's legal surrogate shall sign and date the Order and may either have the form notarized by a Kentucky Notary Public or have their signature witnessed by two persons not related to the person for which the form is being executed or related to the legal health care surrogate. The legal health care surrogate shall also complete the required information on the EMS DNR bracelet insert found at the bottom of the EMS DNR Order form. The bracelet shall be detached and placed in a hospital type bracelet and placed on the wrist or ankle of the person for which this Order was executed.

The original, completed EMS DNR Order or the EMS DNR Bracelet must be readily available to EMS personnel in order for the EMS DNR Order to be honored. Resuscitation attempts may be initiated until the form or bracelet is presented and the identity of the patient is confirmed by the EMS personnel. It is recommended that the EMS DNR Order be displayed in a prominent place close to the patient and/or the bracelet be on the patient's wrist or ankle.

REVOCATION

An EMS DNR Order may be revoked at any time orally or by performing an act such as burning, tearing, canceling, obliterating or by destroying the Order by the person on whose behalf it was executed or by the person's legal health care surrogate.

IT SHOULD BE UNDERSTOOD BY THE PERSON EXECUTING THIS EMS DNR ORDER OR THEIR LEGAL HEALTH CARE SURROGATE, THAT SHOULD THE PERSON LISTED ON THE EMS DNR ORDER DIE WHILE EMS PREHOSPITAL PERSONNEL ARE IN ATTENDANCE, THE EMS DNR ORDER OR EMS DNR BRACELET MUST BE GIVEN TO THE EMS PREHOSPITAL PERSONNEL FOR THEIR RECORDS.

THE HOSPITAL EXPERIENCE

HOSPITAL CARE TIPS (BASED ON SURVEY OF 700 NURSES)

At Check-in

According to Consumerreports.org/health the top tip from a survey of 700 nurses is:

1. **Bring your list of medications with you. This includes prescription, over-the-counter, and supplements.**

2. **You have to become a pro-active patient. You have to become part of your medical team.**

If your doctor is going to examine or touch you and you didn't see him/her wash their hands, it is entirely acceptable to politely say

"I didn't see you wash your hands when you came in. Would you mind washing your hands in front of me now?"

Be insistent if you're unhappy with your care or don't understand something. Ask to see the "Patient's Advocate" or the "Hospitalist."

Forty-six percent of nurses said it would help very much if patients checked the medications being administered to them during their stay.

Now that is what it means to be **pro-active** and being part of the medical team. If you see something you don't understand or agree with then let your voice be heard.

WHAT IF NOBODY LISTENS TO MY CONCERNS?

Fifty-two percent of nurses in the survey agreed that patients should work closely with a patient advocate, social worker, or case manager to coordinate care. But patients usually have to ask for such help, and only 9 percent of patients and 17 percent of their relatives (12 percent overall) in our survey did so. They might not have known they can summon those allies simply by using their bedside phone.

At Check-out

1. **Make sure you understand plans for your patient discharge.**

2. **If you're not satisfied, ask for help from your hospital's patient advocate, social worker, or case manager.**

3. **Insist on a medication reconciliation between home and hospital drugs.**

See your primary-care physician within a week of your patient discharge and arrange for him or her to get copies of your hospital records.

CHAPTER 2
TRUE STORIES FROM CAREGIVERS
WHO TELL WHAT IT'S REALLY LIKE!

EXPECT THIS DAWG!

(Tough love from the trenches)

> As for you, be strong and do not give up,
> for your work will be rewarded.
>
> 2 Chronicles 15:7

Here are excerpts from caregivers that seem to be representative of most of the caregivers I have interviewed. These are firsthand accounts of caregivers and the struggles they had to contend with and the sacrifices they made... these caregivers whom I call Christians.

FROM JUNE ROMAN

The most difficult problem I have faced has been my role change from a daughter, who adored her strong-willed, determined father of deep Christian faith, to the primary caregiver and decision maker for a man I hardly can recognize since his drastic illness that began on November 27, 2004. The best advice that I got was from my husband, who told me, basically, that I could not view my father the way he used to be, but I had to become the parent and deal with the present situation. It was crushing advice, but oh so very true... the drastic personality change, the gutter language coming from my preacher father's mouth, and the total exhaustion.

We use Wedco Home Health—some are great and some are mediocre all from the same agency—depends on the person doing the caregiving... Currently, part of us goes to one church in the morning and the rest of us go to a church in the afternoon because someone always has to be here at home... Not much in the way of entertaining at home any more. In the beginning, our home had a revolving door with Home Health, different therapists (OT, PT, and respiratory folks every day of the week even some weekends). My father's doctor was great, the hospital was pretty good—social workers kept pushing DNR papers that I was not ready to sign, and pushing for nursing home placement which I did not want, but the level of care was okay. They used a lot of sedation to manage behavior, which I was not fond of at all."

FROM DUANE WALLACE

My wife has had AD (acute dementia) for going on 15 years, has been in the late stage for 5 years, was in an ALF (assisted living facility) for 4 years and has now been back home for 16 months... She has to be fed and that can be a real problem at times. She gets distracted easily at times, and is difficult to feed. She doesn't have many teeth, so the food has to be in small pieces, and when she doesn't open her mouth very wide, it can be a problem. I just have to keep reminding myself that she doesn't realize what she is doing, and be VERY patient. When things get really bad, I just put my arm around her and tell her I love her. You have to tell them several times because it takes repetition to sink into their minds.

When she was about 8 years into the disease, she kept having terrible pains under her breasts. Nothing seemed to work to cure them. They would just come and go at different times. Doctors could not find a source of the problem as they kept thinking she was having heart problems. We finally came to the conclusion it was psychosomatic pain. But, during those attacks, she would sit and cry, asking for help, and there was nothing I could do. When she went into the ALF, the pains disappeared. Once in a while, even now, when I wake her in the morning, she will get something that jerks her whole body and almost puts her to her knees. If I didn't hold on to her they would. I am able to get rid of them by talking calm and quiet, and keep telling her that I love her and will take care of her. That always works.

She requires help with everything. Taking her to the toilet, dressing and undressing her all require physical strength, and usually she is uncooperative. She must be held while walking, and getting her in and out of the car. I find that when I put her into the car (similar seats to bucket seats) that I can turn her around, put my knee under her rear end, and lift her high enough to get her onto the seat. I must then lift her the rest of the way into the car. It really works rather well.

I don't think anyone can be prepared for that role (caregiving). My mother-in-law also had AD and we cared for her for 3 years, but it was not the same. To watch someone so very close to you go downhill and know there is nothing you can do except make it as easy for them as possible, is something impossible to prepare for. I was, however, prepared when I brought her home from the ALF. I had become almost an expert at caregiving. At least that is what I have been told.

FROM KAY GENTRY

Dementia... it's all the same to me because it still takes your life away from you.

FROM STEVEN RISNER

I felt like screaming! Usually 3 to 4 times a day, not only at mama, but myself, and the entire world as well, how could she come to this, this seemingly robotic-like thing that was always independent, strong-willed, and undaunted in the face of everything, from surviving the Great Depression to losing a child. How? Why? I became so angry at her, not so much because of this illness that had ravaged her once 'sharp as a tack' mind, but her very way of life itself. So, I read, at night, after putting her to bed, I read A LOT. Everything from newspapers to encyclopedias, for just a bit of escape, knowing it would begin again early the next morning.

I certainly was NOT prepared for what was in store for me. I had no idea that I would be caring for what increasingly became an infant-like woman in her early eighties! Adult diapers, daily bathing, (sometimes more), correct dosing of medications, all at once, and for the rest of her life, however long or short it may have been.

I mistakenly held my feelings inside for the most part, I figured I could handle this as I had handled other serious issues in my life. That was indeed a big mistake, I found out, and am still finding out after the fact. I am trying to 'straighten' out my life once again. Therapy does wonders!

If I could start over, I think I would have tried to have more patience, although I did a good job for the most part. I sometimes would maybe answer to sharply, maybe didn't come to her fast enough, maybe... I don't know, I guess I did the very best I could do, given the situation I was in.

At the beginning of mama's illness, this woman would cuss! I think SOB was the primary word, that was first. Then she would accuse family of stealing from her. And perhaps lastly, was the eating. Immediately following a meal, I would seat her in the recliner, start to eat myself, and she would say, "I'm starving to death." EVERYTIME! It seems so trivial now, but anyway, I would give her something else to eat, she never gained any weight. But my question was always this: "How can you hold so much?"

Her reply... "Old Diabetes takes all my food." I would say no more.

I lost my precious baby doll January 20, 2003, and, like the previous 3 years, I was with her when she left. I can't describe what I felt; I guess I went into complete, emotional shut down, numbness, nothingness, just shock I guess. Actually, I play it over and over in my mind. I don't see how I managed to walk out of the hospital, call family members, make arrangements, and even help with dressing her at the funeral home. I had dressed her every day for three previous years, I didn't figure once more would kill me!

Mama had a great laugh, and a bad singing voice. I would play some of her favorite tunes, and she would start 'singing' right along with them. It was hilarious, and some of the most beautiful bad singing I had ever heard. It was strange to hear her sing along with some of those songs. I remember thinking, "This she remembers?"

When she would have an accident in her Depends, this little old lady would say to me, "I used to change your diapers, now you're changing mine. Ain't that awful. I'm an old pisser." Then she would giggle, and I would get tickled at her. Then she would start laughing, which in turn got me going. We had a lot of good laughs over that.

I would have really benefited from some sort of book that kind of told me what I could possibly expect.

FROM 'DAUGHTER'

Daddy refused to believe that anything was wrong with him and, therefore, the 'official' diagnosis was only several months before he died, although we'd known it a long time.

He had that strength and will power you describe of the depression generation. Six weeks before he died, I was again trying to get him to the hospital. "Daddy, why won't you go?" (a stupid question on my part) But he drew himself up as best he could and replied in a firm voice: "In my considered opinion, there is nothing wrong with me."

Dear God, thank you for giving me this opportunity to care for my parents. One of the **hardest parts of it all**, besides the physical exhaustion, is coming to grips with the fact that **our logic does not agree with our parents' logic.** Even today, I find I have trouble getting my mind around the fact that my mother can no longer get her mind around facts that used to be child's play to her.

If nothing else, I hope we are setting good examples for our children regarding our own care some day.

FROM STEVE RISNER

I want to tell you about a wonderful, beautiful woman who was born February 6, 1916 in Eastern Kentucky. She left home at 13 to attend high school in Berea, Kentucky, worked in a munitions plant during WW2, owned several businesses, raised 2 sons, and helped raise two grandsons. She was an avid grower of vegetables, flowers and any other living thing that needed help getting started. This woman was my grandmother, and I was one of the grandsons she helped raise.

Zelda R. Risner Havens was NOT a complainer. Having several diseases, including crippling arthritis, diabetes, angina, and others, she just kept on going full throttle, that is up until the age of 81, when one day out of the blue, she gave me her car keys. She said, "I think I had better quit driving." That was it, no discussion, no more driving for her. Weird.

Then other little things, like the showers 2-3 times a day, mind you, 'Mama,' as I called her, was always a very clean woman, but not to this extent. She then began to leave the stove on, put on way to much hair mousse, forget where her money was, forget who had been in to visit, things like that.

We took her to see her doctor, and after several tests it was confirmed; she had Alzheimer's disease. Wow, this independent woman, who always worried about other folks' well being, was going to need someone to help with her own.

That's when I moved back in, gave up a ten year job in radio, and became her total caregiver. Now, not long after I had moved back in, she fell and broke a hip, total replacement. While in the hospital, she had a stroke, partially paralyzing her left side. With the help of a fantastic physical therapist she started walking again with the help of a 'gait belt,' and we went back home.

Back home her mental state became worse. If I went out of the room, out of her sight, she would call for me, and none too calmly! When I went back to her, she just said, "I just wondered where you'd been, I hadn't seen you in a long time."

It was this way constantly, day in, day out, 6:30 am till around 9:30 pm every day. It was enough to make me often think, "I can't do this!" But, do it I did, with no help from her surviving son at all. Her first born son, my father, had died in 1983, and that was certainly devastating to her, and of course my brother and myself. My brother was working, and was not good at dealing with that type of thing either. So, it was just me. My step-grandfather (her 2nd husband), was there also, but his age was working against him as well. So, I did it all, bathing, feeding, medicating, the works.

This woman was not easily entertained either, and I did not want her to just sit in the recliner with nothing to think about, so I decided to do the following:

1) Play music for her, CD's, cassettes, whatever. Mama liked Gospel music and Loretta Lynn, and even Diana Ross. That's what she got. I even found some Big Band tunes for her.

2) Play movies that she may have seen years ago. It was comforting for her, I think, to see films from the 30's and 40's, and it helped that I enjoyed them too.

3) On warm days, we went out and sat on the front porch. I always put sun-block on her, I didn't want to deal with sunburn on top of everything else.

4) I wanted Mama to be as comfortable as possible, and I found that 100% cotton clothes were best, as well as washing clothes with Dreft detergent. It costs more, but she did not scratch so much. I found out that some of her meds caused the scratching too.

These things, and so many more, I did for a little over 3 years, full time, very rarely getting a respite. There was no help, and nursing homes were not an option. I just couldn't put her there, couldn't.

I am now caring for another family member, not with Alzheimer's, but a broken leg. This type of care seems to be my destiny.

FROM GARY ANONYMOUS

My wife has Huntington's disease and needed caregiving when she was only 47 years old. She is now 62. I had promised her I would allow her to stay home as long as I could, and that involved changing the house. Our living room became her bedroom, I hired home care aids, got financial assistance (I lived in Minnesota at the time), and made the house safe for her. The one thing I became very frustrated with and I would suggest as a caregiver's tip: **In dealing with a disease that is progressive, get help on evaluating the needs at 6 months, 12 months, 18 months**

etc. It seemed like when I would add something to meet a need, I was always too late. A stair lift was installed, and by the time we were going to use it, we were almost beyond the ability to. I think it was used less than a dozen times.

This past spring I finally had to place her in a nursing home, and that is part of the reason for my move to Kentucky; to start living again.

FROM ANNA WHITES

In 1991, my husband and I moved to Eastern Kentucky with our one year old daughter to care for his grandmothers. Granny Ann passed away when our daughter was 6 and our son was 4, but Ma-Ma lived until Amanda was 12 and Lawson 10.

During that time, she lived down the road from us. She had progressive congestive heart failure and became less able to care for herself over the years, but strongly resisted her children's' suggestion of a nursing home. Looking back, I don't know how we did it—starting out in our careers, young children, all that driving, all that money (food, "babysitters", medicine, co-pays!!!!), but we survived.

We felt very, very alone, due to lack of help manuals or even suggestions from her doctor or friends. Couple with that, the understandable resentment because the rest of her family, 3 children, including Pierce's mother, and his 2 siblings, didn't want to do much to help. It was the hardest thing I have ever done, but I would not take back those 11 years for anything. Our kids shared a special bond with Ma-Ma. We are still recovering from the financial burden (it slowed our careers down, and caring for elderly grandparents is expensive), but it was worth it.

FROM SALLY C. ALLISON

Since 2000, my husband and I have been the primary caregivers for my mother and my mentally handicapped sister. In 2005, we added my husband's mother. We were lucky to have enough bedrooms to accommodate everyone, so we did not have to move, but we were at a loss to find the information really needed to guide us down this new road of life. I did have a cousin whose mother had Alzheimer's, and she was able to pass information along to me, and I could call her for advice. But for the most part, like you, we have learned by trial and error and a lot of patience.

Due to my mother's sleepless nights, together with her constant motion and activeness, I finally had to put her into a nursing home, but I have continued a diary. In the beginning, it was just for my relief, to write things down. But it has evolved into an insight into the nursing home care problems, rules, etc., and what I can do from the outside to continue to know that my loved one is getting good care from strangers.

After my mother-in-law moved in, we got a new set of problems because she had a slew of medications to be taken 2 times a day. She had a heart condition, diet restrictions, and physical needs—everything almost the opposite of my mother. I started another diary to add things about her. I started a daily record of food and liquids. I tried to make sure she ate every 4 hours.

Then, in the spring of this year, my mother-in-law was also diagnosed with the beginning of Alzheimer's. So far, she is still with us. Her physical health continues to be more of a problem than the beginnings of dementia. As her dementia progresses into full blown Alzheimer's, I do believe she will probably exhibit an entirely different set of issues, and we will again learn what to do as we go.

My mentally handicapped sister is an entirely different story, and even though saying she is mentally handicapped makes it sounds as if she would be the hardest to take care of, actually she is the easiest.

Since 2000, when all of this caregiver opportunity started for us, we have experienced so many things; I don't know where to start. Although all caregivers are alike in some ways, I feel that circumstances, live styles, financial needs, physical needs, etc. all affect the way you help your patients during this period of their lives.

FROM KIMBERLY STEWART

(Kimberly brings four and a half years experience from a nursing home environment and also two and a half years experience as a Hospice Volunteer. From her extensive and dedicated experience, she submits the following.)

Most caregivers have the illusion they can do it all, for everyone, all the time, and do it well. This works for them for a short time and then they burn out, regroup and organize their plans, or they seek help from others. Caring for someone is a tough job and everyone is not cut out to do it, and not everyone has the emotional stability to handle the stress and demands of Caregiving.

Caretakers have a 24/7 job... they comfort, they clean, they care for, they speak for their family member. They often put their lives on hold (sometimes for many years) in order to care for their person. This, at times, causes fatigue, stress, anger, sadness, exhaustion, and resentment. Some caretakers would say it's fulfilling and rewarding, but most are not honest about what they are really feeling.

My observation is that most caregivers do find a lot of positive rewards in taking care of someone, but they also have a lot of other emotions that most will not discuss. They will not discuss their feelings because they do not feel it's socially acceptable, so they go through their many days thinking they can get through it without melting down in front of anyone.

I have seen caretakers who decide they've had enough and walk away and leave their family members to be cared for by strangers. Most caregivers have no experience in being a caregiver, and when they look for help there is very little available. Information is available in so many different sources and at different sites. One book has one piece of advice, another book has more advice. Social workers give referrals to caregivers on where the best nursing homes are, in-home help, Medicare, Medicaid, etc. There is so much information without a map on how to find it or interpret it once you find it.

Many caregivers say it's like a puzzle, you get pieces of information and you try to piece it together to form a whole picture. I find it hard to understand why there are so many people going through the same things and there is so little complete information on how to be a caregiver without giving up your own life or giving up on your loved one.

Sometimes, the family member begins to feel like they are a burden to the caregiver and would rather let their health decline then to be a burden to their family member. They feel like they have nothing to contribute to the family and that they have no purpose in living so long. They express how hard it is for them to go on living in a world they can't keep up with or wish to any longer.

Everyone they love has passed away, gone away, or is emotionally away and they feel like they have lost everything of their younger years. Food looses all attractiveness since the taste buds die out and diminish in the aging process.

Caregivers need to give attention to providing nourishing, healthy meals that consist of mainly fruits and vegetables and protein sources. In Lexington, the Good Food's Co-op has a part time dietician that can assist with planning out a diet appropriate for each person. She takes into all factors about the person and their specific needs.

FROM ANONYMOUS

Here is the real deal, but I am blessed everyday...

I had always tried to plan ahead. Ten years ago my parents and I discussed how their later life care should be. I said, "What are your wishes?"

They said they did not want to go to a nursing home, but if I could not care for them then they needed to know that so they could financially prepare for that and save money for long term Elder Care Insurance premiums, which are quite pricey. Dad already had the funeral plans prearranged, even the obituary was written.

We agreed that when the time came, I would care for them in their own house since they had cared for me throughout my life. When the time came, I would sell my business and devote all my time to them. It was agreed that my wife and I would move into their house.

Everything seemed so well planned and tidy. I could see my wife and me living with them as a happy family unit, going out to dinner once a week, and maybe taking in a play from time to time.

I know that, at some point, people must die, but that notion was still not clearly defined in my mind. I just stored it with other 'foggy' notions that I had.

As a retired counselor, I felt like I at least had a leg up on the psychological issues that might arise. I felt pretty content for the moment.

I will spare you a lot of detail about how dad went from a robust, healthy 98 year old man, to suddenly clinging on to life. This was the result of cardiomyopathy and some meds that the cardiologist prescribed that made him worse, literally killing him. His docs, at first, would say things like, "I wish I could be as healthy as you when I reach your age" or "You are perfectly healthy for a man your age." The cardiologist said he thought a pacemaker might make a big difference even at his age. It was at this point where things, little things, seemed to keep going wrong like the pacemaker could not be installed, and much more.

Now dad was in the hospital and I honored my care commitment. That weekend, my wife and I moved everything we owned into their garage and the upstairs of their house. We pushed all belongings into one room and we had another smaller room to sleep in. A third room, we were going to remodel for our TV room. We even began pulling some wallpaper off. It's been over a year now, and not much more has changed. Torn wallpaper still dangles down. We still live amongst the clutter of things brought from home, and we still talk about the remodeling... soon we will get our lives in order, I tell myself.

Within two weeks, my counseling background showed me that we were both in clinical depression. I did react quickly to that, and made appointments to the doctor for meds to help us. Still we would find ourselves just staring at the wall for periods of unknown time, no feeling, just numbness, not understanding where this funk was coming from.

My parents' health changed quickly. As I got to visit several of his docs, I was at first surprised at how dad would love to recite this ritualistic 'woe is me' mantra to them, repeatedly. It would go something like "I just don't know what will happen if I die because my wife won't be able to take care of herself. It will be a hellova mess... just her." He would repeat this to every Hospice worker, every person that walked in the door. Here I have just given up my business, I am already living in a small room of the house, and this is the thanks we get??? These people that he tells this to, fixate their stare like a laser right at me. I just know their minds are asking, "How could we do such a thing... abandoning these sweet elderly people?"

Then there was how he loved to tell all the ladies that would visit, "I have already given my house to my son, so I am at his mercy. He could put me out on the street if he wanted." He glances a sorrowful look and squeezes their hand even tighter. The actual fact is, my dad has never deeded over the house to me, I am the one that could be in the street. Just one brain infarct, and he might give house, and everything, to the 21 year old nurse he fell in love with at the hospital, but that is another story.

I hate misrepresentations, half truths, and outright manipulative lies. My stress level hits new highs. *I rescued my patient from near death three times but he doesn't remember any of it.* The first time was from a catatonic state of depression. And twice by disregarding his docs advice and reducing medications. He was taking 325mg of aspirin, which was causing a significant increase in bleeding during catheterization. The urologist told me bleeding is normal, and with some people more than others, don't worry about it. This time the urine collection jar shows 20 oz of fluid, about half of which appears to be blood. The last save was the time I backed off from the digoxin for his heart. That medicine was spiraling him deeper into nausea, and took away his appetite. The doctor's office said, "It's normal for a patient on digoxin to feel worse for a while before they begin to feel better. Keep him on the digoxin." I took him off digoxin because he was dying anyway. He now is healthy enough to mow the lawn, which I let him do (with supervision).

Mother continues to decline. When I started she seemed almost normal, but bit by bit she declined. Now she's in acute dementia, semi-ambulatory, and incontinent. She sometimes doesn't know who I am or who her husband is. Now she can't communicate, and makes this incessant grunting noise every time she breathes. That can be nerve wrecking. Sometimes the noise sounds like someone struggling for a breath of air, but she makes these sounds purely from habit. Sometimes I find myself starting to mimic her without thinking. I catch myself and reel my brain back into reality. She loves to follow my wife around the kitchen, constantly getting in the way, and literally just one step behind her, a behavior characteristic of dementia. When we finish our chores and can escape upstairs to our room, we just lay down and stare into space... waiting for the next emergency. Mother is up and walking around at all hours of the day and night (maybe sundowner syndrome). Her walking cane comes down hard on the floor with each step... thud... thud... thud... How will I ever get some sleep? My mind struggles for peace and sleep, I hear a crash... mother has fallen. This time nothing is broken.

I am at a loss to describe how I feel except to say it's like someone just sucked the life out of me. A phrase I have also heard from other caregivers. The power of the grip that this depression has is uncanny. I take meds, exercise, and read Bible scriptures more but, now winter is here. I feel myself struggling from its pull like an invisible evil menace that keeps trying to draw you into its deep abyss of nothingness.

I have tried to examine what my internal struggles are all about. For me, the role of caregiver showed me what a vast difference in fundamental ideologies existed between my patient and I (or at least that what I perceived). He was atheist, I was Christian. He was a manipulator, I tried not to be. He was continuously embellishing his life's accomplishments ad-nauseam (another characteristic behavior of aging), I am the opposite. His actions betray his words. With me, my word is my bond. On and on, the list goes.

I just wanted a patient I could respect for having, what I consider, good ideals and family support. I don't appreciate hearing him use the lord's name in vain every time something doesn't suit him. I don't know how many times I have heard him say, "Well, I will be G... damned!" I suspect some day he will get his wish.

It's hard for me to overlook his narcissism. I try to advise him on health issues, but he only listens to either a doctor or nurse in a short skirt. He only hears what he wants to hear. I can only work in the background to keep his health up. Any overt criticism I make becomes fodder for some kind of confrontation with his doctor or hospice. He seems to like pitting me against the medical field. I try to walk this tight rope between the two.

As a counselor, I am also seeing my dad exhibit some disconcerting behavior, which I am sure he is not even aware of. It apparently derives from some childhood sexual and gender issues that ultimately reinforce some strong adult manipulative behavior that is demeaning to both the male and female gender. I won't go into this because I do respect privacy on such a sensitive topic. As a caregiver, you must be alert to subtle behavior changes in your patient, understand them (changes) in terms of their origin, and adjust your feelings towards acceptance (assuming these behavior quirks are non-threatening of course). Acceptance comes from understanding, forgiveness, and love.

Mother is the gentle lamb. She just keeps on going and going. Her diapers have to be changed every few hours and she hates that. She lashes out at me to quit it, and commands me to stop it. When I try to bath her, it's the same thing, but ten times worse. She lashes out like I am killing her... the water is too wet... it's too cold... she is just not going to have any more of this from me! I continue and after all the verbal abuse, she is dry and now smiles, and thanks me. She is happy again... until the next time.

Everything is made more difficult because dad tries to maintain the control he used to have. He wants to question every nickel and dime spent, but I take a firm stand. It's all about control. He loves it when the chaplain from hospice or the minister from the church visits and he can trap them in a debate about 'proving the existence of God.'

Now, the very health of myself and my wife begins to waver. She is having back problems from muscle strain from overuse and now may need to have her gallbladder removed; I just had a spinal operation (decompression) to relieve pinched nerves and sciatica. Why are our bodies breaking down? Some medical articles point to stress. There was a point at which my parents were actually healthier than we were. What an odd situation... our world really was turned upside down. But these are issues that we can get back under control... I think.

But now it's back to the everyday stuff... changing mother's diapers every morning. How many times have I wished that we could just sleep late on a Saturday morning? No, we can't do that. As I cut the diaper away, the stench of ammonia from a pound of urine soaked diaper mixed with the essence of fecal material almost knocks me off my feet. It's almost more than I can handle at times. As I start with the wet wipes to clean off her bottom she lashes out again, "I don't want this! I don't want you doing that so quit it!" My mind wants to lash back with, "I don't want this either, but I am doing it for you so shut up!" But I bite my tongue, smile, and talk to her in soothing baby talk. I finish changing her sweat pants and socks,

53

bag up the diaper, and clean up anything else. The diaper bag gets temporarily thrown outside along with the stench of the urine tainted pants. That is on a 'good day.' On a bad day, there will be diarrhea to contend with, it will be smeared prolifically, like a painter wanting to leave his/her indelible signature. Of course, that means it's shower time, then verbal abuse of the caregiver, cleanup, and often a repeat of what we just did because the anxiety of the shower often causes her to drop some more 'calling cards.' Eventually she wears down and I tuck her into bed so she can sleep. I am worn down also.

In the morning, I give her a hug and take her in for breakfast where she will spend the next hour slowly eating and sleeping with her oatmeal. In three hours it all starts over again. In time, she will lose her motor signals, and won't be able to stand. That will

progress on to difficulty swallowing, and the process of life change continues.

At night, I catheterize my patient for urine. The stench here is almost unbearable at times. He sits on a paper towel that is spotted with smears of feces. He wants to use that same towel, day after day, because that is another penny saved, and waste not want not, etc. He grew up during the Great Depression. My repeated requests for him to use fresh towels clearly carry no medical significance. I purchased a urine test kit for indicating bacteria. I thought I would try to stay on top of that. Years earlier, I had used that for helping my mother know when she had a UTI (urinary tract infection). Then she would call the doctor for an antibiotic Rx, and we stayed on top of that game never letting it get out of control. For dad, the test showed positive for moderate-high levels of nitrogen fixating bacteria. I called his urologist doctor. The urologist tells me to quit my testing for bacteria and just catheterize him twice a day. I have heard from others that this seems to be the urologist's modern approach to controlling infection... contain it but don't try to stop it. Dad's Hospice nurse took a lab sample on two occasions. The lab results were positive for a bacterial infection and a short trial of antibiotics was given. Of course, I knew that was destined to failure because his diapers are always contaminated badly. How can he sit with his penis in a feces coated diaper and NOT be contaminated? Neither the nurse nor doctor seemed to register this concern. The nurse explained the last failed attempt to kill the infection was because the "lab did not correctly identify a resistant strain of bacteria, so this time we will stop the infection because we know what it is." I am politely chastised for overreacting and hospice suggests I stick to the procedure (which doesn't call for preemptive treatment, but only after the fact response... like when the patient develops chills and fever and a death rattle, then call us). I feel helpless, but agree to do the best I can. Today, however, was the exception, and the catheter immediately started an avalanche of semi congealed blood. The infection was back. I thought it would never quit. As a caregiver,

these are some of the situations you might possibly get into.

The solution for soiled diapers is simply to change them... but dad can only accept this instruction from either a person with at least one MD degree, preferably two, or a cute nurse that will hold his hand. Go figure. Strange (maybe not), but true. Everything defies logic in this business.

My point is, despite all the chaos, God is the only unmovable, unwavering rock that stays true for me. Aside from that, Hospice has truly been a blessing and they deserve everybody's (and all of America's) support.

These are some of the situations I never even thought about when I became a caregiver. I envisioned still holding on to my private counseling practice and another small business in some kind of part-time mode, but that was not to be. This job literally keeps you hostage other than stealing a couple of hours to do some quick grocery shopping or banking. And through it all, you wish your efforts would be appreciated by your patients, but they are oblivious to everything. They seem to think of you as being on an extended vacation in their home at their expense.

My patient thinks he still sees and hears well. He knows nothing about the mess he leaves after every meal from spilled food or breakfast syrup from his pancakes making the table sticky like flypaper. He thinks he even cleans his plate as he runs it under the faucet and sets it aside to dry. The syrup is still dripping off the plate. At lunch and dinner my parents are served wonderful home cooked meals made by my Ukrainian wife. These are full of natural fruits, vegetables, meats and cheese. I personally serve dad's favorite ice cream for dessert. I believe there was one occasion when I did hear him say, "That was a good dinner." I feel sorry that he doesn't even acknowledge my wife's meal that took hours to prepare, but he is tuned into the radio headset that he wears almost 24 hours a day. He is in his own safe place. If I ask him a question, he winces like he's been shot as he removes his headset to answer. His unspoken communication is "don't you dare interrupt me!" The first thing he says to the social worker is, "I feel lonely... nobody to talk to." Yeah... right.

As caregivers, we feel so underappreciated and communication can be difficult at best . Mother can't understand a thing spoken to her, and father is infatuated with himself and his great deeds to mankind. He only will 'token' listen, which to me is one of the greatest insults. Often he turns around when I am in the middle of a sentence and walks away, uttering some placebo like, "Well that's fine, fine." I remember one day, telling him my wife was sick today, before I could say another word he's saying, "Well fine, fine" and walks away. But then I think that this is sort of what Jesus went through in a different time and place. Nobody likes a prophet in his own town, everybody knows that. I guess the next step is to look forward to my crucifixion. I am joking.

On the lighter side, there are moments, like the time I had my patient at the doc's office. We are waiting for our turn to sit down at the file clerks station. Another lady was seated in the chair in front of us. My patient turned around, his back side about eye level with the lady, and just lets go of the most humongous line of watery farts. He wasn't even aware of what he was doing because he can't hear very well... it happens all the time with him (hence the expression of endearment "old fart"). The poor lady looked angry, but seemed too pale, weak, and possibly shocked to even complain. She appeared almost catatonic; anyway what can ya say to a 99 yr old man with impaired hearing? I was trying to do the chameleon thing and blend into the wallpaper.

So, Mr./Ms. New Caregiver, this is what it is was really like for us (and continues). For others it is much worse. Their patients may be abusive both verbally and possibly physically combative. Some of them have tics that make them shout out obscene verbiage. Some of them outlive their caretakers whom have become casualties of the stress from relentless demands.

Take comfort, for you caregiving can be much better because you have the benefit of wisdom from those that walked the path before you.

I would like to plan for a vacation with my wife, but know that is impossible. My wife describes this experience like being in prison. Yet this is really our gift, our stepping stone towards the opportunity to learn true caring and what love is all about. I recognize I still have a long way to go in my lesson book, but I thank God that we were judged worthy to be given this opportunity.

I still look forward to my journey as being a pilgrimage for my life. I think about scriptures "through his stripes we are healed" and think that in a similar vein "through our stripes" we become presentable to God... that one day we may enter by that narrow door, the Kingdom.

A FINAL HEADS UP

The last very important thing that probably isn't even on your radar screen at this point has to do with how physically heavy your patient is. One of my patients is 96 lbs., the other one (the healthy one) is about 150lbs. I am athletic and weight over 200 lbs. Normally, I can lift my 96 pound patient up from the floor or bed with ease. But when their health erodes to the point where I was picking up 'dead' weight, then the picture took a real turn. I can still do it, but it is not easy. I know you are already trying to put this in perspective by figuring that you may have picked up an 80lb bag of oats at the farm or an 80 lb bag of concrete mix, and you conclude it wasn't too difficult. What are a few more pounds? Okay... first, the mechanics don't jive with that analogy. You can figure that whatever your patient weighs in the ambulatory stage, you can double that to get

Ben Blyton

an idea of the net 'effective' physical effort when they are totally limp. I really don't know how caretakers with heavy patients manage. My hat goes off to them, as I salute.

> My point is, if you decide to take on this role of being a caretaker, you need to plan ahead for when your patient becomes non-ambulatory and you are lifting dead weight. This is a very important insight for you, but only if you read this, of course ☺. You need to do much planning ahead for this or consider the possibility of a nursing home as a last resort.

Mr. /Ms. Caregiver, are you ready now? Seriously, if you can deal with what you have read in this chapter, then you have a gift. Let that guide you in making the right decision to become a caregiver. Let your light become the light of the world! (PS- If it was easy then everybody would be doing it, right? ☺)

FROM LOIS L

I would say to anyone thinking of doing this, it's the opportunity of a lifetime to really get to know your parents in ways you never did. You will be so blessed by it. By the time my dad was sick and in the hospital, it was the most natural thing in the world for me to rub his head and hands and kiss him and show him all the love I couldn't growing up. It didn't matter that I had become the parent to him for a little while. Toward the end, I was a 67 year old child loving her father and, thankfully, we had made the most of our living together that we possibly could. I had no regrets.

FROM ELIZABETH ANDREWS

When Johnny and I were married, we were very active in our church. That was where the majority of our friends were. We would hang out on trips, events at church or just dinner. We had so much fun and when Johnny and I were at home alone, there didn't seem to be anything lacking. In January of 2007 I began to notice that Johnny was having lapses in memory and seemed "foggy." Other times he would be fine. I made an appointment with our family doctor to see if maybe he was beginning Alzheimer's' or had had a stroke. He was checked over and tests were run but they could find nothing. He seemed to get progressively worse. I couldn't leave him alone, so our friends at church came to lend a hand. I could never tell them enough how much I appreciated their help. I was also contacting every senior center in the area to find out if he could be placed there. He was becoming so weak that eventually it was not an option. I have always been someone who could solve any problem – the go-to-guy, if you will. Finding a solution was not easy and things were changing so quickly I was in a panic. In February he was placed back in the hospital and that was when I began to feel that I was fighting a losing battle. And losing I was, but I would not give up until one of his doctor's told me there was nothing they could do... he was worn out!

I remember one morning shortly after I brought him home, we were lying in bed talking and he suddenly got very quiet. Then he asked me "Am I dying?" I was never so calm as at that moment because I wanted him to be strong. I said quietly, "Yes, are you afraid?" He waited only a moment before replying "A little." I told him not to worry, that I would be with him and his grandparents would be waiting for him. We never spoke of it again.

I had papers drawn up for his power of attorney and will. He could barely sign them, he was so weak.

On April 4, I had him moved to a hospice facility and he died within a week. Friends from church were there at the hospital and at the hospice facility.

After Johnny passed, going to church was one of the hardest things I ever experienced. I would walk into the building or even driving to church hurt tremendously. I pushed back from all our friends and became a recluse. I went to work and came home. I didn't want to be with anyone.

I have relocated to my hometown. Johnny has been gone three years. I hope I am able to move forward – slowly.

FROM BEN BLYTON

COMMENTARY: Understandably, by now you may be having second thoughts about this caregiving thing. Most everybody does sooner or later, but let me share this fact concerning all the caregivers that wrote to me in response to a newspaper column: NOT ONE SINGLE PERSON SAID THEY REGRETTED THE EXPERIENCE!! Everyone has a hard time at first, and then makes sacrifices of the life and times they once had. You lose friends, your freedom, your privacy, your will, and whatever pleasures you can think of, they too become a casualty. This is just a natural part of the social structure of life. Your patients will never understand your world just as you will never understand their world. They will never understand your sacrifices, and when your experience comes to an end, when you are ready to graduate, you realize you have been given a priceless gift. You have learned to love that which took your life, but gave it back to you. If the world could learn this lesson, there would be no war and no famine. Feel blessed and KNOW that God has chosen you for this gift.

DON'T ASSUME HELP FROM THE FAMILY

SIBLINGS OFTEN SAY "NOBODY ELSE SEEMS WILLING TO HELP"

Recognize that this behavior syndrome is caused by two main elements:

1) Lack of communicative understanding and 2) lack of a structure.

Do this:

a) Identify manageable and doable jobs into however many categories there are potential helpers. b) Assign one person (probably you) to be the boss overseeing that everything gets done within reason and does some duties. Everybody needs to participate in some way even if it's just a minuscule amount. This builds structure and facilitates communicative understanding.

THREE THINGS TO KNOW ABOUT NON-HELPERS (family, friends)

1. Non-helpers in a family are passive as long as someone else is doing the job (this translates as "don't expect any volunteers").

2. Non-helpers totally underestimate the difficulty of the job.

3. Non-helpers don't have a safe place in the overall structure of the caregiving experience they don't know where or how to contribute in a positive manner so they default to what they perceive to be "constructive criticism" which ends up being counterproductive to a team approach. (That's just a formal way of saying your brother or sister ain't gonna help ya one bit, but they will gladly criticize everything you do.)

The underlying idea is that no one wants to be a heel. They just need to be walked to the water trough and hand-fed once or twice before they can actually be part of the solution. Sometimes even that doesn't work.

Be sure you state explicitly what a sibling's job duty is and praise them when they actually do it.

If they still refuse to help, just know that for whatever reason they are fighting with their own demons and tell God you would like some bonus points for your extra work. He is good with giving extra points.

CHAPTER 3
THE TEN COMMANDMENTS OF CAREGIVING

As we have opportunity, let us do good to all people,
especially to those who belong to the family of believers.

Galatians 6:10

1) BE READY TO MAKE FIRM, FIRM, FIRM AND QUICK DECISIONS

The second most favored topic was a plea for good advice, aka a 'plan' in the beginning of being a caregiver. In this chapter, you will find my **Ten Commandments of Caregiving**, followed, of course, by the most common mistake every new caregiver makes. I decided to make this the real number one 'must' do, because without it, none of the others will get done... and you can take that to the bank.

The crux of the entire issue is that you have GOT to separate the warm, fuzzy, 'Mr. Nice Person' feelings, from the wisdom of that cold-hearted 'Caregiver.' Mr./Mrs. Nice Person wants to believe the pleading and assurances of his/her parents who demonstrate responsible, logical behavior at this time. Mr./Mrs. Nice Person agrees to let everything just be for now. "We can wait until we get closer to witnessing impaired functioning before implementing unpopular changes," he/she reasons.

Let me ask you, if your inability to act quickly on wisdom were to result in the accidental death or suffering of your patient, an innocent bystander, would you ever be able to sleep again? Could you ever excuse your failure to function responsibly? This is the toughest part you may have to face, but sooner or later the inevitable patient deterioration occurs, surreptitiously at first, but then it's suddenly in your face. Are you going to be a caregiver that will ACT or REACT? INNOCENT LIVES DEPEND ON YOUR CHOICE. Be prepared for plenty of dialoguing to sell your ideas. This MUST be a one-sided discussion (your side).

I know you have already thought about how your new caregiver life will be, but you are going to miss that by a mile. Instead, I want you to anticipate empathetic communication challenges. *At each turn, how will you change a frown into a smile?* How will you deny your patients strongest and often vehement protests without getting into a confrontational battle? IF... you are always armed with a few suitable clichés, then putting your FIRM decision into action is easier. For example: "You have to leave the kitchen now so we can get it cleaned and ready for you later." Of course, whatever you say, you should also simultaneously be backing it up by gently leading the patient toward another room or area. Or use the 'wall clock' as the authority: "Well, the clock on the wall says it's time to take our nap now." Ya get the picture?

THOUGHT TO REMEMBER

YOU DIDN'T TAKE ON THIS RESPONSIBILITY TO BE POPULAR BUT BECAUSE YOU CARE.

Now go out and prove it.

---

2) SECURE ALL THE CAR KEYS—NOW!!

Okay, so it's not going to be easy to ask for your patients' keys when they adamantly claim they can still drive proficiently. I couldn't do it at first. Then, there was a car accident, but thankfully nobody was hurt. Still, I didn't ask for the keys.

Then, there was a fainting spell at the grocery and a 911 call. This time, I took quick and decisive action, but look at how stupidly irresponsible I was. Others could have lost their lives because I was not making the tough decisions.

Explain it this way to your patients: "When I made the commitment to become your full-time caregiver, I also had to assume the role of making management decisions. I understand that you are having trouble giving up your last bit of independence, but it is something I do because of my love for you. There is no further discussion on this issue. Maybe you would like to ride with me when it's time to go to the grocery?"

3) GET POWER OF ATTORNEY NOW!—A BIG MUST DO

Okay, I know you and your patients have already agreed to transfer power of attorney when the time comes, but here's the fly in the ointment: When the time approaches, several things are likely to happen. First, the aging parent's way of thinking will most likely have changed. Often it is toward paranoia, which means they don't want to let go of POA (power of attorney) because they feel less secure. They may worry that you will start making donations to every charitable group that comes along, or maybe buy a new TV, etc. In fact, what will most likely happen as the patient ages is that they will be the ones burning the mail order pages and giving large donations to charitable representatives that have learned to 'tune in' to their personal needs.

Secondly, you assume that the moment you get POA, you can keep the tribe fed by writing checks at the local grocery... wrong. Well, eventually you can, but first you will have to file 'original' documents that your attorney has drawn up for you to be POA. It seems like everyone wants an 'original' document. Hospitals also want the original document, and even pharmacies. Now, once you present the original documentation to your bank, it still will not be a done deal. Often there is a required waiting period. This could be ten business days (I have never understood a business day but I think it's however long a business needs to take when they have your money) or longer. That's a long, long time if the cupboard is bare.

Anticipate some real objection from the patient to giving you POA. To help their comfort level, suggest that you will jointly meet with their attorney to have him provide whatever legalese is needed to make the patient feel secure, but at the same time allow you to function, unimpeded, as POA. Any good attorney should know how to do this.

Once you have POA, you need to add your name to the banking account as POA. Then, I suggest you get a bank debit card issued to you in your name. For instance, I have a bank debit card issued by my own bank but with the Visa logo. I use it as a credit (not debit card). This will give you the flexibility of transferring monies from one account into another for bill paying, plus you can use it like a regular bank credit card e.g. Visa. Ask your bank for details.

PS: I would also have the attorney update any living wills. Always carry a copy of your living wills, POA, and copies of any recent, pertinent medical files in your car. The hospital may need this stuff just to admit your patient.

4) DO IT NOW!

Take care of any personal needs you have been putting off such as getting a tooth filled, getting any elective surgical options taken care of.

The reason: After a short time as a caregiver, you WILL be in some reduced state of mental functioning. That is a given. In due time, you might stare at the wall or sleep for hours on end with no motivation for doing anything. It's coming... you have been forewarned... and it will still get ya! But the good news is that since you know what to expect you can go to UR doc and get some happy time meds (seriously...do this...one sign of depression is the denial that anything is wrong...deeper depression is the insistence that nothing is wrong).

Make those doctor appointments you have been putting off now. Also have your doctor note your frame of mind. Tell the doctor that you are now in a caregiver role, and soon may need evaluation for antidepressant meds (more on that later). You want time to begin the evaluation right now, so when you hit depression city he can prescribe meds on the spot. Normally there is about a 4-6 week evaluation period from the time you tell a doctor that you are in need of an antidepressant to the time when they will be released to you.

5) REMOVE AREA RUGS

Understandably, this will be difficult because of all the memories that go with them. The danger, of course, is that the aging patient often begins to lose muscle memory bit by bit. Sooner or later they will trip and fall. Not good. Tell the patient you are putting the rugs away for winter storage or sending them out for cleaning, etc. For the difficult to let go situations, I recommend rolling the rug up and covering it like you are waiting to send it to the cleaners.

It may take weeks, or even a month or two, but sooner or later they will just forget about the rug. Then store it in the garage or wherever. I was unsure on this at first because my patient protested so much, but when mother fell (luckily, she was unhurt) that was enough.

I know you want to be the perfect caregiver that keeps everybody happy all the time. That won't happen, so please change that mindset now. I tried to keep everybody happy too. I agreed to keep the last large area rug that was hand braided by my grandmother. As hard as I tried to put spin on that issue, I failed. I let my mother keep this rug, with all its memories, as I constantly worried about someone tripping on it or my incontinent mother wetting on it and how would I know? As I write this, I must confess what a failure I was on this one issue. I have just hauled that big rug, with all its memories, out to the curb. Yep, you guessed it... mother just dumped on it big, big time. I believe it was the milk of magnesia that loosened her up. I only gave her an ounce one day and one ounce the day before, then wham! ...when you least expect it. I can't even imagine how she accomplished this without filling her diapers. The diapers were supposed to be my primary defense for this sort of accident.

> One point for you to absorb is no matter how well you plan for things, the patient will occasionally find some way to thwart your best efforts. Well, this is just part of the aging process, and I accept that.

If I practiced what I know now, that rug would have been rolled up and wrapped for storage despite all the protests my patient could have mustered up! Let my experience guide you towards smoother sailing.

6) NO MORE LIVING ON A SECOND FLOOR

There are always people telling me that their patient has been living on the second floor for years with no problems. Some say buy a Stairmaster. Okay, there are always exceptions to everything but the safest approach is to put everybody on the first floor. Of course, a basement or lower level will have to have an appropriate lockset to prevent the patient from having a potentially fatal stairway fall. Again, I didn't think mother's health was a liability yet. Wrong. At work, I got the call from 911 asking what hospital I wanted my mother taken to. She had fallen upstairs, hit her head, and was bleeding profusely. She recovered, but that was enough for me to move both of my parents' beds downstairs that very day.

I realize that it is best to keep patients in their familiar surroundings, but there are exceptions, and this is one. Put the patient downstairs and you, the caregiver, move upstairs.

Stairway elevators can work, but they require additional safeguards to prevent the patient from falling when entering or exiting the lift. Of course, there is no such thing as a fool proof system. It is just a question of how much risk are you willing to take for a short term gain. *They are best suited for someone younger than 70 whom has the faculties to accurately control their balance.* After the age of 70, life changes are too unpredictable. Your patient may be fine getting in and out of a stairway elevator one day and the next day they fall head-first down the stairs. Now you have allowed a preventable accident and you have wasted a lot of money on the elevator.

Once more, please let the guiding principal be that if they were in 'dependable' (and that's the operative word) health, then you wouldn't be taking care of them.

7) CHANGE YOUR MINDSET NOW

It's so easy to look at seemingly healthy parents and be lulled into that fantasy vision. I mean, they can communicate rather normally at first. Dad assures me he will drive extra safe, and it all seems so unnecessary to upset him for no firm, visible cause. Right? I mean, I can't even make a case against changing the status quo. What right have I to tell my parents what they can or cannot do? I tell myself, "Maybe I should wait until something a little scary happens so then I can have substance to support my case." This is the mark of a follower, not a leader. You do NOT have the luxury nor the right of being a follower. You must take charge!

Before you know it, your patient will have an accident or stroke. Mental functioning can change in a heartbeat, and often without you knowing it. You cannot wait for the car wreck, the stair fall, or hip break from tripping on that pretty area rug. Remember, almost any kind of fall for a person of frail health could be fatal. If they break a hip, the chances for a survivable outcome are not too great either.

Both you and your patient object to change, not only because of different value systems, but also because of different experiential environments. Simply translated, that means that you and your patient will be at odds forever, until you develop the winning strategy.

The winning strategy is when you get your 'must do's' done and your patient is are cool with everything you did... pretty much anyway.

They will never be happy with change, so just do the best you can. Remember, it's your ball game now—not theirs.

So much has been written about the gentle art of persuasion that I don't think you need to hear it again. You know what to do. Do it. You will backslide from time to time, and that's normal. When you do, you must work hard to regain control. Don't just throw in the towel and become a victim also. Caregiving is about real world emotions and feelings. Your character is what you do with these emotions and feelings. *The strategy now, is to play to win, and your patients are going to put a full court press on you to see that you fail.* Although, they aren't aware they are doing any such thing, of course ☺.

8) PROTECT YOUR PATIENT FROM HAZARDOUS CONDITIONS

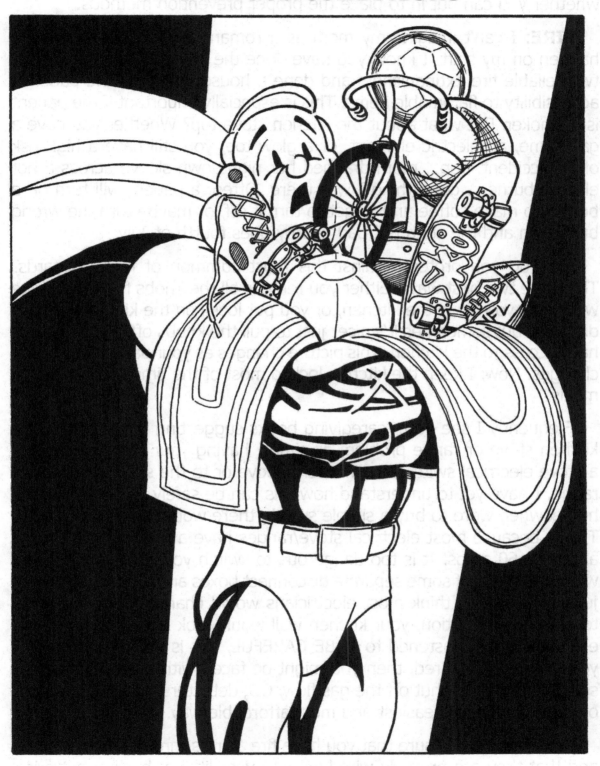

Somewhere between then and now, your patient will do something dangerous that was foreseeable and preventable. It's just a race to see whether you can put in to place the proper prevention methods.

FIRE: I can't imagine my mom as a roman candle. That just won't happen on my shift. I know you have done the obvious, bought at least two reliable fire extinguishers and done a house check for the patient's accessibility to flammable items. This is especially important if the patient is a smoker. But what about the kitchen stove top? Whether you have a gas flame, an electric element, or a glow top, you still have a high risk of an accident. Yep... mom dragged her nightgown sleeve across a hot electric burner... good thing I was there. Often, a patient will turn on a burner to make coffee and forget to turn it off, or maybe turn the wrong burner on and the cloth hot pad nearby goes fourth of July.

How do you protect against this most common of home hazards? There are two best ways. Either you remove all the knobs from the range whenever you leave the kitchen, or you put locks on the kitchen doors. I did both, but sometimes it's nicer just to pull the knobs off and let people have access to the kitchen. This picture changes as your patient's behavior changes. Now, I keep the kitchen locked most of the time, except during meals.

Frequently I see other caregiving books suggesting a quick fix to the kitchen stove or range problem as simply having your electrician install a stove electrical switch out of reach, above or to the side of the stove/range. I have yet to understand how this can be safely done. If you, the homeowner, were to buy a simple switch, there would be a fire for sure. This is because most electrical stove/ranges have a max current flow of about 40-60 amps. It is too dangerous to switch your range on and off without the use of some separate disconnect boxes and a contactor circuit just to be safe. I think most electricians would charge about $400-699 to do this. In addition, your kitchen wall would look hideous with all the electrical (s)crap fastened to it. BE CAREFUL, this is not an easy job. If your range is gas fired, then you might be faced with expensive electric solenoid valves to shut off the gas flow, CO_2 detectors, etc. Again, taking off the knobs is the easiest and most affordable way.

Remember to be sure that you have fire alarms throughout the house and that they are properly wired with 10 year lithium backup batteries.

If they are stand alone units, make sure they have the 10 year lithium battery. Buy the cheap ones if you have to. Get them and pray they work. Sometimes a prayer is better than a hope.

9) PROTECT YOUR KITCHEN AND BATHROOM FROM BEING FLOODED—A BIG $$$ RISK!

It will happen sooner or later. Your patient will turn on a faucet for some reason, walk away, and the water is flowing at a full clip. In a short time, your floor will be flooded, and then the sub floor, and then any rooms below that. Having been involved in home inspections, I can tell you this is one way to establish mold growth that may ultimately involve removing extensive parts of the house... not cheap in this day and age. **FAILURE TO TAKE ACTION HERE MAY COST YOU THOUSANDS OF DOLLARS LATER!**

The solution is simple. First reduce the flow rate by a third (by that little valve under the sink) on both the hot and cold side of the supply water. Then, if you are working with the kitchen sink, you remove the strainers and replace them with new ones. You can get these from the hardware store. Tell the salesman you need to be able to completely remove the center boss pin that normally allows for the big rubber stopper underneath the strainer to stop water flow for soaking dishes. Tell him you want to throw away the rubber stopper and center pin. My home depot guy said, "I think this plastic strainer will work, but the center pin won't come out, sorry." I included this because so often sales people are well intentioned, but are not really focused on success. I bought the two strainers, and a big pair of pliers easily broke off the center pin. Now you have a strainer with holes for easy water flow and that cannot be used as a stopper for the sink. Of course, your spouse will complain that they can't pick up the strainer without the center pin to hold. That will pass to ☺!

Now, for the bathroom sinks, you have a lever operated stopper. Get under the sink and press the release clips that will allow you to slide the sink stopper completely out of the sink. Throw this away.

You have now protected the value of your home more than you can ever imagine. Good luck and sleep better.

10) EMERGENCY CONTACT NUMBERS

Make a list of people that are capable and willing to provide service and other caregivers in these areas:

RELIEF CAREGIVERS

Find as many as you can (which will probably be one or two), because chances are, when you get ready to use them, they will be working for someone else or any number of things according to Murphy's Law.

Find at least one person that you feel will be reliable enough to serve at a moment's notice in case of an emergency. Of course, you should offer them a premium pay rate for being 'on call' so to speak. If your patient's needs become more unpredictable, you might consider paying this 'on call' person around $5/hr just to 'be readily available' should you call. Then, if you do call, you should pay them around $25/hr for their services. Of course, you would only pay the 'on call premium' during the brief time that your patient is in crisis resolution. That's cheap insurance when you need help.

In general, you can expect to pay $10 per hour and up for a 'sitter.' A sitter is a person who will know how to change diapers, give sponge baths, cook meals, and maybe do the washing. That rate is in Kentucky, but many people are caught so off-guard with caregiving. They will pay practically anything sometimes. I have been there and done that also. I understand. Don't let any caregiver in Kentucky say the going rate is $15 or $20 per hour. You are the buyer, and what you offer sets the going rate in your household. Other seasoned caregivers are also paying $10 per hour, and most of the time, they really have little demand placed upon them. Also, I have two patients, but unless there are special demands such as "don't let the patient move out of your sight," one sitter should be able to handle both for the same fee or slightly more if you declare their wages. One sitter I had decided that she should get twice as much for just watching over two people. She wanted $20/hr. I told her she is absolutely worth it and I wished her good luck as she was leaving.

To find a sitter call your local elder care facility. Then contact your church. If you place an ad in the paper or on the internet you don't know what kind of background you are going to get. Usually word of mouth to some church members gets around pretty quick.

OUTSIDE NURSING AGENCIES OR INDEPENDENT HEALTH CARE AGENCIES

Contact at least one, and have any preliminary paperwork already filled out. This agency might be able to dispatch an RN or aide to work with your patient's constipation problem for example (assuming you are not able to). These agencies generally charge around $125/hr for an RN to visit a patient. Some have minimum clock time charges also. Remember, when you need help, get help now, and worry about paying the bills later. Your patient will thank you.

You need at least one home health care agency that is of the 'stand-alone' type. This means they have their own medical doctor so you don't have to find your doctor in the middle of the night in the event of an emergency. To your patient, this is very important because he/she may not be able to wait until the next day when your family doctor is back in the office and can write Rx's and order tests. The alternative is to use the 911 call and let the EMT's take your patient to the hospital (note: if you don't have insurance, the base actual billed rate on the EMT service is about $800—more on that later). I am sure they will also work with you on a payment plan if you have a fixed income, but check for your locale. This could become an important issue if your insurance, or lack thereof, does not cover EMT runs, your patient's health status is not stable, or you anticipate several calls to 911 during your care.

UTILITY REPAIR SERVICES

Maybe it really is a 'dark and stormy night' in the middle of winter and ice causes falling tree limbs to knock out power to your neighborhood. This could take hours or days to fix. Who ya gonna call?

Remember, most utility companies only have service obligations to restore power to the mast head (where the overhead power lines go down or underground lines go up a pipe to the electric meter) on the outside of your house. If you had the entire mast head brought down by a tree limb, you will have to find an electrician willing to be there and work before the power can be restored. In the case of something like a lightning strike, you may need extensive help from an electrician. If money is no object, you just hit the yellow pages and tell the first contractor these magic words "cost is no object." For the rest of us, electrical and plumbing rates, especially in an after-hours situation, can run anywhere from $75/hr to $400/hr. Electricians and plumbers usually work in pairs also ☺.

The point is, please have established contact with a repairperson whom others in the community have high regard for (or at least have nothing against).

Tell the contractor that you are a caregiver, yadda yadda yadda, and would he be willing to not exceed the price of _____ per hour, plus the cost of materials? (I would think $80-$125 per hour for an emergency call out on a dark and stormy night is reasonable but not $400).

COMMIT THIS PHONE NUMBER TO MEMORY

911

THE MOST COMMON CAREGIVER MISTAKE

In psychiatry, there exists a phenomenon that has puzzled scientists for centuries. We know that it involves interactions between the brain and one's environment. It involves the repeated and predictable patterns that we all make. Some say, it eschews out of man's higher learning centers in the prefrontal cortex for programmed behavior. It is universal and self-inflicting. I submit to you that Steven Covey (author of *The Seven Habits of Highly Successful People*) would explain it this way: "We all think we see the world as it really is, but we do not.....rather we see the world as we are."

From my years of study, I have refined the root cause for the caregiver's most common mistake. I will reveal it to you on the following page. (Note: Sensitive minds may want to avoid pain by shifting into ol' denial mode.) The caregiver's most common mistake is a pattern and it's known as...

STUPIDITY

85

It's our pattern for failure. I know I am being a bit hard on you, but it's really just tough love from me to you. You can thank me later.

Yes, it's truly amazing how I can tell you 10 things that you must do to survive caregiving and you will do precisely none of them in a timely manner. Like myself, I let my heart override objective decision making. I failed to communicate to my parents that, as a caregiver, I would be making decisions many times against their wishes. Failing to get their understanding, I tried the next best thing (I thought). I decided to act as mediator when we all agreed there was a problem. Then, I would have the evidence and group support to make changes and still be loved like a puppy. Dumb, dumb, dumb on me! How stupid could I be?(don't answer).

Remember the old adage "once bitten, twice shy?" For me this became "constantly bitten, still stupid." I promise to do better.

That is flawed logic! Is it okay to wait until a patient wrecks the family car maybe causing loss of life to innocent bystanders before I can prove that taking the keys away is justified? Is it okay to wait for my mother to fall down the steps before I can justify telling her that she must live downstairs from now on? My experience has shown me that, even after the fact, your patient will not change their outlook on giving up those keys or whatever. Now I can understand why. It is because you and I assume our patient will always have a rational mind, forgetful, but rational. A rational mind begets rational behavior right? Not in dementia. Forget everything you know based on logic. *You will never be loved like a puppy again. Get over it and do the work that God sent you here to do. Don't fail him... love him.*

Why are we all so needy that we risk the lives and safety of others just to redeem ourselves with our patients when we need to take an unpopular action? We want to be loved by our patient for the rest of our lives, don't we? But the truth is... in a short while, our patients will most likely no longer remember us. Perhaps they will think we are the enemy, or at best not remember what it was all about. *This is the time in your life that you open your heart to God's love. Believe it. Know it, and never doubt it.*

I can tell you this... and you will think about it... and you will agree mostly... but you will be powerless to change your pattern for failure. I was unable to change things before a wreck AND a fall had occurred. I wanted to be loved not despised (and I did not have this book to read). Now, please go do the RIGHT thing...force a change to succeed!

CHAPTER 4
R U RED E? EL I B THEN
LETTUCE GIT R DUN!

(Early language of KENTUCKY VALLEY SETTLEMENTS)

> Keep alert, stand firm in your faith, be courageous,
> be strong. Let all that you do be done in love.
>
> 1 Corinthians 16:13-14

BEFORE YOU MOVE IN

'Satus locus'

(I think that means 'starting point')

A TOUGH LOVE CAREGIVER AGREEMENT

(if you don't have some form of this, you might regret it later)

"Why would anyone want an agreement? I mean, I have known my parents all my life, I trust them."

At some point your parent's brain deterioration will produce changes that they will deny. Suddenly you become super bad because you want to take the car keys away, or move them into bedrooms on the first floor of the house. Don't think they are going to take their new changes lightly. Often that is when the parent reads the riot act to the caregiver and threatens to kick *them* out.

I strongly recommend that back when you and your parents sit down to discuss final care that you tell them you will be their caregiver and you will probably have to make job and income sacrifices to do this, but you will gratefully do it and welcome the opportunity to give back to them.

The Tough Love Contract, Part I

This is a non-binding signed document which you write that reminds the parent they have given you the right to make decisions on their behalf.

If you don't have something (anything) in writing, you will most likely end up sacrificing your day job only to have your parents tell you later to bug off because they didn't like some condition you have imposed such as no driving, no cooking, they must live on first floor, etc.

I would say something like "I am going to be making a big sacrifice to take care of you. I am looking forward to it. But in order for me to do my job, you must assure me in return that I can make the final decision in anything that I need to do to maintain your safety and well being. I need you to sign this simple one line agreement that you will do this." Explain that the only reason you are asking them to sign this is because a year from now they may not remember the agreement and hopefully they can understand that.

An agreement gives you hard copy proof that they have given you power. It could come in very handy later if things go South in the relationship. It gives you a rock to stand on.

Make copies and keep in your bank lockbox. With all the confusion going on at home, you will never find important documents when you need them. You might even frame it and hang it in plain sight, your choice.

This agreement will also give you great peace should you ever have to put your parents into a state or private nursing home because they refuse to follow their agreement. Without this, you might always be in a verbal dual about what they want and what you want. If you don't let them have their way then "you must leave this house immediately." I have been told of that happening from time to time.

Remember, your patient's mind can go downhill fast and the changes in behavior can be a big shock. You can be your parent's hero/heroine one month and the next month you are something

unspeakably foul and being cursed at. If you waited to this point, forget the signing and just do the best you can until the ship sinks.

Caregiving is a catch-22 in some ways. You are often damned if you do (enforcing safety) and damned if you don't (overlooking clear and present danger). For example, allowing repeated and erratic driving may be considered criminal negligence should either the patient or a bystander gets hurt. If your sweet, innocent patient takes the car out and causes a personal injury you can pretty well assume that your patient, yourself, your pet, and anybody within sight will be the object of a lawsuit. I have heard of one patient who had six spare sets of car keys cleverly hidden from their caregiver. You may spend all of your patient's money and all of your money defending your patient and yourself. If the case goes south for you, then your patient may lose all his/her property in a settlement.

You cannot afford to risk getting into a position of liability or negligence ! ! !

This agreement helps you to more easily, pull the car keys or whatever without losing your caregiving role. Just pull the document and tell your parents "you agreed to my decisions, I have made great sacrifices for you and now it's your turn to make sacrifices for me."

In the unlikely event they absolutely refuse to sign, you now have early warning that your path is going to be rocky. You could be the best intentioned caregiver in the world and still get sued for negligence because of your parent's abusive behavior. The stress will be constant, and your job and personal life will suffer.

The ugly truth is that you are going to eventually have to give up your day job, suffer chronic depression, endure marital stress, lose most of your savings and at various points in time your internalized stress will be a contributing factor to numerous deteriorating physical, emotional, and mental changes. Not to mention that when you do emerge from your completed caregiving experience you will likely discover you will never ever be the same person again... (a condition almost as bad as this run-on sentence, sigh).

I can never forget the moment when my mother had fallen (upstairs) and hit her head. She was bleeding profusely, rushed to the hospital, and ultimately repaired, with a long painful recovery. That might not have happened if I had enforced my rules and made her live downstairs in a safer environment, but she had soooo politely promised me that she would be very careful if I would just let her climb the stairs to her room.

She was just so sweet, I mean how could anyone say no to her plus she did *promise* to be careful. So really now, I wasn't all that much to blame, was I?

Almost every caregiver I know has, at one time or another, fallen into this trap with their parents. Each side was well intentioned. But as a caregiver you must realize that your patient's ability to assess and evaluate danger continues to diminish with age. It won't be noticeable at first and you are suckered in. There are times when the caregiver becomes the patient's greatest danger.

Each caregiver has an implicit duty to take the high moral road and, leaving emotions aside, do the responsible thing to protect their patient.

This is what you can look forward to many times over if you are not able to take **full** control of the safety of your patient. It's irresponsible on the patient's behalf and irresponsible on your behalf to not implement full safety control. Remember, they are no longer able to objectively assess the dangers in the world around them. If you can't do it, then you must walk the path you choose.

The Tough Love Contract, Part II

This is a collection of three binding legal agreements (refer to the section on Estate planning).

Before the caregiver can be effective they **must** have empowerment authorized by the patient giving the caregiver (or other family member) **POWER OF ATTORNEY** (POA), **MEDICAL POWER OF ATTORNEY** (MPOA), and a **LIVING WILL** (LW).

I can't overstate the importance of having these three agreements. The pitfall is that your patient, presently healthy, will argue against giving up control to you. That is to be expected. Your patient will stall for more time. Then, one day, you notice small changes in your patient's behavior and before you know it, they no longer can demonstrate legal capacity; they can no longer sign the three documents listed above. Consider your goose thoroughly cooked now. You can do nothing until you hire an attorney and try to get legal guardianship status (no easy job).

When you reach out to your patient during the early stage when they still have legal status, remember the scriptures "speak only to those who have ears to hear." In other words, if your patient won't "pay the fee" (sign the documents), then they can't "ride the train" (be taken care of).

It is with great love that I reach out to you with the following advice: If your patient will not grant you the authority you need, then consider discussing placement into a nursing home when the time comes.

I know that this may seem contra to your mission of service, but sometimes we can best serve by putting our patient in an environment where they cannot hurt themselves or others.

All too often the caregiver thinks that things will change and the patient will gradually see the light and turn over the POA to you. They might even suggest that too. **Be forewarned, "that dog just won't hunt."** You may give up your career, your health, and much more just to discover that in the "end game," you have been shut out and your patient no longer can make legal decisions. In fact, they might even "abhor" you or no longer know you. Now you are the victim—you are jobless and in poor health.

God wants us to learn to make the right decisions that someday we all may be able to care for each other in a loving way. Sometimes these lessons are difficult and come with a great price. Others may feel our lesson is to learn compassion through our own suffering. The correct lesson is the one that you are led to choose through careful prayer. Making a decision to put parents in a nursing home is sometimes a necessary and compassionate choice. Ask for guidance through your prayers.

YO DAWG! TO BEGIN, LET'S FOCUS ON SOME BASICS

(more articulate language of today)

YOUR GOLDEN RULE ABOUT WISDOM:

Learn from the mistakes of others

LIFE LESSONS: THINGS I 'SHOULDA, WOULDA, COULDA'
DONE DIFFERENTLY

I just love those three little words... they are like permits to be irresponsible.

In the last book my mother passed. By the time this book is finished, either my father will have passed or I will (just joking!). Here are things I wish I could have done differently.

I wish my favorite little words had been: I will, I won't , I can't. Despite my best efforts at planning ahead, I still totally missed my opportunity at preplanning. These areas include not being ready with dad's investment portfolio, not having already put into place a more austere budget control, and most of all not having realized from the git-go that I cannot still operate my own office and be a caregiver (but in theory it shoulda worked perfectly).

Caregiving is an imperfect world—it tests the patient and the caregiver.

At times, I can't help but feel that this was what it was like to be a Roman gladiator. You courageously fought against the odds with rules that could be changed on a whim. Victory was balanced on the thin edge of your impromptu game plan. Failing to quickly and decisively act would be the last curtain call for you.

Once I made the decision to close down my office and move my books out, it still took a month of work just to review all my files to see which I could or could not throw away. I should have closed the office down 6 months ago, but I kept hoping somehow I could make it work. You most likely will be repeating my mistake by now... not. Learn from my mistakes. Get pro-active now!

Somehow we are still living like pack rats. We seem to move our baggage from one room to another and then back. This gives us the feeling of moving forward, hopefully towards neatness which I have decided belongs to the unobtainable state of nirvana. Where does the time go???

I SHOULD HAVE PLANNED MORE FOR THESE AREAS:

1. Repairs to the house

2. Reviewing with our attorney issues about probate court

3. Cleaning out the garage from all the never used stuff my wife and I brought with us when we moved in

4. Cleaning out all the stuff after my mother died. She had only about half the books I had, but she had cornered the market on handmade clothing.

5. Completing unfinished business that I never anticipated, e.g. confirming that a burial plot had in fact been prepaid and prerecorded.

6. I had never anticipated the ups and downs of working with a great company such as Hospice. I wish I had understood the real pecking order and how decisions were made so I could have been a little more effective in supporting my own choices of care management with regard to medications, etc.

7. I should have spent earlier times studying my patient's documents, especially his investment portfolio, and whether it was even remotely appropriate for us. Turns out it was not even close to being appropriate. When the market tanked in late 2008 so did all the financial resources… didn't count on that. Nope… that one bit me like a snake in the grass). Last but certainly not least, I never thought to consider that as I transition to becoming a caregiver, I just coincidentally happened to be in the age range where health issues become almost commonplace. For example, I never dreamed with all my exercising, I would be at that age where blood clots can happen… and did. That put me in the hospital for a week and made a cripple out of me for months after that. Who knew? I "shoulda" known, but tell me how I "coulda" known something like that would happen?

Do a reality check on yourself from time-to-time to see if you are in a delusional dream state. It's a luxury your patient can't afford.

8. I should have realized that kicking depression requires active

commitment... it doesn't just happen (unless you can stay on meds). Our emotional states never really got much higher than mild depression. We still find ourselves staring at the walls at times or finding a total lack of desire to do anything, but this also saves on renting DVDs. This was alleviated significantly by joining an exercise facility where I have a schedule for exercising three times a week. This provides structure and helps to insure commitment.

Exercise outside the home as often as possible. You just might live longer. In fact, according to a recent study, a caregiver should exercise at least thirty minutes every day to offset the daily stress of being a caregiver.

YOUR GOLDEN RULE ABOUT SENIORS:

You cannot trust the senses of a geriatric patient, period.

My patient amazes visitors with his apparent mental clarity. He still gets distinguished awards from groups he has served with in the past. Clearly he/she should get a pass on everything, right? I mean, just being old should be entitlement to whatever the patient wants, shouldn't it?

Wrong! My patient promised (after taking some timed response motor skill tests) that **he would never drive again**. "Fine with me and it's a done deal," I happily replied as I gloated over my easy victory. "Caregiving is not so difficult," I thought to myself.

A few days later my patient was involved in a car crash driving to get his favorite BBQ chicken. Fortunately, nobody was seriously hurt. I mentally kicked myself for being so irresponsible.

This time I made my patient promise to really, really, really never drive again. "That should do it," I thought. The next day, I got a call from the hospital... seems he drove to get his favorite num-nums to eat for supper and fainted at the store.

The actions of your patient will be the consequences of your actions.

This time there was no discussion, no more promises, I just rounded up all the car keys. I felt a new sense of empowerment and from then on each time I resisted the 'status quo' and opted to do the 'right and responsible' thing I felt my strength grow. I felt my commitment as a caregiver to my patient become stronger and more meaningful. I felt truly useful and needed.

For the newbie caregiver, on our best days, we can barely see through the fog of all our preconditioning, rules, and charms to assess the reality before us.

Doing nothing is so easy to default to and that always makes everybody happy until... sumpthin' hits tha fan.

I recommend setting forth a set of basic rules for your patient such as no driving, no going upstairs alone, no cooking, no falling, etc. **As your patient's mind begins to revert more towards deductive reasoning, they will fail to heed some of these rules.** This gives you a measuring stick to take action for which there cannot be any second chances given. You are doing this to protect them. They will never understand and will defend their clarity with great vehemence at times. Remember, there can be no passes, second chances, or 'get out of jail free' coupons; just rein in your control.

Making tough and unpopular decisions reveals a kind and compassionate caregiver. Anything less is inexcusable.

SETTING A BASELINE FOR YOUR PATIENT'S HEALTH

Let me emphasize that you need to become more knowledgeable about anything that affects your patient's health. Go to the nearest bookseller or pharmacy and buy one of those 'complete drug listing' manuals. Read up on any meds your patient is currently taking and any that he/she might be taking in the near future. Know what side effects to look for and what combination of meds might be harmful. Learn at what times to take meds and without which foods. For example, the effects of some meds are significantly altered if the patient has had grapefruit at any time during the day.

As quickly as possible, you need to get as much medical info as possible in order to establish a baseline of the patient's current health. This will give you, and other health care providers, a reference point for comparison.

Purchase some file folders, a couple of log books, and several different colored markers at your local office supply store.

You primarily need to know your patient's blood pressure sitting down, the pulse rate sitting down, weight, any allergies to medicines or environment, a brief description of the patient's overall frame of mind (happy, sad, moody, depressed, up and down mood swings, anger spells, etc.), the general outward appearance of their skin turgor, muscles, and their facial expression (both eyelids open the same amount, smile is even and symmetrical, normal hair loss, speech not slurred, etc). Use colored marker to highlight different levels of concern as you make entries in your log book. For instance, "frequent coughing spells" in the log book would have a red highlight color. This would mean it's a high priority item to speak with his doc about because it could be a bronchial infection. I think you get the point. Maybe choose another color for the "to do" items.

When you trade watch shifts be sure the next person (usually your spouse) can look at your log book and instantly seen what items are flagged and what your comments were. Trust me, there will be times when you are so tired you just can't focus on reading... that's when those easy to see colors bail you out as you search for the red highlight that tell your foggy brain "wake up... this is important."

Oh... don't forget to observe your patient's eating routine in detail (just once). For example, my patient always seemed to have a normal appetite and her swallowing ability was okay. Then, we went through a period in which she began to complain of stomach pains at mealtimes and she didn't want to take any Alka-Seltzer. I was puzzled. Everyone I talked to was puzzled. My doctor friends came up with a lot of scary things, like esophageal cancer, that might in a round-about way be causing the problem. Long story short... I watched her throat very carefully as she drank her liquids. Yep... I bet you are already in tune with me and thinking the same thing. Could it be a Schwannoma of the epiglottis?

I chewed my finger nails in anticipation of what might follow. It was then I noticed that with each sip she would gulp air and force down a swallow. Why? I dunno, but she did, and that forced not only the drink down into her stomach but also a lot of air, which was creating the stomachache. She had more gas than a hot air balloon. I solved the problem by making her drink through a straw. For some reason, this broke her newly acquired habit and her symptoms went away.

My point is no observation is too small.

Look, Listen, and Think.

Please, make a point to get out your phone book and locate all the services in your community that relate to caring for the older ones (Eldercare is the proper term that we should use to disguise having to say 'caring for the old ones'). Look for headings such as *Senior Citizens* (my favorite synonym), *Health Services*, or *Community Services*. Look for any service, committee, or program with *Alzheimer* in the title. Actually, the Alzheimer's group is a good bet because they are widespread. Their national number is 1-800-272-3900. If nothing else, just make a point to stop by and pick up a few pounds of the free literature they have available, say "howdy!" to whomever is there, and be on your way with all the errands you have to run. They won't bite (well... the short one working there might).

PS: Ask them about the 'best friends program' and if it's right for you.

Also be sure to read the list of resources towards the end of this book. These have been handpicked for U! You must make the call... I don't hear you dialing your ear dawg. Get on it!

PRELIMINARY STUFF TO DO TODAY

HOME SAFETY

Many caregivers are supporting and caring for loved ones in their own homes, while others are caring for loved ones and living in the patient's/parent's own home. Typically, most homes are not designed for caregiving.

Take some time to look closely at each room where your patient may spend time, paying special attention to the bedroom, bathroom, and hallways. With advice from a patient's healthcare team (that loosely translates to yourself), you may need to make some changes for the comfort and safety of all who live there, keeping these points in mind:

SAFETY

Are there handrails to help move from one room to another?

Is there a raised toilet seat for easier sitting?

Are there grab bars near the toilet and bathtub for safety in standing and lowering?

Are there non-skid mats on the bathroom floor and in the bathtub to prevent slipping and falling?

Are there night-lights for safety in moving around at night?

Are there working smoke alarms and fire extinguishers throughout the home? Do you periodically check to ensure they are operating properly?

Are emergency numbers—Fire, Hospital, 911—and contact numbers by the phone and on the phone and in another convenient location? That's 3 locations minimum not just one, happy location. I just had 911 tattooed on my hand. No more brain struggles there. Clever, huh? Git R' Done!

If your patient is disabled, you will want to ensure that he or she:

1. **Uses a cane or walker in a safe manner**... but first I want you to examine the item closely for defects, poor assembly, etc. Hey, it's not hard... just use some common sense. I mention this because just the other day I saw a geriatric lady using one of these walker-shopping carts at the grocery. It just collapsed on her as she was going out the door. She took a bad fall. A couple of cross braces were not securely locked into position. A walking cane can be hazardous if the rubber boot at the bottom is missing. Always check your equipment. Ya wouldn't want yer cane to misfire now, would ya?

2. **Have a clear path through each room**... there are no rugs or raised room dividers to trip over and no slippery floors. You can carpet the bathroom with non-slip padded throws to help prevent falls because of a wet floor. Don't allow moisture to become trapped under any kind of pads, tiles, or over-lay material for

more than a short period. The result could be mold that is expensive to remove and causes respiratory problems in some people. A nice wooden parquet floor might be in trouble unless properly sealed against water infiltration.

3. **Is the patient secure in his/her wheelchair?** If your patient is weak, a tray that attaches to the wheelchair can prevent falls and provides a place for your patient's drinks, magazines, etc.

4. **Insure that the patient cannot fall out of bed**... be cautious because they may try to climb over or around rails and end up falling or suffering a twist (spiral) type fracture... not good at all. When the time comes, and you need to use bed rails, be sure to get full rails and not half rails.

EQUIPMENT

I have marked with *** the items I have found most important to my experience, things I wish I had done from the git go.

*** A bed that is lower to the floor than normal, and later a bed with side rails when the patient weakens.

*** A walker and/or cane

*** Bedside commode (You MUST get the kind that is surrounded by handrails on at least two sides (three is even better).

*** No spill drinking containers. I have great success with my 102 year old patient using a standard plastic container with a no-spill plastic straw available from Kroger's. I would avoid using the kind with a side handle for easy carrying. I tried them (non-spill proof) but when your patient carries them the left-over liquid inside runs out dribbling a trail wherever they walk. They all look kinda freaky. Most (except the Styrofoam ones) can be washed in the dishwasher. I keep a couple on hand and use them for protein drinks, Gatorade, and cranberry juice. Keeping your patient happy and hydrated should be your motto.

MOBILITY

*** Have area rugs been corralled? Round 'em up and move 'em out!

*** Is it easy to walk or move from room to room without running into furniture?

*** Are there multiple night lights for safety when moving around at night?

COMMUNICATION

Quick, easy, and readily available ways to communicate with others are a must for you and your patient, especially in an emergency. You may want to borrow or purchase:

A cordless speaker phone with speed dial memory so you can simply hit one button in an emergency and get help without compromising the safety of patient.

Phones with a super large digital display for easy reading and with ring and voice enhancer. These are helpful for people who have hearing problems.

A cellular phone, if you and your patient travel or spend time outside the home (you need some way to always be able to make a 911 call if necessary).

*** A medical or home alert system that will summon help with the push of a button by the patient if you occasionally leave them alone. My patient wore his around his neck. He took a nap, rolled over, and triggered the button. Within a few minutes, the big EMT van pulled up with five firemen. They were polite about it, but the insurance company had to pay about $800 for that error. Take false alarms seriously.

*** An intercom or baby monitor so you may listen to your patient when you are in another room. I purchased a base transmitter for the patient's room and two receivers. One receiver for carrying with me and the other is permanently stationed in our bedroom and is plugged into the wall outlet. I used "the first years" brand unit from Target for about $35.

*** A bell or special alarm that your loved one can ring to ask for help without yelling, or to signal a 'rush to me now' emergency. I use a Target doorbell transmitter and receiver.

*** A voice amplifier to facilitate communication with someone that is hard of hearing. I use a Radio Shack voice amplifier that can be worn around the patient's neck and connected to a pair of headphones worn over the head. Vanity will be your biggest deterrent here. Dad thinks he can hear far better than he really can, and mother doesn't want to disturb her hair coiffure. Hearing aids work fine for people that still possess the dexterity to insert them correctly into the ear canal and then exhibit even greater skill to locate and manipulate the tiny power switch (about the size of a proton) on each unit. No wonder these people get dementia. I think I would be brain dead just from the mental anguish of trying to insert those little buggers in each ear and getting the acoustical smack called "feedback" when the tiny volume control first kicks in. Remember when your school principal would talk into the microphone before turning the volume down. It's still a good way to waste a few grand for the less nimble patients.

A word of caution: I have never seen such skillful salespeople as the ones that sell hearing aids. You will be eating out of their hands from all their flattering praise. My patients dropped several G's on new aids which they rarely, if ever, used. They were really glowing from all the attention and pitch from the sales personnel.

HOW TO PHYSICALLY LIFT A PATIENT

There are many variations and gear for this, but here's my simple approach:

THE STANDARD LIFT

For the leaner patient, I recommend standing in front of and facing the patient. Lift them by placing your hands under the armpits while also putting light lifting pressure against the thoracic cage... just don't put all the loading on the patient's shoulder joint. At the same time, you angle your own elbows inward to be supported upon your own upper trunk. This gives you a good mechanical framework and might save you from a back injury. Of course, you begin with your patient in a sitting position and your own knees slightly bent as you reach under your patient's armpits and pull them towards you. You, simultaneously, begin to straighten to the completed lift position.

For the more durable size patient, you have several options depending on their size. Sling-like devices that you put around the back of the patient are commercially available at most health stores. These usually have gripping handles that allow you to pull the patient toward you as you begin your raise.

Another variation is to substitute a long beach towel for the sling. The patient is in a sitting position. The caregiver encircles the buttock of the patient with the towel, and with a hand gripping the towel on each side of the patient, follows through by pulling up on the towel and at the same time pulling the patient in toward his/her chest.

THE 'V' LIFT

For the really disabled patient, you can rent or purchase a 'V' frame on rollers that has a sling seat and gearing to make the most difficult lift possible. I would try to rent rather than buy.

TWO-MAN LIFT

Depending on the situation and the size of the patient, there is the 2-man lift wherein one person is situated on opposite sides of the patient with the patient's arm extended around each lifters neck. The lifters use their inside hand to grasp a towel slung under the patient's leg closest to him. Each lifter uses their outer hand to maintain a firm grip on the patient's arm. The lifter's shoulder is taking up some of the load. On a three count, both lifters use their arms to a maximum lifting advantage. Please use your good judgment on whether the risk of your lifting is worth the risk for the situation at that time.

WHEN LIFTING IS NOT AN OPTION—THE ROLL

Sooner or later, you will be faced with how to change the diapers on a patient whom is either too heavy or too weak to stand. For this, you need to do a 'roll.' I am amazed at how quick and easy the Hospice bath person can do this with my now weakened patient. What I learned, I pass on to you now.

Place one of those rectangular green sided mats on the bed. Roll your patient onto his/her side (90 degrees). Now bunch up half of the matt and place parallel alongside patient's posterior (butt) side. Roll the patient back onto and just over the mat (188 degrees). Then pull out the bunch. Now, the patient is centered over the mat. Remove the loose fitting pants, cut the diaper, and roll patient to each side to remove the diaper.

Using a diaper with tabs (I recommend this for bedfast patients) clean patient's private parts and sanitize as best as possible. To re-install a clean diaper, again roll the patient 90 degrees to the side, lay the diaper down with the long axis parallel to the patient and just roll them back into original position with their backside on top of the diaper. Bring up tabs and fasten.

If using standard issue diaper (no tabs), just roll patient from side to side as you bring the diaper into position.

THE ESTATE
THREE THINGS YOU MUST KNOW *NOW!*

This is one of those areas that often get overlooked by the caregiver for one reason or another. My internal excuse was fear of trying to understand legal stuff... gives me a headache. I was very fortunate to have access to a leading estate attorney who nurtured my wife and I along this bumpy road. I have laid out the top three things I want you (the caregiver) to get done as of yesterday. Please learn from my mistakes.

AN INTERVIEW WITH AN ATTORNEY SPECIALIZING IN ESTATE LAW

What are the top three "to do now" things for the new caregiver?

Well, the legal things are important, but they are not necessarily the most immediately critical things. First of all, caregivers need to have authority to do anything. The primary importance is that the individual (patient) themselves make the proper arrangements and many people don't do that. Here is my list of the **TOP THREE THINGS** to do right now:

1. **POWER OF ATTORNEY (POA):** Every caregiver should have a valid POA which authorizes the day to day taking care of business matters such as paying bills to filling income tax returns to property management, etc.

2. **LIVING WILL (LW):** Everybody should have at least **two health care documents.** One is the statutory "living will." Not everybody does that, but they should. A lot of people don't understand that a Living Will only applies in two situations: one is where the patient is terminally ill and about to pass. The other

is where the patient is in a coma. If the patient is not in either of these conditions then the will is not called for.

3. **MEDICAL POWER OF ATTORNEY (MPOA):** The other most important document they should have is the MPOA. I prefer to keep the medical power of attorney separate from the general power attorney because sometimes different people are needed to serve those functions. For example, one person may not wish to be responsible for making the healthcare decision but they might gladly take on the job of taking care of the day to day business. **Making sure the right people are doing the right jobs is a big part of the legal assignations.** The more thought you put into this, the fewer headaches you will have later.

It is important that the person who is designated as the legal medical surrogate (or caregiver) has clear legal standing (POA) to have access to medical information; otherwise they won't be able to get anything done.

Of course there should be some information provided by the patient in regards to where the checkbooks are, special bank accounts, pension fund addresses, insurance contacts, legal document, etc.

If your patient won't give you power of attorney then there is another process that you can resort to. You would apply for legal guardianship which requires a certain procedure be followed to determine if the patient is truly incapacitated and involves several evaluations which include a medical evaluation and a psychological evaluation. The decision of those results is made by a small six member jury. If the jury determines incapacitation then the surrogate (caregiver) is appointed the legal guardian and that allows you to take care of all the aforementioned items.

THE ESTATE—INFO YOU SHOULD APPLY ASAP

What can go wrong if a caregiver just neglects to do anything at first (like I did)?

Well, when it comes to business things, somebody has to take care of paying the bills and taking care of maintenance, etc. If the caregiver neglects to provide reasonable support then there could be legal claims filed against that person for failing to maintain the property, paying bills, etc. This would generally be a civil suit but could also be a criminal suit if criminal intent was determined. (Now you know that pleading ignorance is not an excuse. ☺)

As a caregiver you have both implicit and explicit obligations to the patient. Be sure you have the legal power to deal with the situation.

What happens if the patient dies before granting power of attorney to the caregiver?

The power of attorney and similar documents die with the patient. The only authority is the representatives of the estate. If there is a will, the authority is going to be the executor. If there is no will, the estate will be administered and settled by the court. The first responsibility is to pay all the final bills, pay all the taxes, and take care of any unfinished business and then distribute the assets to where they should go.

If there is a will... asset distribution will be already specified.

If there is no valid will... "Intestate" in legalese... intestacy statutes apply.

If there is no will or "intestate," then there is a statute that says things will pass down through a certain order because there are different tax consequences involved, not only for the estate, but also for those who inherit the estate. Under the Intestacy law, in which the state basically creates a "will" for the decedent, there are several layers of distribution involved, but typically half of the estate will pass to the spouse and the rest to the children.

Federal laws leave the creation of "Intestacy" laws up to the states. Consequently, these laws and the judicial decisions will be different from one state to the other. For example, in Kentucky, the above generality is applied.

If there is a valid will, but it is incomplete... partial intestacy applies.

This is another reason to get very familiar with your patient's legal affairs. A will is updated maybe every five years. In the meantime, more property or assets may have been acquired that have not been placed in the will. A similar situation would occur if the will only covers certain assets groups such as all the 'personal' items (jewelry, cash, bonds, etc.)

but the real estate is omitted. Under the statutes of Intestacy, the omitted assets would then be distributed to the heirs in the manner set forth by the state statutes.

If there is a will, but it was not filed with the probate court within a specific time... the entire estate will be distributed according to the Intestacy statues.

Who decides which person will be the executor of the will?

That choice is made by the patient, designated in the will and appointed by the court. The executor does not decide what the distributions are because that is already specified in the will. The job of the executor is to round up the bills and get everybody paid, settle the tax issues, and follow the directions of the will.

Who decides which person will be the administrator?

It's always the principal (the patient). If the principal waits until they are incapacitated to do anything, then nothing will be effective because a person has to have legal capacity to sign these kinds of documents. If the patient signs the document and is deemed incapacitated, then the documents won't hold up in a court of law.

What can I do if my patient does not have legal capacity?

You need to apply for legal guardian status. But realize that this can sometimes get complicated when it comes to proving someone's incapacity to make rational decisions thus inhibiting them from signing legal documents.

Can the administrator and the executor be the same person?

Generally speaking no, unless there is an incomplete will, in which case the part that was not covered in the will is assigned to an "administrator" and the part that is covered by the will already has an "executor" elected by the patient and stated in the will. Generally speaking, it is often preferable to have different people serving these two functions according to their skills, accessibility, etc. In addition, the will carries a higher degree of responsibility (see last question below). The person chosen as the executor must be willing to take on greater responsibility.

When it comes to medical documents, the patient often wants all of the children involved so that no one person would have to carry that decision making burden by themselves.

When it comes to the executor, who pays the bills, one might want to appoint a family member who is not 'proximity' limited. In other words, appoint someone close by, but who also possesses the basic skills for bookkeeping.

What is the most common mistake a caregiver can make in estate affairs?

A person doing nothing, no planning, and just being oblivious (that was me again). I guess the second worst situation would arise from not spending enough time planning who should be assigned to do this or that job. Selecting the best person should involve what skills the person has, how far away they live, what their personal preference might be (for example, you would not want to designate someone to handle the medical affairs if that person is afraid of that area to begin with or can't bear taking on that much responsibility), and how much time can they realistically devote to the task. There are more considerations, but this gives you an idea.

Of course these are just guidelines that you need to mention to your 'principal' (or parent) since they are the one to make the actual choices. Be sure that you have open dialogue with your patient so that you can be part of the decision making process AND that you have your patient's knowledge regarding where all their pertinent documents are kept. If you can't find their documents, then you can't do anything to begin with. In other words, you are stuck at square one with nowhere to go.

What is the difference between an administrator and executor?

If there **is no will** (Intestate), then an *administrator* is appointed by the court to administer the estate of the deceased person. If there **is a will**, then that document designates an "executor" (as specified by the patient) who "executes" the provisions stated in the will. The executor also has the ability to sue or be sued on behalf of the estate. If nobody wants to be the executor of a legal will, then the court can appoint an administrator of the will (the same as in the case of having no will).

For Kentucky, what is the time period for filing a will?

The statutes say 10 years, but in reality it usually is less than a year.

What determines a valid will?

Essentially, a valid will is a document that describes the distribution of assets and is signed by two credible witnesses that are not heirs to the estate and by the testator (the one creating the will and is generally the patient).

Is it safe to just buy a "will kit" and do it yourself?

You can do that, but I like to say it's about as safe as "taking your own tonsils out." You see, there are so many complexities involved in the law that it becomes very difficult to use a kit for anything other than the simplest of all simple wills.

What type of attorney do I need?

An "Estate" or "Elder" attorney comes to mind first, but there are others also.

THE STOCK PORTFOLIO

WHAT U SHOULD KNOW

PORTOLIO MANAGEMENT- LESSONS FROM MORGAN STANLEY

An interview with Roger Collins, Vice President, Morgan Stanley Smith Barney, Lexington, Kentucky.

(I am not vested with Morgan Stanley Smith Barney in any way.)

For a new caregiver that is placed in a situation that involves taking over their parents portfolio, and assuming that the caregiver has very limited experience in investments, and they need to make a decision on what to do, what are some of the main points that you would like to emphasize to the caregiver? What do they need to know, what do they need to do?

I think there are two major things to be done. First you need to look at the assets that you inherit and evaluate the tools that you have. Secondly, you need to look at the problems that lie ahead of you. For example, if you need to consider nursing home care for a parent you are looking at about $53-54K per year. A second parent doubles your debt. There are other expenses that usually have to be factored in depending on that patient's individual needs. Also, you need to factor in an inflation rate of 4-5% per year."

As far as the portfolio is concerned, the client caregiver should sit down with a portfolio manager (financial advisor/broker) and talk about the assets you do have and talk about the financial expectations you have. You then discuss with your manager how you can best leverage your assets to give you the performance you want. He/she will discuss the various types of investment instruments that are available and help you to weigh the pros and cons of each.

Roger talked about some of the tools that he likes, such as "covered calls." I will spare you the details, but suffice it to say there are many investment methods available to help you reach your goal. Keep in mind that everything carries some degree of risk. As a caregiver you need to decide how much risk you are willing to take with your portfolio and discuss this with your financial advisor.

Are most stock brokers also financial advisors?

Well, they are here.

So if a caregiver came in to see you then you would be able to provide financial advice as well as serve as their stock broker?

That is correct.

When we talk about portfolio management you mentioned that you like to find high yielding stocks, but in this market there is a lot of volatility so where do you see investments in this market?

Well, again, it all depends on the assets the caregiver/client has to work with and how many debt obligations he/she has to satisfy, but I like investments in companies that are known for their growth more than their dividends, like IBM, P&G, and similar. I also like Utilities.

When someone asks you to manage their portfolio do you get actively involved? It seems that if you are trying to manage hundreds of accounts you can't possibly micro-manage every one of them unless you have free reign?

Well that has a lot to do with the client. Some clients just don't want to be involved and give me authority to use full discretion. Another way is actually one that I feel more comfortable with and that is to call the client every time I do a trade. I want the client to know what I am doing and have an idea of what the risk/benefit is for them (i.e. Does it make sense to do this trade?).

What other advice would you like to mention to the new client?

ell, I think everyone should know what the cost of doing business is. That cost can reflect a number of variables such as trade volumes or it can reflect a direct percentage of the amount of assets involved. In short, everybody should understand what they are being charged for. You should take time to sit down with a broker that you may want to do business with, maybe go to lunch, but just be sure you feel comfortable with that person. Be sure they answer all your questions to your satisfaction.

How do you keep your client up to date with their portfolio?

Well, besides the summaries they receive in the mail, I like to have them come into the office each quarter and we go over their portfolio. It's just so important for a caregiver to take an active interest into how their investments are performing and have a chance to voice their input. Caregiving can often have serious financial needs associated with it, so it's important that I can educate my client on what we feel is the safest pathway to achieve the results we need.

A couple of thoughts from me are:

- Choose a seasoned broker from a reputable firm.

- Stay away from penny stocks unless you just want to have fun... like buying a lotto ticket. Never use them for serious financial fulfillment hopes.

- Spend some time discussing your investment needs with your broker. Get involved!

- **Utilize information tools on the internet** to keep you informed on a daily basis.

Some examples include:

1. Dividend Detective, which allows you to look at which companies are paying the best dividends.

2. Market Watch (www.marketwatch.com)

3. Wall Street Journal (online.wsj.com/home-page)

4. The New York Times (www.nytimes.com/interactive/2008/10/08/ business/economy/20081008-credit-chart-graphic.html) This site has five market indicators that I like including the LIBOR index.

5. Business Insider (www.businessinsider.com)

6. Bloomberg News (www.bloomberg.com/news/economy)

7. The Baltic Dry Index (www.bloomberg.com/apps/quote?ticker=b diy&exch=IND&x=15&y=11) This gives you an idea of how much shipping trade activity is going on.

8. The VIX index (www.cboe.com/micro/vix/introduction.aspx) This give you an idea of the volatility in the market.

9. The TED spread (www.bloomberg.com/apps/quote?ticker=. tedsp%3Aind) This gives you an idea of how difficult it is for businesses to get loans; a very important indicator.

10. The Flow of Funds Account of the United States (www. federalreserve.gov/releases/z1/Current/z1.pdf)

It can take some time getting used to the terminology, but it is the factual assessment of the US economy before the spin politicians cripple the facts. This might be a good exercise for you and your financial adviser to go over.

There are a great number of market commentators. I happen to like Nouriel Roubini (www.roubini.com), Meredith Whitney, and H.S Dent (www.hsdent.com/blog).

Please do not believe everything you read, especially any public government information on housing, retail sales, trade, and everything because the data has been corrupted or "spun till the cows came home." (They often redefine their yardsticks.) All publications put their own twist on things. **Go for the general overview.** If the headlines say the market went up because the home sales were up... don't believe it. Most of the time the market rises or falls for reasons an outsider (you & me) will never be privy to. It's usually due to computer algorithms, the secret work of "quants," high frequency trading (like thousands of trades a second) or often it's pegged to the value of a currency relative to the US dollar (like the EURO/USD ratio).

Do your own investigations... believe no headline... trust no government... believe the facts and trust your common sense. Hold steadfast to your principals.

A common example of spin might be the "New Home Sales" report from the gov't which often includes sales for which contracts have been written, but never executed... this is pure gov't spin. In these times, many written contracts are not being executed so that hidden, unmentioned caveat is very important in assessing the true facts of just how healthy the housing market is in this example. To make things more challenging is the fact that various government stimulus programs are always being kicked into the quagmire and it's often hard to know if "employment," for example, is really up and helping the economy or was it because of the temporary effect of census workers, or the gov't hiring system allegedly allowing the same census worker to be counted two or three times as a "new" hire. Retail sales are always up in the spring so the spin comes from whether it is being compared to the previous year (y/y) or the previous month (m/m). If you "spin" the data you can make the crash of 1929 look good. In fact, Wall Street did just that, as evidenced in this quote from Business Insider's article compiled by Dan Alpert, "They (Wall St. Investment Trust executives) say that the current rise in security prices is firmly grounded on the improvement in business conditions that began in December (1929)." That was pure nonsense. A few months later the market collapsed and took over a decade to recover. The "big crash of '29" really occurred in 1930.

Look at market indexes (they don't lie, but they are dull), use your common sense, use your broker's advice, no 'penny stocks' and roll your dice.

The last thought I want to leave you with is to plan for the big "what if." This might include currency devaluation (like a sovereign government issuing a new currency such as monopoly money) or returning to a standard based currency (it used to be gold, but now it might have to be aluminum or calcite). This economy is going to be tested in many ways... you need to be a step ahead.

CHAPTER 5
124 TIPS AND IDEAS FOR SURVIVAL:

MORE MUST DO ITEMS

> Be devoted to one another in brotherly love.
> Honor one another above yourselves.
>
> Romans 12:10

I was going to try to list these in order of importance, but realized that would only apply to my patient. Other caregivers have different priorities. The present numbering system is random or really just God's will at that moment.

HEALTH TIPS (HTIPS)

HTIP #1: WHAT U NEED TO KNOW ABOUT G.E.R.D—important

GERD stands for Gastroesophageal Reflux Disease or sumpthin' like that. It is very common with the geriatric group. It is really a syndrome that represents many symptoms. It can closely mimic the features of a heart attack... complete with chest pain, numbness in arms, yadda yadda. In fact, there is no real definitive way of differentiating from a real ticker attack and GERD when you are not in the laboratory. Taking a dynamite pill (nitro gly.) should alleviate the GERD promptly, but please do whatever your doc advises. I have no legal or moral authority to tell you what to do. I only suggest what I would do.

This is one of those symptoms that you will hear from your patient time after time. They usually say "I have a discomfort in my chest and I can't explain it" or "I feel pain near where my heart is" (as they point to their right side of the chest, ☺). Know your patient's medical history so you know what to react to and what not to react to.

Even though my patient has some past history of cardio problems in the past (left sided cardiomyopathy), he also has a history of heartburn. When he thinks he is having a "coronary," I give him one nitro pill under the tongue. If it goes away, then it was probably GERD. So far it has always been GERD. Your knowledge can save you countless trips to the emergency room for nothing.

HTIP #2: CHOKE HAZARD

Avoid serving your patient foods that have long stringy fibers (such as asparagus) or stringy forms of protein (such as chicken). With chicken, you can cut up pieces into 1/4" squares or even puree with tomato soup. Stringy fibers are a common cause of esophagus blockage. This info comes from the endoscopist that treated my patient. Should this occur on the weekend (naturally) he recommends taking the patient to the hospital emergency room (and wait there).

HTIP #3: ASPIRATION PNEUMONIA

Avoid serving your patient unless they are sitting up. I know this isn't always possible, but what we are trying to avoid is the potential life threatening situation of acquiring aspiration pneumonia. Some factors that put patients at high risk for this include those with dysphagia (difficulty swallowing), smokers, patients with a bad ticker or viral disease, patients with excessive mucous, alcoholics, druggies, and just about anything.

One caregiver related how her patient acquired aspiration pneumonia from eating ice cream. I could only speculate that the patient might have had bacteria laden mucous that the ice cream caused that to spill over into the trachea. The patient ultimately died.

The point is you never know what can trigger food, or mucous to spill over and cause pneumonia. Be vigilant if your patient is at high risk. If you notice that something has gone down the wrong pipe (maybe patient starts coughing). Even if the situation seems normal, continue to stay vigilant. The actual formation of pneumonia colonies may take several days and suddenly you have a critically ill patient.

A major warning sign is a high fever. Know what your patient's normal oral temperature is so you can compare. Fever is not the only sign.

HTIP #4: PREPARE YOURSELF TO BE PHYSICALLY FIT

The two main reasons are: 1) It will help to alleviate your stress/depression state and 2) you will need plenty of strength when you have to lift a patient that has collapsed or fallen and can't get up. **Remember a 'dead or limp lift' requires twice the effort of a 'live lift.'** Of course, you understand that the vernacular 'dead lift' doesn't require anyone to actually be dead... just unresponsive.

And for you macho guys... yeah I'm guilty too... just because you weigh a lot, lift weights, and think you are in shape, be prepared for a surprise. The real danger in not having a strong back which requires a lot of 'helper' muscles to also be in good shape. The act of bending over puts a tremendous leverage disadvantage on the lower spine (L3-L5 region). Some studies have indicated that the structural disadvantage of that region is like stressing it with five times as much weight as you are actually lifting. That is why an unconditioned torso can be a candidate for the ol' slipped disc and worse. That usually means you are out of commission for some time and will have to have someone feed you and your patient. Wasn't supposed to be that way was it?

It happened to me trying to lift my mother who only weighed about 100 lbs. Eventually, I had to have a spinal operation for pre-existing stenosis. I never would have thought it possible which is what I can pretty accurately predict for you (unless you are proactively thinking and making risk assessments on everything you do).

HTIP #5: DEHYDRATION... FEAR THIS! (Often accompanied by a blood clot)

Yeah, yeah, in the summer time we hear about needing to drink more fluids... I mean come on, how important a threat can dehydration be reeeaally?

I always keep a sharp eye on my patient for any signs of anything not being right. I am a health advocate, exercise at my physical therapy center about five or six hours per week, and on the weekend I do a twelve mile inline skate just to relax and prove my good fitness. My patient is 102 year old, sleeps most of the time, and eats only tiny portions at mealtime. Guess who became dehydrated? ME! I absolutely could not believe it! HOW? WHY? In fact, I had noticed that when I did the pinch test on my thigh it took longer than one second for the skin to return to normal. I thought immediately of dehydration, but erroneously ruled that out because I had not done this pinch test in over a year, so I wasn't sure what my normal baseline looked like and more importantly I really felt just fine up to this point.

All the wisdom in the world can't help the person who does not heed the advice.

The short version of this is that within three days of feeling the first symptoms, I had to make the 911 call and be taken to the hospital. The ER determined that I was dehydrated and put in an IV. I had acute kidney failure, and had a blood clot in my right leg in the femoral vein.

My 102 year old patient is now at home, while his caregiver (me) is embedded in the local hospital. Something is wrong with this picture. I was caught totally off guard. Upon standing, my presenting symptoms were feelings of extreme bilateral weakness in the quads (thigh muscles), immediately followed by a feeling of fluid pressure building up in the legs (due to the clot blocking venous return I presume), and after walking about 20 yards I was ready to faint (orthostatic hypotension). The pain was intense. Relief only followed when I laid down either voluntarily or involuntarily.

I also had some kind of back inflammation thing going on, so I decided to take ibuprofen 800mg every four hours. The next day, I was no better. The next day, I had to call 911.

Somehow I had gone all the way into the later stages of dehydration without even suspecting a thing. How, I puzzled? Next, the Ibuprofen was exactly the wrong thing to take (as any NSAID would be). As my kidneys were failing, the ibuprofen caused the shutdown to escalate much more rapidly. I still have a lot of questions about what happened, but I can share this much with you (be especially mindful if you are over the age of 55). Here are my guidelines:

1. Don't ever take your state of hydration as a given fact.

2. Avoid the over-use of NSAIDs (especially in hot weather)

3. Use Tylenol (acetaminophen) for pain control

4. Hydrocodone or tramadol are okay for higher pain levels.

5. Monitor your own and your patient's weight regularly.

6. Always carry a bottle of water with you.

7. Do the 1, 2, 3 pinch test regularly

(1, 2, 3 pinch test: select an area to pinch on your thigh, arm, or forehead. If the skin at any one of these area does not return to normal within 1.005 seconds, you can suspect dehydration. Since skin turgor can vary with age you need to know what is a normal baseline for you or your patient. A second is mentally counted as "one thousand and one" and somewhere there will be an exception to everything).

I was told that dehydration occurs over time, so you might not even notice anything abnormal at first. Then, one day, the perfect storm occurs. You have just had a hard workout but being the clever person, you thoughtfully took a couple of Aleve for joint pain before workout (as usual) and later that evening you took some ibuprofen just to be on top of everything. The next morning, everything seems normal at first... you get up from the breakfast table... wait... what's that pain I feel? I feel kinda lightheaded too. I better lay down for a rest. You barely make it to your bedroom before collapsing on the bed. You reach for more ibuprofen.

I just read that General Petraeus (straight from the rigors of Afghanistan) passed out during a Senate hearing yesterday. The stated cause was dehydration. Now, if dehydration can catch that fitness nut (with apologies) off guard, it can do the same for you or your patient. You should drink eight glasses of water a day. Set a goal that you can keep and do it every day (or I'm sending the General to see ya). I drink two glasses at each meal and then something in between so I know I must be getting about seven glasses per day. You can count the water in your bowl of soup or the milk in your breakfast cereal as a cup.

This is the real storm... fear it. It can be painful and very, very costly.

HTIP #6: PERIANAL CLEANING–important

On occasion, I instruct my patient to wipe his perianal area with Clorox wipes when I want to be certain any sign of UTI is controlled. Sprays, lotions, creams, gels have the disadvantage of requiring either direct hand contact with contaminated areas that can be vectored under fingernails or not being a real bactericide. Poor cleaning can lead to UTIs. This might be a little harsh for people with sensitive skin. If that B U, then choose something milder. Visit a medical supply store and look at other options. Find what is easy to apply yet effective. Moist towelettes will work, but they generally are not bactericidal which is okay as long as you aren't having UTI problems.

HTIP #7: UTI's—ASSESSING THE SITUATION

Again, I am not a medical doctor. I am just a doctor of happiness. If my patient has a UTI (urinary tract infection), how would I know? Well, 90% of the time you will observe your patient complaining about not sleeping and having to get up and urinate all during the night (although that can also be a neurogenic bladder problem). Ask your patient if they feel a "burning" sensation when they urinate (a strong indicator). Look at a sample of your patient's urine collected in a clear jar. Collect as much as you can because often there will be 'normal' sediments that look milky that may pass with the urine. If you can easily read newsprint through the bottle of urine, that's a good sign. If it's cloudy, that may or may not be a good sign. If the patient had veggies lately, there might be cloudiness due to oxalates, urates, and other veggie by-products. What to do? Note if the urine has a strong ammonia odor, that's not a good sign. On the basis of three of these being present: Burning, cloudy, and ammonia odor, I would make a presumptive positive call that significant bacteria is present. In fact, if the odor when you empty the container of urine into the toilet is so strong it makes you want to gag, then I consider that also a presumptive positive call by itself.

Going a step further, I personally make it a point to keep on hand a vial of urine test strips, available from any medical supply store. They look like little cardboard strips with little pads stuck along them. They are designed to be briefly dipped into the urine. The pads will change color and tell you what is present. Some strips will test for more than you need and you pay a premium for this. I just really need to see the amount of "nitrites", "leukocytes," and "protein," but mine also came with a pad for "glucose." Test strips are another tool to give you a solid commitment to address a possible infection. Strips with a pH pad can also be helpful because most UTI's have urea-splitting bacteria that cause the urine to go alkaline (pH above 7.0); just another bit of info for assessment.

Because your aging patient has a more fragile system, it is imperative that you **act** immediately if you suspect an infection. What now? This is totally your call. I would recommend you get your patient in to see a doctor ASAP. Unfortunately, that can mean a several day wait period. Not good. And remember that most docs (and Hospice) will want a sample to send for the lab to identify the little buggers causing the UTI, which means a three day delay.

Hopefully, if you present your observations, especially if you are using the urine test strips, your doc's physician's assistant might go ahead and issue a prescription on a presumptive basis while the lab takes it's time.

I personally try to keep some antibiotics on hand just for the occasion. Levaquin and the whole class of flouroquinones are good "broad based" antibiotics, which means they will kill either gram negative or gram positive germs. I don't even see any need to identify what kind of germ you are dealing with if a broad based antibiotic will kill it. I think, unless your patient has a history of multiple refractory (difficult to kill) infections it is a waste of time to assess what the name of the germ is... just administer Levaquin for three days... fix it and forget it. Name that germ 'gone.'

I know hospice is really big on wanting to know just exactly what the name of the germ is... they do a lot of lab work... and always would come to the same conclusion... give the patient Levaquin, DS Cotrim (sulphonamides and trimethoprim) or something similar. I asked them why they need to send the sample to the lab for analysis. They said "so we will know exactly what kind of germ it is and administer the most effective antibiotic." Sounds right on until you realize that any broad spectrum antibiotic will work and even the nurses' own spec sheets will

show Levaquin at the top of the list of most effective killers. The exceptions are rare (less than 1% in my experience).

They just waste about a week arriving at the same conclusion. Part of that delay is because if your patient is under Hospice care and your patient has a suspected UTI, then more people will be involved in the chain of command... or more cooks in the kitchen. I feel that valuable time is lost in chasing windmills. I advocate immediate treatment (usually one Levaquin per day for three days only) and only then, if no response is seen within three days, would I ask for a culture type. Even if the patient really doesn't have any infection, no harm has been done. Time is of the essence for geriatric care. Also, if you go the long route down to actual culture typing... somewhere along the way... Murphy's Law will be invoked and that key lab technician has just left for a week of vacation... or the medical director is gone for a long weekend or a new sample is needed (it happened more than once to me, "the lab just lost my sample"). I like to work fast and effectively, and the fewer people I have to count on the better.

Also, don't forget that antibiotics for our canine friends will often work just as well and are a ton cheaper. The only difference is that you might have to settle for a first or second generation antibiotic instead of the latest Cadillac on the market, but who cares? Sometimes a side effect is that the patient may have a bad bark for a few days... just kidding. I also like the Cephalosporin class of antibiotics because they can penetrate tissues well. For routine infections, I really like the simple but effective Ampicillin 500mg (which is a penicillin). I like to keep antibiotics on hand so I can act immediately.

I personally don't worry about outdated antibiotics. The truth is that most of the common antibiotics (like the classes mentioned here) are chemically stable years beyond their expiration date. I personally use some meds myself that are as much as ten years old (more on that topic next).

HTIP #8: IS IT SAFE TO USE MEDS BEYOND THEIR EXPIRATION?

In a study done by the military a few years ago, over one hundred drugs were examined for safety past the expiration date. According to the *Wall Street Journal* (March 29, 2000) and reported by Laurie P. Cohen, the military found that **"drugs as far as 15 years past their expiration date were still safe and effective."**

"The expiration date, required by law in the United States, beginning in 1979, specifies only the date the manufacturer guarantees the full potency and safety of the drug—it does not mean how long the drug is actually "good" or safe to use. Second, medical authorities uniformly say it is safe to take drugs past their expiration date—no matter how "expired" the drugs purportedly are."

The exceptions include nitroglycerin, insulin, liquid forms of antibiotics, and the tetracycline class of antibiotics (and grandma's egg rolls). All your normal antibiotic pills and aspirins, and pain relievers are safe for years beyond their expiration date.

HTIP #9: DOES YOUR PATIENT HAVE DIFFICULTY SWALLOWING PILLS?

You may find that your antibiotic or other meds only come in a large size pill which your patient can't swallow very well. Try this: grind up the pill with something heavy (a hammer or bowling ball will do. Don't worry about contaminating the antibiotic... it is not likely to happen because few, if any, microbes can survive on a steel or plastic diet). Place in a tablespoon (leave out the bowling ball) and cover with applesauce. If your patient complains about the after taste, I like to administer a spoon of honey... and then maybe a spoon of honey to help my patient.

HTIP #10: HOW TO CHOSE A LONG-TERM CARE NURSING HOME

There may come a time when you have no other choice but to put your patient into a nursing home. The following is a web site for any nursing home in the United States (supposedly). I was impressed with this site. All I had to do was type in the area code I wanted to examine and presto!... a complete listing of nursing homes.

Go to: www.Medicare.gov/NHCompare

HTIP #11: MALE CATHERITIZATION 101

The two main reasons a male geriatric patient needs to be catheterized are to control infection and to open flow around an enlarged prostate. There are other reasons of course, but a normal healthy patient will eventually need catheterization. Most patients can be taught to do their own. The sick ones need someone else to do theirs.

I have done over a thousand catheterizations. I will now share what I learned and suggest some things to be cautious about.

Urinary infections will occur as a normal course of events. First, the aging immune system (and caregiver) becomes weaker from the workload. Second, the bladder often becomes more flaccid (without elasticity) and has a tendency to compartmentalize. When the patient urinates one compartment may be emptied, but not the other.

An un-emptied urine compartment at body temperature will be excellent for incubating most species of bacteria. This bacteria may climb back up the ureters (the piping from the kidneys) and into the kidney where there are hiding places for them. **Left unchecked, bacteria can be terminal for the patient.**

To keep bacteria in check, most urologists will recommend that the patient be catheterized twice a day. For my patient, I do catheterization once per day, but I also use cranberry juice with each meal to lasso rogue bacteria in the kidneys.

There are many different types and sizes of catheters. My patient uses a Coude type. This has a curved tip to facilitate passing around an enlarged prostate. It is not for leaving in the patient. The diameter is usually determined by the urologist and will be small enough for the patient's urethra, but large enough to stop urine from running down the outside of the catheter. I somehow can't imagine a person with a urethra so large that even the smallest catheter wouldn't firmly seal. I mean, I tested one (the smallest) on myself just to see what the patient felt. I felt like I was giving birth or whatever. Maybe the Jolly Green Giant... yeah, that's the guy that needs a large cath.

Your patient may need an indwelling cath at some point, especially if he happened to be admitted to the hospital for several days. This type of cath typically has a balloon tip to keep it in place. To remove it at discharge time, the nurse will inject glycerin into the cath whereupon the balloon will dissolve, allowing the whole cath to be easily pulled out. I am telling you this because elderly patients are often discharged when they are still in a delirium state. When the nurse was out of the hospital room, my patient seized the cath tubing and started pulling it out 'the old fashioned way.' He growled and tugged and tugged some more. The balloon tip was holding it in place and tearing the endothelial cell walls causing copious bleeding over everything like a scene from a Steven King novel.

Of course this was on a night shift on a weekend and no cath-savvy medical personnel were to be found. A few frantic phone calls found a urologist that talked the aide through the glycerin extraction. Remember that patients are apt to be in a state of altered awareness just from being in a hospital setting plus the medications.

Expect deleterious and unpredictable behavior from any hospitalized patient. Go through your list of "what ifs" and try to anticipate what might happen next.

I have done this over 1000 times for my 102 yr old patient. I've been through some pretty scary times in the early stages, but I've learned a lot. Hopefully, you will extract something useful and perhaps even life saving.

Generally speaking most seniors, even with handicaps, can catheterize themselves. Your urologist, or the internet, can provide instruction.

An enlarged prostate that restricts urine flow is another reason for catheterization.

Earlier I had mentioned that you will always be dealing with professionals in the health care field disagreeing about the proper sanitation measures and frequency of the procedure. **Don't be afraid to trust in your own wisdom.**

Hospice is especially prone to lay out some pretty elaborate precautions for eliminating external contamination. It sounds good, but doesn't fit into the real world model (for me). In fact, I was given a bunch of literature by one of the nurses which actually contradicted their procedure. I can't fault them because it's really a case of C.Y.A. What else can they do without major changes to their S.O.P (standard operating procedure)?

Previously, I mentioned that sometimes you will be faced (no pun intended) with copious bleeding due to inflammatory conditions of the urethra and/or prostrate. This can be really scary, but my patient had pretty normal health with normal clotting factors and a normal immune system. The urologist said occasional 'bleeds' were normal, but I kept looking for a reason. Bingo. In my patient's case, I found that once I had reduced his dosage of aspirin back down to the standard 81mg, the bleeding problem pretty much went away. That was great news.

Don't be afraid to question your patient's medicines and interactions.

The next problem I was encountering was becoming more and more frequent. The urethra was blocked by either the enlarged prostate or an autonomic response of the urethra muscles that extend for some distance up and down the urethra... not just at that bladder stricture. I noticed that often my patient would anticipate the insertion of the catheter and subconsciously start tensing his fists or fidgeting with his legs. Sure enough, that proceeded to block the urethra. How on earth can I deal with this??

Of course you could just shoot the patient, but think of the paperwork involved. Nope. I tried a number of things that might be distracting, but eventually it boils down to technique. In real estate, you hear that it's all about location, location, location. Well, with catheterization, it's all about technique, technique, technique. **Remember that success depends upon a smooth and continuous insertion of the catheter.** Initially, I was encountering the enlarged prostate and would then have to twist and turn the catheter until I could find the way around this blockage. I have learned that upon inserting the catheter, I needed to simultaneously begin rotating the shaft of the catheter counter clockwise. Invariably, this allowed the catheter to slip by the prostate and on towards the bladder.

In the rare event you have not made a flawlessly smooth motion, you will note that the urethra muscles may instantly block you. To circumvent this, retract the entire catheter from the penis and reinsert. I don't understand the exact mechanism, but I sense that there is some sort of sensory stimulus that seems to be initiated at insertion and as long as this motion is not interrupted by erratic movement of the catheter the insertion will proceed without event.

Once, I had a nurse from Hospice do the catheterization while I was away. She encountered blocking of the urethra. My patient was getting nervous, she was getting nervous, and finally she suggested that a urologist be called in (at 10 pm at night). My wife insisted that she relax and keep trying in a smooth motion. It worked, to her great relief. Of course my patient had some urethral bleeding for the next few days from the trauma, but it resolved on its own.

What I learned about the importance of the smooth and continuous movement may prove invaluable to you during one of those 'crises.' One last bit of valuable wisdom I learned from my experience was that the type of lubricant you choose for the catheter has a lot to do with the success of a smooth insertion. Previously, I used the KY gel lubricant. I noticed it was always forming a stickiness along the plastic shaft, even before I finished the insertion attempt. I switched to the KY liquid lubricant. It works great. Be sure to apply it to your gloved fingers, then spread it up and down the catheter until the shaft of the catheter is completely covered. Now you are ready for insertion.

From a practical standpoint, given my patient's normal health, I was able to make the entire catheterization procedure a very routine and doable thing. Again, I would use the same catheter for several months. I would often use the same set of rubber gloves. I would, of course, wash everything with a brief rinse from the faucet. Beyond that, infections were kept well under control and the entire procedure was done in a few minutes depending on how much urine I had to tap (usually 10 oz.).

I don't mean to beat a dead horse, but this is something your patient encounters every day, mate. I like to have a supply of antibiotics on hand to stop those occasional infections. A broad spectrum antibiotic such at Levaquin covered 99% of infections in my patient's case. Often the nursing service, Hospice or etc. will want to take samples first to confirm an infection and then spend some more time figuring out the best antibiotic (it always turns out to be Levoquin). I find that unnecessary, but I am sure they have to go through that long process because of liability. I would just give my patient one 500mg Levaquin a day for three days and the job is done.

Oh, how do I know when he has an infection warranting treatment? Simple... when you can't stand the ammonia smell of the quart sized container of 'cloudy' urine you have just collected, then consider it teaming with bacteria even though your patient may not show any physical changes.

As I mentioned before, I also keep on hand a roll of litmus paper to check for presence of an alkaline pH of the urine and keep a vial of test strips (available for your local medical supply outlet) that will indicate nitrite, leukocytes, and other goodies. Those first two are the main indicators for the presence of bacteria. That along with the presence of a pH greater than 7 (alkaline, but generally in the range of 7-8) will give you a pretty good idea.

Lastly... I know many readers are holding their breath waiting to tell me that not all bacteria produce the ammonia smell or alkaline pH. You are correct. Have a dog biscuit. Most of the time you will be right on target treating with Levoquin whenever the smell gets really rancid (with or without the other litmus indicators). Remember... if the smell knocks you over and you can't read a newspaper through the glass urine container, your patient probably has a problem. Act on it 'post haste' or 'right now.'

Sometimes you may encounter a strange smell like that of a skunk or a strange color in the urine, like pink or even purple. These all indicate bacteria interactions. Keep in mind that some cloudiness is permissible because this may be due to various salts and chemicals from the last meal. For example, oxalate salts are common with a lot of veggies. Actually, the when I catheterize my patient, I find that the last few millimeters coming down the tube are milky white. Don't be alarmed because it is a mix of things including some white cells that are shed in normal day to day functioning. Just remember that a real knock down smell would tell me to administer an oral antibiotic ASAP. Some patients can't swallow a large pill. I usually grind any solid pill into small pieces and smother that with apple sauce, which makes everything slide right down.

If you ask me how I get antibiotics when most docs won't prescribe them without a patient consult, lab work, yadda... yadda... I can tell you that some veterinary supply houses may sell them to you without a Rx. The antibiotic is the same and the price is much, much less expensive. Also, I have been known to go to the internet for Canadian pharmacies for less restricted purchases. I only mention this because fate always seems to precipitate a crisis on the weekend when the doc is unavailable. In lieu of this, I have known caregivers to use their Urgent Treatment center for antibiotics for their "sinus infections."

GENERAL TIPS

Tip #1: DEVELOP YOUR SENSE OF HUMOR AGAIN

This is very important for your own mental health. Start with reading humor books or comics. Remember that you laugh when you can see a different point of view. The more points of view a person can see, the more stable a platform they have to judge things by.

Tip #2: INSTALL SAFETY GATE TO LIMIT ACCESS TO ANY STAIRS

This is a must when you have anything other than a Ranch style house. Expect to have to physically modify it to accommodate your needs. It must do more than keep a puppy from going upstairs or downstairs. I had to add a lock and steel cables to keep my patient from hacking her way through it with her best scissors.

Tip #3: NEVER EVER ARGUE, DISPUTE, OR RATIONALIZE WITH DEMENTIA

It's so tempting to want to try to 'rationalize' with your patient. Save your time—Forget about it!

Tip #4: NEVER BE CRITICAL

This does no good in the immediate time frame and will ultimately cultivate a negative relationship lacking in trust and communication.

Tip #5: SPEAK SOFTLY BUT... (Ha... forget the big stick)

This speaks for itself... zzzzzzz. Your patient responds most readily to tone of voice and facial gestures.

Tip #6: ALWAYS SMILE AND OFFER ENCOURAGEMENT

This is very important. Treat your patient like a 3 year old and expect same behavior. Praise them, support them verbally and with a loving touch.

Tip #7: BE SURE TO NOTE THE DETAILS OF YOUR PATIENT'S CURRENT HEALTH—BREATHING, BALANCE, HEARING, VISION, SMELL, TASTE, ETC.

Take a full inventory of your patient's health. Later, you will use this as a baseline when discussing aspects of your patient with the doctor or RN.

Look at the condition of their finger nails from time to time. Notice if they need trimming. If their nails are yellowing with longitudinal ridging, suspect Diabetes Mellitus. Something that looks like a small blood blister under the nail bed may indicate Lupus or a heart condition.

If you see a longitudinal dark brown line, suspect Addison's disease. If the nail bed has a brown coloration, suspect renal disease.

Tip #8: BE ALERT TO SWALLOWING PROBLEMS

These can come out of nowhere and cause anxiety. Use applesauce to put a pill in or, if appropriate, crush the medication and put into the applesauce. I do this will all my patients meds. I do recommend checking with your pharmacist first.

If the swallowing problem has to do with food, then use a food processor and just smash it into a puree. I also serve cottage cheese, protein drink, and bologna salad from Kroger's. It tastes just like ham salad, it's inexpensive and ready to go but you may need to request it. They'll order it for ya. I usually order it and then get at least five pounds so they won't get stuck with the whole lot. Have them package it in one pound containers. I freeze and de-thaw these when I need them. You would never know it was frozen, and this is one of the few salad-type entrees you can do this to.

Tip #9: BE ALERT TO THE PATIENT DISCARDING MEDS WHEN YOU AREN'T LOOKING

Your patient's are sneakier than you might ever imagine, so don't think they won't spit out their pills when you aren't looking.

Tip #10: BE SURE TO HAVE ADEQUATE LIGHTING IN THE PATIENT'S AREA

I use those energy efficient bulbs to reduce electric cost. The lighting is for you as much as it is for the patient. You need good lighting when you visual inspection of your patient daily looking for signs of bed sores or irritation.

Tip#11: INSTALL GRAB BARS EVERYWHERE THE PATIENT FREQUENTS

This is a must do if you want to prevent your patient from falling and obtaining a serious injury. I put three on the shower/tub, one by the toilet, and elsewhere as needed. I recently saw a new suction mounted grab bar that was very impressive. At under $30, they are ideal for smooth tub/shower liners. The upside is they can be easily moved around to suit your needs (plus I actually used one to pull a dent out of my Avalon ☺)

TIP #12: INSTALL BATH TUB NON-SKID 'STICK-ONS' (I DON'T MEAN THE KIND WITH THE TASSELS EITHER)

I used non-skid stick-ons from Home Depot for stairs. They are super wide and long. You can purchase the little star shapes, etc., but I like to go overboard with huge wide rectangular strips.

Tip #13: INSTALL NIGHT LIGHTS IN BEDROOMS, HALLS, & BATHROOMS

Redneck night lights, such as Bud Lite neon signs, are okay too and provide ambiance. You know I'm joking, right?

Tip #14: INSTALL DOOR CHIME/BELL ON PATIENT'S DOOR

Depending on the stage of dysfunction that your patient is in you may find it critical to know when the person leaves and returns from their room, especially at night. If you don't hear the return ring, check to see if Patient has fallen or fainted.

Tip #15: INSTALL SOUND TRANSMITTERS AND RECEIVERS IN THE PATIENT'S ROOM

I went to a Target store baby department and found what I wanted. I recommend you buy two receivers for each transmitter (or two receivers and a transmitter for each patient). The reason for the second receiver is that one can be permanently fixed in your own bedroom powered by the wall outlet and the other one, powered by batteries, you can carry with you at all times. I had good success with "The First Years" by Learning Curve. The only drawback is that the volume control thumbwheel, even with ridges, is so slick you will have trouble turning the unit off or on.

TIP #16: PLACE A 'FALL MAT' BESIDES THE PATIENT'S BED

Some nursing homes use these. They may be difficult to find, but an office supply store should have something durable and cushiony, like the mats that cashiers stand on all day. I found a 3X5 mat with beveled (sloping) edges on the internet for $115 for. It may sound pricy, but it's much less than repairing a broken hip.

Tip #17: LOWER THE HEIGHT OF THE PATIENT'S BED

This is the way I approached the issue of fall safety. I removed the top mattress and replaced it with a 3" thick dense 'memory foam' cushion that contours to the body. I purchased it from Sam's Club for about $129. (This memory foam was defective because it didn't help my patient's memory one bit ☺)

Tip #18: PLACE 'EMERGENCY CAREGIVER' BELL OR SWITCH IN PATIENT'S ROOM

This is a great idea for emergencies but ONLY if the patient has adequate cognition to understand how and when to use it. I used a wireless doorbell transmitter from Radio Shack. I strapped it onto a block of wood using red tape for visibility and placed the door chime receiver in my bedroom. Instruct the patient to use it only for emergency situations.

Tip #19: PLACE A LARGE, EASILY READABLE CLOCK IN PATIENT'S ROOM

It's important to help the patient keep oriented as much as possible. Don't invest much, because soon it will be useless also.

Tip #20: PLACE SIGNS AT SELECTED AREAS

These are signs that tell the patient what to expect or what day it is; general, simple, but helpful information. For example: "Kitchen closes at 7pm." "Refrigerator closes at 7pm" (then lock it with something).

I use these on the kitchen door, which I have to keep locked except when in use. The signs will only work for a period and then the patient won't understand them. Use whatever aids you can for whatever period you can. Be flexible and look ahead towards the next event.

Tips #21: INVITE FRIENDS OF PATIENT FOR REGULAR VISITS

This is a must do item. Actually, anybody will do. They just want to chat with any and everybody.

Tip #22: PLACE FAMILIAR OBJECTS (MEMORIBELIA) WHERE APPROPRIATE

This helps to orient their mind with the use of chronology. It is common for a patient to feel lost or confused (even by the caregiver). Things from their past may help to reassure them.

Tip #23: INSTALL SLIDE BAR OR DEADBOLT LOCK TO CELLAR STAIRS

Install what you can... anything is better than nothing. A slide bar is the easiest, but make sure the patient can't open it.

Tip #24: SERVE FOODS THAT ARE NOT BLAND

This is because the patient's sense of smell often is the first sense to go. This alters their sense of taste. For instance, flavors can no longer be distinguished when the sense of smell is gone. Making something yummy means you have to hit the basic tastes. These are sweet, sour, salty, and yucky (I'm not entirely sure about the last category, but I think it's right ☺). As long as the patient has a tongue with the basic receptors, they can enjoy the basic tastes, but everything else tastes the same. Here's a real example: My patient likes to make his own breakfast at 6 am every morning. He always eats waffles that are simply toasted in the toaster.

I forgot to check the stock of waffles in the freezer one night. The next morning, I arose early to get them but met my patient in the kitchen. He said to me, "I think there is something wrong with the toaster because I can't get the other waffle out."

What in fact he did was mistake the 3 oz. sausage patties in the freezer for waffles. The 'waffle' in the toaster just fell apart and died in a pool of fat. He had gotten the other sausage waffle out and placed onto his plate. It was just raw meat covered with syrup, and he had eaten about 75% of it. I asked, "Why are you eating that raw sausage?"

For him, the sausage had no appreciable taste, only texture, which by then was similar to a syrup-soaked waffle (a true story).

Tip #25: EARLY DEMENTIA—COMFORTING TALK, LATE DEMENTIA —COMFORTING SMILES

Even though your patient may not seem to be understanding a thing you are saying, they often pick up on your intent and attitude which can be very reassuring to them. Just pretend to understand whatever they are saying and smile, but do it with sincerity. In the later stages, smiling and plenty of hugs is about all you can provide.

Tip #26: COVER HOT WATER HANDLES COMPLETELY WITH BRIGHT RED TAPE

This is simple, but really makes life easier when ya can't think. It's good for the tired caregiver also. Sometimes, when I feel numb from it all, I am glad I don't have to use any more brain power to remember which handle is hot or cold. You will have days like that too, smile.

Tip #27: COVER COLD WATER HANDLES COMLETELY WITH GREENTAPE

Ditto again!

Tip #28: SET THERMOSTAT 3-4 DEGREES HIGHER IN THE PATIENT'S ROOM FOR APPROPRIATE PATIENT

Remember that most patients have a reduced metabolism and need additional heat. The exception might be the more robust patient who might not need the additional heat, or even need a cooling fan.

Tip #29: RESTRICT THE PATIENT'S ACCESS TO THE TELEPHONE

Expect the unexpected. Your patient might accidentally dial Alaska, but if someone there is willing to talk, I guarantee your patient is willing to... never mind a $300 phone charge.

Tip #30: RESTRICT THE PATIENT'S ACCESS TO INTERNET

Your patient can really have a field day if they get hooked up to some off shore casino or 1-900-sex talk numbers where the phone charges might be as high as $50/minute or more. Casinos use credit cards and the sky's the limit. The financial risk here is too great to take. Your computer must be in a lockable room or you must have program controls that prohibit the user from accessing certain types of sites that you specify.

Tip #31: RESTRICT THE PATIENT'S ACCESS TO MEDS

Some patients will try to eat meds like candy. I keep them out of their reach on a top shelf. They like the brightly colored ones the most.

Tip #32: INSURE THAT ALL ROOMS OCCUPIED BY PATIENT HAVE FIRE/CO$_2$ ALARMS

Tip #33: KEEP SEVERAL SMALL FIRE EXTINGUISHERS IN PLAIN SITE IN EACH ROOM

Tip #34: MAINTAIN GOOD FIRST AID KIT WITH PLENTY OF WIDECOMPRESSES, BANDAGES, TAPE, CAYENNE PEPPER, ETC.

Tip #35: EXERCISE CAUTION WHEN USING ELECTRICAL HEATERS

A special note of caution here: People with dementia often have reduced ability to feel heat. While using an electric heater to warm up a room can be a good idea, a mobile patient can bump into them. The result could be possible second and third degree burns on your patient's legs. They might not even be aware of their tissue damage, but your visiting social worker might want to report you for abuse.

The other danger is that dementia patients may have no sense of danger. I have found an electric heater running full blast and sitting in the middle of a pile of newspapers or on those old, tissue-thin sewing patterns (for the patient who thinks someday they will do sewing again).

Tip #36: REMOVE/IMMOBILIZE ALL 'FLOOR SNAKES'

Extension cords, temporary cords, dirty clothes, and literally anything lying on the floor can trip a patient or caregiver time and again. Pick them up now or cover over with wide grey duct tape or black 'Gorilla' tape. THIS IS IMPORTANT!

Tip #37: KEEP SEVERAL UP-TO-DATE PHOTOS OF PATIENT

These are good to have in case your patient wanders off and the police need a description.

Tip #38: KEEP EMERGENCY MEDICAL INFO 'VIAL OF LIFE' IN REFRIGERATOR DOOR

I keep this in the frig door shelf... not the freezer door either. Your 911 rescue team will appreciate this too. The 'vial or life' packet should have a list of medications the patient is on, any allergies, and living will directive. 911 teams are alerted to look in the fridge for this info (or at least that was the intent).

Tip #39: AMBULATORY PATIENTS NEED TO WALK AND WALK AND... WALK

This is essential for reducing the rate of decline of mental and physical attributes, as well as significantly helping to maintain the peristalsis of the G.I. tract.

Tip #40: CHECK DEHYDRATION—A COMMON PROBLEM

So how do you check for dehydration? In a young person, you just pinch their skin on their arms and see if it stays 'tented' or not. You knew that, right?

But the skin on an older person can be too thin for the pinch test to work or they can be so obese that you might not be able to tell. Here is a well kept secret, divulged just to me (and about a million nurses): Pinch the skin in the middle of the forehead. It's simple, but effective. Who knew?

Probably the best way to gauge dehydration in an end stage patient is to simply keep a record of their liquid intake and determine the relative amount of urine left in their diapers.

Tip #41: KEEP A NUMBER OF BOXES OF LATEX EXAM GLOVES IN KEY AREAS

Exam gloves are available in materials other than Latex should you be allergic. Latex is the most commonly used and available in either powdered or un-powdered varieties. We personally dislike the powdered type because it leaves a bad residual powder smell on our hands. We use McKesson Medi Pak #20131300 powder free latex exam gloves with 100 per box. They are strong, durable, and rarely tear.

Tip #42: ENCOURAGE GROUP PRAYER PARTICIPATION AT EACH MEAL

Tip #43: USE A 'RELIEF' CAREGIVER AT LEAST TWICE A WEEK FOR YOURSELF

You need to exercise five days a week for optimum mental health (and physical health also). The secret to success is to make it a ritual that you do whether or not you think you need to. One purpose of exercise is to flood the brain with endorphin neurotransmitters to calm the mind and minimize the production of harmful cortisol derivatives.

The other essential aspect for respite caregivers is to give yourself some quiet time or quality time to visit with friends, etc.

Tip #44: CONSTIPATION—OLD TIMEY PREPARATION FIX

Mix equal parts of applesauce, wheat bran, and prune juice. Mix well and keep in the fridge. Every morning, take one tablespoon. (donated by Jackie Graves, RN for Second Presbyterian Church-Lexington, Kentucky). My wife & I tried it. It was safe.

The 'UKRAINIAN RAINMAKER'—beet salad—another great recipe for constipation relief. This is from my wife's homeland of the Ukraine so it's got to be good! The active ingredients are the beets. Their mechanism is not well understood (not at all might be more accurate), but I must warn you that your patient might be scared when he/she spots what appears to be blood coating his stool (not their chair). The first time I tried this, it scared the PJ's off me because I thought the beet mucin was blood. I knew I was a goner! For the record, there was no blood. The bright, red mucin-like coating seems to work like 'Teflon,' if you get what I mean. Also, you will note that the stool itself is softer as though there were some sort of oil emulsification process going on (perhaps like Mira Lax?).

THE RECIPE:

1. Boil beets (2 or 3) for 40 min.

2. Discard water and cover the beets with cold water for about a NY minute.

3. Allow them to cool down and then grate the beets (coarsely)

4. Add as desired:

   a. pickles & mayo

b. apricots, nuts, & mayo

c. canned green peas & mayo

(Use either a, b, or c, but do not mix the combinations... I'm not sure why.)

Tip #45: TAKE THE PATIENT AWAY FROM HOUSE AT LEAST ONCE A WEEK

Go to a movie, if possible, or to the park, a restaurant, or even to the grocery where they supply 'walkers' with wheels and a basket. Soon you will no longer have this option, and tomorrow may be too late.

Tip #46: USE A LARGE INFO PLACARD ID OR DOOR LOCK

Some patients just have a propensity for wandering off. This can often be very time consuming to find and retrieve the patient not to mention the possibility of injury or death. A name, address, phone number to call ID tag is fastened to the patients clothing. Use adhesive labels, or pin clasp fastener. Another solution is to install a door latching system that cannot be operated by the patient, e.g. digital lock (very pricy) or simple padlock (inexpensive but more annoying). Design your own but git R' done!

Tip #47: PROTECT THE PATIENT FROM DEPRESSING NEWS

The patient runs the risk of misinterpretation and imprinting stimuli for depression in the subconscious. I only speak about happy events or nothing at all. It's pretty quiet around the house now (just kidding), but I try to inject humor into everything as much as possible. However, I do think it would be appropriate to discuss the patient's feelings about death in order to help reassure them. For example: If their fear is about whether their spouse will be cared for properly, then you can explain how this will be provided. This is reassuring news.

Tip #48: DO PETS POSE TRIP HAZARD?

There are many reports about patients tripping over a dog or cat sleeping at the top of the steps. For advanced dementia, you must keep pets separate from the patient except during supervised times.

Tip #49: FIND WHAT RELAXES THE PATIENT, MUSIC, WATCHING TV, READING, ETC. (AS LONG AS IT'S LEGAL ☺)

Tip #50: INSTALL REAL 'DAYLIGHT' BULBS IN THE PATIENT'S READING AREA

This can help with mood disorders and 'sundowner's syndrome.' These bulbs are the 'bluish' bulbs and can be purchased in either the normal bulb shape or like a neon tube type.

Tip #51: PRESSURE SORES—USE MEMORY FOAM FOR ALLEVIATING PRESSURE POINTS

Pressure sores can sometimes be a real problem. Prevention is easier than trying to treat after the fact. I used a "memory foam" (3-4" thick). This will go a long way towards alleviating pressure points between the patient's body and the mattress (forewarning: some new memory foams must be aired out for a few days before using because they stink).

Tip #52: PURCHASE TWO DIFFERENT COPIES OF DRUG INFORMATION BOOKS/MANUALS

I like to keep one by my bed (read it until I fall asleep) and the other in the kitchen area. (These are the only two areas in a house correct?) You need to study the meds! Often, one manual will be able to fill in info that the other manual didn't list.

Tip #53: PURCHASE AN ADDITIONAL BOOK OF BIBLE SCRIPTURES

You can never have enough. What more can I say? He is the

Way... learn how now.

Tip #54: RENT/PURCHASE PORTABLE TOILET AND PORTABLE TOILET SEAT WITH RAISED HANDLES

This is very useful for changing diapers actually. The handles give the patient something to hold onto while you cut the diaper and remove it from the patient. Then turn the patient around and have them sit on top of the closed toilet seat while you remove their sweat pants and put on clean socks and the diaper. Later, you will be doing the diaper change entirely on the bed.

Tip #55: SET THE HOT WATER TEMPERATURE FOR A MAXIMUM OF 115-120 DEGREES

I set the temperature at the hot water heater by locating and removing the two screws on the small, 4 x 8 cover plates fastened on the side of the tank.

One access port has the thermostat. **Disclaimer: This job should be done only be a licensed union electrician and accompanied by a licensed union plumber and maybe a couple of state code inspectors to insure maximum safety.** Change the set point to the desired range of 115-120 degrees. Then, just give them your check book and get a paper route for the extra income you will need.

Tip #56: PURCHASE WASHABLE CHAIR COVERS

Or you can retrofit your home's interior with white plastic lawn furniture... it's so easy to clean and will attract some new and different friends fur ya ta visit wit.

Tip #57: PURCHASE OR MAKE CORNER PROTECTORS FOR FURNITURE

These can be bought (I just can't remember where), or, to save $$, I just use a big plug of pre-softened bubble gum, then a colored felt marker to match furniture color. I have heard rumors that my mountain friends can do all that with one plug of 'bacca. Git R done!

Tip #58: LOCATE AND ATTEND LOCAL CAREGIVER'S SUPPORT GROUP

I know it is hard to find time to attend, but I highly recommend it. You need to meet others that you can reach out to from time to time. Having friends that understand what you are going through is priceless.

Tip #59: LOCATE ALZHEIMER'S 'BEST FRIENDS DAY CARE CENTER'

Tip #60: LOCATE COMMUNITY CARE SERVICES FOR ALZHEIMER'S PATIENTS

Tip #61: EACH DAY FIND ONE NEW ASPECT ABOUT YOUR PATIENT THAT YOU CAN LOVE.

Tip #62: EACH DAY FIND ONE MORE SMILE FOR YOUR PATIENT

Tip #63: EACH DAY, TALK WITH GOD ONE MORE TIME

Tip #64: LEARN DIFFERENT WAYS OF COMMUNICATING

For example: Act out laying your head down to communicate "it's time for your nap."

Tip #65: EXPRESS AGREEMENT EVEN WHEN YOUR PATIENT CAN NO LONGER VERBALLY COMMUNICATE

Of course, only agree when it is appropriate, not if the patient is trying to say, "I'm going to bite you." Be rational about it.

Tip #66: LOOK HAPPY AND SMILE OFTEN... IT MIGHT EVEN BECOME INFECTIOUS

Tip #67: EXPLORE NEW HOBBIES YOU CAN DO AT HOME... TRY EXPRESSIVE HOBBIES

Experiment with water colors, clay modeling, pattern cutting, etc. These can build rapport and trust between patient and caregiver.

Tip #68: EXPLORE AROMA ESSENCES TO STIMULATE SENSORY AND GUSTATORY RESPONSES

These often stimulate the patient to recall memories. With each one, ask the patient, "What does this remind you of?" Pleasant memories will bring contentment to your patient and reduce their anxiety. *Note: This does not include the use of 'weed' or other mind altering aromas.*

Tip #69: PRACTICE '3 MINUTE CAREGIVER MEDITATIONS' THREE TIMES A DAY

Keep squaring that number each day and ya might get your 'wings' real soon ☺. Just do the best you can when you can.

Tip #70: WALK WITH A MOBILE PATIENT EACH DAY

Let the patient use your walker occasionally ☺. Walking stimulates the entire cardio-vascular system potentially heading off serious health problems from poor circulation.

Tip #71: REDUCE WATER FLOW RATE AT EACH FAUCET BY $1/_3$

Under the sink there should be a separate valve for the hot and cold.

Adjust accordingly. This is to limit the potential for sink overflows and high water bills. Just one faucet left on for an afternoon can add an extra $120 to your water bill!

Tip #72: THROW ALL YOUR PATIENT'S SOCKS AWAY

Go buy new ones all the same color and size. I recommend the kind that comes just above the heel by a couple of inches, black, and a loose, stretchy weave (I like Dr. Scholl's Socks for Diabetics; you can get 2 pairs at Wal-Mart for less than $5). *You want a sock that is easy to get on and off the patient several times a day as you change their diapers.* To me I was very frustrated when trying to handle the patient and I reach into the 'sock' box and can't find two socks that match. Important.

Tip #73: BUY SWEAT PANTS FOR YOUR PATIENT TO WEAR AT HOME

Do not buy the nylon or plastic kind. Buy soft cotton, but NEVER IN BLACK OR WHITE. These colors generally do not show 'spotting' from urine as well as other colors that produce better contrasting effects when 'spotting' upon. Grey is a great color for showing wetness.

I find that if I go to Wal-Mart and ask for men's sweats I get my best deal. These are about $5 per pair, in soft cotton or something. The men's sweats fit my patients, both male and female. You need at least 6 or more per patient because you might have to change them as often as you change their diapers.

Tip #74: KEEP NUTRITIOUS 'LIQUID MEALS' ON HAND

I keep plenty of 'Slim Fast' or similar (carried by Sam's Club, most pharmacies, and grocery stores) on hand stored in the garage and a case in the fridge. Expect to pay about $22-27 per case at Sam's Club and up to $36 per case when bought in smaller packs at the grocery.

This is for one patient. For the other patient, I keep her favorite vanilla flavored shake (distributed by Sam's Club under the name Member's Mark 'Balanced Nutritional Drink.' It is a competitor to Ensure but much less expensive) in the food pantry out of reach. That patient could founder herself on these drinks if I kept them in the fridge where she could get at em' all the time. These drinks insure that my patients get a well balanced meal along with their home cooked food prepared by my wife.

I personally no longer use 'Boost,' which is popular, but I found that my patient was spilling small amounts everywhere and that stuff is almost impossible to wash off wood flooring after setting a while. Trying to communicate with the company was not fruitful either. Our antebellum flooring is speckled like it has chicken pox everywhere. Not pretty.

Tip #75: BATHE THE PATIENT REGULARLY

As long as you keep changing their diapers on a regular basis and give your patient at least one full tub shower/bath per week you should have no problems. The biggest threat is from wet diapers that have been left on for too long. Wet diapers, especially in the summer, can quickly cause cell toxicity from ammonia released by bacteria. What you end up with, are patches of skin that are reddened, sore, inflamed and subject to easy penetration by bacteria as the patient scratches at the itchy skin.

Tip #76: USE A STRAW OR 'SIP-A-MUG' TO REDUCE DROOLING BY YOUR PATIENT

Tip #77: IF YOUR PATIENT IS A SMOKER, START REMOVING A CIGARETTE PER DAY AS LONG AS YOU CAN CONTROL THE SITUATION

I know you are already asking, "What's the point?" Well, you don't want to hear your patient struggling to get each breath as they battle drowning in their own inflamed lung secretions... not a very good 'Kodak moment.' On the other hand, your patient may insist on smoking. Spell it out for them, and if they still want to smoke, then this becomes one of those 'quality of life' issues. Another technique is to make the experience not so enjoyable. Try adding a couple of drops of cod liver oil into the tobacco on each cigarette. Do what you think is best.

Tip #78: KEEP SEVERAL PAIRS OF LARGE FINGERNAIL CLIPPERS IN CONVIENENT LOCATIONS

When you have the opportunity to trim nails you generally can't find the nail clippers. While you go look for them the patient walks off. Cleaning nails is especially important if your patient is in the habit of using his/her fingers to dig around the anal supply duct to facilitate a constipation problem. Then they spread germs everywhere and to everything they touch.

E. coli (and other buggers as well) can thrive for as long as there is a food source and moisture. Wooden floors allow them to thrive because there is usually some moisture condensing on lower levels, not to mention spilled food particles. On the other hand, wood has a natural antibiotic, lignin, which seems effective in controlling the spread of bacteria. I use clippers, determination, and ear plugs to trim my patient's nails. The ear plugs are for the screams of "You are killing me!"

Keeping the nails cut back reduces the sheer volume of fertilizer that can be stored under them.

Tip #79: KEEP ANTISEPTIC TOWELETTES FOR CLEANUP AFTER FERTILIZER SPILLS

I keep something like Clorox towelettes on hand for these jobs. You need more than a fragrant towelette, you need a 'killer' towelette!

Tip #80: FOR DRY MOUTH

Patients sometimes get this and most medical supply stores carry a glycerin based applicator you swab the patient's mouth with. Alternatively, I have given the patient a teaspoon of honey with the instructions not to swallow for as long as possible. The honey works by the ol' osmotic gradient or something. Anyway, it can pull in moisture from everywhere. Others in the house might become mysteriously dehydrated no less, to the chagrin of the patient. Okay... just kidding.

Tip #81: A TAX ISSUE

If you hire a caregiver for respite, check with your states laws regarding how much you can pay out before you are required to pay additional Medicare and social security costs. Yes, I find the government will go to any lengths to squeeze money out of dying patients and caregivers. It's no wonder that most respite caregivers will work for a little less and want to be paid in cash! Hint... hint...

Tip #82: HOW TO MAKE YOUR OWN PROTEIN DRINK SUPPLEMENT

Okay, call me cheap, but protein drinks can get to be expensive, particularly when your patients live years beyond expectations. Here is what I do. I buy a product carried by Sam's Club (and health stores) called 'EAS' for energy-athletics-strength. The package claims 100% whey protein. Whey is made from milk and is the 'Gold Standard' for protein. Athletes use it for muscle enhancement because it is so high in amino acids, especially in the branched chain ones. I supplement this with multivitamins to supply the minerals.

The main difference between whey, Boost, and the Balanced Nutritional drink is the former is all protein and the two latter are mainly minerals, some protein from casein, and sugars. That is why EAS should be used as a supplement with other sources that have minerals. I buy the six pound bag of EAS and it outlasts the Boost and the BN Drink by 3:1 or more (if you do the math, you should find the ratio is really much higher at 10:1, but I always siphon off some for myself). I mix it with either water or milk. Whey has a nice 'sweet' taste of its own.

The cost is about $23 for a 6 lb. bag at Sam's. Cost wise, a serving of whey + multivitamins= about $.10, while Boost is over $1. That's a big... big difference!

Tip #83: TIP FOR GETTING THOSE LATEX EXAM GLOVES OFF

You can save money on non-patient applications as well if you use the same pair of gloves more than once (like for cleaning). This is particularly suited for the gloves without the stinky powder in them. It's easy to pull them off, but then they are inside out, and sometimes it takes a while to return it to the outside in position again. Here is what I learned from some nurses. With your palm up, lift the glove edge near the center of your palm and blow (like a balloon). At the same time, grasp with the fingers of your other hand and pull the glove off. Finally, the crowning moment of glory arrives when you complete this with that characteristic loud 'snap' as the latex glove flies off your hand and smacks the closest bystander.

This takes some practice, but when done right, it's so simple. You will be amazed that you didn't discover it earlier. (Also, it shows that you are not a newbie, but a seasoned veteran caregiver using tricks from the 'old school.' You can walk tall now!)

Tip #84: CONTROL FOR ACHES & PAINS

Here, I am referring to everyday sort of aches and pains. For example: If your patient has been sitting in the wrong position all day and they have a sore neck, or (like this morning) your patient tried to get out of bed and got halfway out, with their legs touching the floor and then gave up because of pain in the hip area from hyper flexion. I find that the over-the-counter product, Aleve used in moderation, does wonders. If the problem is chronic joint pain from arthritis, I would ask your doctor for a prescription of Ketoprofin cream (sold under the name of Orovil or sometimes just formulated by the pharmacist on the spot). This is a vanishing base cream with the active ingredient, Ketoprofin. Ketoprofin has also, reportedly, been very good for treating fibromyalgia.

I find the cream useful, but only use it from time to time because it's pricey (about $50 for a couple of ounces). It's worth trying once just to see if it helps you or the patient. The only contraindication for Aleve (or any of the NSAID meds) is that the patient does not have kidney problems or is pregnant. Naw... I didn't think so mate.

Tip #85: A GREAT BREAKFAST FOR CONSTIPATION PROBLEMS

I give my patient a bowl of oatmeal accompanied by a tasty cup of her favorite drink, which has her meds dissolved in it along with Mira Lax, which is completely tasteless. She is a real champion after that. I keep my patient on Mira Lax, about 1/3 cap full, for a daily maintenance routine. I have known others that have taken it for a couple of years with no side effects. It is entirely tasteless. I would be alert to giving too much and causing diarrhea, which then might result in a potential electrolyte imbalance. For that reason, I would always consult with a physician before using it on a long term basis. I personally think this product (Mira Lax) is a huge help in eliminating fecal impaction problems. Since using this product, my patient has not had a single recurrence of fecal impaction. It does not come out runny, just soft, and I use wet wipes to clean up with. Anything beats fecal impaction! For now, this seems to have stopped the pain of constipation. Yea! (PS- have your doc write a Rx for the generic form of Mira Lax and save $$)

Tip #86: HOW TO STOP A SMALL BLEEDING CUT

Sometimes you may nick or 'wing' the patient when trying to trim their nails because they try to pull away at the very moment you clip with the clipper. This may cause a nuisance bleed (a small bleed that doesn't want to stop). Here are two techniques I have used successfully: The first is to use a clean white paper towel and compress it over the cut for five minutes (you can tape it in place also). I have found this to heal quicker than a standard band aid. For one thing, the fibrous surface induces the blood to clot. Also, the lignin in the paper acts as an antiseptic. Lignin comes from the pulp of a tree.

The other technique is to use a tea bag compress for five minutes. The tannin in the tea is a natural coagulator for blood.

Tip #87: HOW TO REMOVE ODORS FROM A ROOM

I know that every caregiver at some time has dealt with the urine smell that lingers in a patient's bedroom. This technique works very well providing you get the right onions. Slice a large onion (white) in half and put one half on the north side of the room and the other side on the south side of the room. By morning, the urine odor will be gone. (My next book is on how to rid your house of onion odors... just kidding ☺).

Tip #88: HOW TO REMOVE URINE ODORS FROM CLOTHES

Of course you could pre-wash, and then wash, and hang your clothes outdoors in the sun for several days, but as a caregiver you don't have time for that. Here is one solution that I like: Instead of placing normal soap into your washing machine, I suggest using Lestoil. Your clothes will, however, trade the scent of urine for pine, but I can deal with that. Also, the Lestoil, unlike Pine-Sol, contains a strong dry-cleaning chemical, so let me warn you that you may need to test your items for colorfastness. I am beyond that. I want results. My patient's top pullover came out of the washer with big splotches of color change. I told her it was very trendy now, but in the 60's we called it tie-dying. She is cool with that.

I can't leave without giving this last remedy because it works so well. Lightly wrap your stinky items in either cloth or wrapping paper. Bury in the soil anywhere above the freeze line (usually at about two feet down). Wait two to four days, depending on amount of smell, and then dig them up. Hint- bury a bone beneath the packages and in two days borrow the neighbor's dog... point to the location and say, "Bone... dig." Seriously, the soil is chock full of friendly molds (like aspergillius, mucor, alternaria, and penicillium) and mutant bacteria that can cleave the nitrogen atoms off ammonia at thirty paces.

Tip #89: HOW TO REMOVE URINE ODORS FROM A RUG

Sooner or later, if you have not removed your rugs by then, your patient will have an 'accident' and urine will get planted into your rug. Here is what to do: First take rug outdoors and make a swale (cavity) where the urine was. Pour in hot water with some dishwater detergent (Calgon) at one tablespoon per gallon of water. If you have it, add some Borax. Get rid of as much of the unbound urine as possible. Then pour vinegar directly onto the stain area and let sit until it's almost dry. Then, add baking soda and let it dry. Vacuum it off and the smell is gone. Well, almost completely gone. I found that once my carpets got blessed by my patient several times, I just had to throw them (the carpets) away.

Tip #89a: HOW TO REMOVE URINE ODORS FROM PET FUR

With your pet happily sedated, use fine shearing clippers. Do all, save for maybe a Mohawk ridgeline. Wash with tomato juice and rinse clean. Style as desired and place briefly in safe, bright sun. UVa + UVb + what's left of our ozone blanket will complete the sanitization process. Be careful not to leave Fido out in the sun for too long.

Tip #90: HOW TO DEODORIZE THE OUTDOOR GARBAGE CAN

I can tell you that on a hot summer day, with our garbage can full of diapers (tied in baggies), the odor will knock your socks off from ten feet. The solution is to keep a gallon jug of Pine sol besides the can and add a cup as needed. Now, is my name Martha or what? What a relief to me and the neighborhood. Alternatively, just don't get within ten feet and put a basketball hoop over top... need I say more Wildcat fans? Using the baggies it gives a whole new meaning to the term 'foul shot,' huh? (I know...it's a guy thing).

Tip #91: ANOTHER WAY TO STOP SMALL BLEEDING CUTS

I keep a bottle of cayenne pepper around for this use only. For a nuisance cut that won't stop bleeding, cover the wound with a thick layer of the pepper, cover with something like a paper towel, and firmly hold in place. Within just a minute or two the bleeding should stop because of the high amount of vitamin K in the pepper. Vitamin K is a natural clotting agent for the body. It doesn't sting either (unless you eat it).

Tip #92: ESTABLISH YOUR OWN INNER SANCTUARY

"I would tell the new caregiver to make sure they have a place in their home where they can get away from everything and everyone and that would be respected as your private space." (Submitted by Lois L.)

Tip #93: DON'T BEAT YOURSELF UP

"One of the hardest things has been for us to decide when 911 needs to be called. With dementia, things can be exaggerated so much you don't know when to really be concerned. also their inability to explain how they're feeling. So, sometimes you let things go and watch closely for awhile when maybe you should have reacted sooner. At those times, you need to be gentle with yourself; you're doing the best you can. Don't beat yourself up over what you didn't do. Just take it from there and go on." (Submitted by Lois L.)

Tip #94: CHANGE YOUR ATTITUDE

When I began to think of my caregiving at home as my ministry right now and how important that is, my attitude about giving up other things (such as various degrees of freedom) began to change.

Tip #95: DON'T EXPECT OTHERS TO UNDERSTAND WHAT YOU FEEL

"Don't expect too much of others in the area of understanding something they have not experienced. Be realistic."(Submitted by Lois L.) This is one area where I hear so many troubling complaints. Often the caregiver is mystified why a brother or sister doesn't ever want to volunteer to help out. The reason is simple. First, they don't understand the tremendous strain you are under, and second, they think as long as you are doing the job their phone is not ringing off the hook then there's no problem. Sometimes a clueless sibling feels that if he/she points out the mistakes you are making that this will be well received information most worthy of an "OMG sibling, how thoughtful of you!." Now for some reason a caregiver will always hear this differently. I see this all the time. If you, as caregiver, would like some help, it is imperative that you clearly make your case and, in NO UNCERTAIN TERMS, tell the clueless sibling what you want to happen. If you have POA, you should have some bargaining power. Don't beat yourself up if you do not get the response you are looking for either. Some people, for whatever reason, just cannot produce the behavior we would like to see from them. They will be judged in due course, so deal with it. If caregiving were easy, then everyone would be doing it right? (Hmmm... may not be the right cliché, ya think?)

It is also worth noting that you will find most, but not all, senior citizens over the age of 70 will not like this caregiving manual for a number of reasons. This is because their logic and rationale has changed; they see everything in a different light. Again, this is why caregivers and their patients create such high interactive stress. Conversely, I have not had one single complaint about this manual from any of the many, many caregivers I have interviewed. In fact, they all echo the same advice and feelings. Go ahead and be the first to complain... then we can play transference and counter transference until the cows come home... just kidding.

> My point is... don't seek your patient's input on whether this material makes good sense... no way Jose'!

Tip #96: RECOGNIZE THE WARNING SIGNS FOR YOURSELF

"I do try to take care of myself and realize when I'm feeling I don't want to go anywhere for a couple of days, that's a sign of trouble for me. I make myself get out and walk through the mall, or call someone to have lunch. I try to have a book going all the time, and that helps me escape mentally. I email friends and relatives; that's another escape." (Submitted by Lois L.)

This topic is so important because depression will bite like a snake in the grass. Before I know it, I am staring out the window at nothing and enjoying it... or I just want to sleep... just a little more sleep. When ya git bit... don't go lifeless, go exercise, or read the scriptures while you walk. Promise yourself you will begin doing some exercise now for an hour and then you can reward yourself by coming back and staring out the window. I find once I get moving, I don't want to resume staring out the window, but I enjoy knowing I could if I wanted.

Tip #97: POST A DNR DOCUMENT NEAR THE ENTRY DOOR

I am assuming that you want a DNR order, but you may not and I respect that. The need is for the EMT team so they don't unnecessarily try to use those big zillion volt 'shocker' paddles over and over, trying to create the world's biggest French fry.

Tip #98: I TEST MY PATIENTS MEDS ON MYSELF

This may seem a bit controversial, but I think in some cases it is well worth it. For example: When my patient was complaining about what might be causing some new dizzy spells, I searched the literature for all his meds. The side effects for all of them included dizziness (and about everything else you can think of). To find the culprit I took the latest med he had been prescribed myself. To no surprise, I felt dizzy too. I took it a couple more times, and it was clear this was the med.

The reason this was important was because it quickly ruled out heart and pulmonary issues as the most probable culprit. Eventually, my patient's system adjusted to the medication, and the dizziness went away.

You, most likely, will also find some antibiotics are not as gentle as we are led to believe. This will help you interpret your patient's health when perhaps they cannot communicate anymore. Again, let common sense rule.

Tip #99: KNOW WHAT TO DO WHEN DEATH IS NEAR

If the patient is expected to die at home, the caregiver should know whom to call, such as hospice, or a doctor (or not call... such as an ambulance). Have the phone numbers already written down.

Tip #100: KNOW WHAT TO EXPECT WHEN DEATH IS NEAR

Some signs include loss of consciousness, the skin becomes pale or bluish, and breathing becomes erratic followed by confusion and sleepiness. Secretions in the throat often lead to what is described as the 'death rattle' and can be reduced by repositioning the patient on their side. By the time this occurs, the patient is not aware of any breathing noises and may continue for several hours. At or very near to the time of death, there may be uncontrolled muscle 'tics' or involuntary movements and possibly a brief seizure. Note that the heart may actually continue for a few beats even after breathing stops. During this time there may be involuntary chest movement and then a frightening seizure.

This can really be scary the first time you see it. While all this is a bit unnerving, it should be seen as a natural part of the process of dying, like the body receiving a passport before the soul can be released to heaven.

Tip #101: WHAT TO DO AT THE TIME OF DEATH

You should know who will make the death certificate out. This must be an authorized individual. It might be a doctor, nurse, medical examiner, funeral home director, or someone assigned from Hospice. You should notify this individual beforehand about when you expect death to occur. A death certificate will be filled out and you should make at least a dozen copies for the ensuing barrage of notifications that must be handled involving insurance claims, accounts, and other holdings. Of course, schedule a meeting with your family attorney ASAP.

Tip #102: HOUSE NUMBER MARKING

Mark your house number in such a manner that it can be seen from the street (when the EMS team is still a half block away). It should have reflective tape or coating. I prefer a marker that would stand about 3' tall so that grass you haven't had time to mow won't conceal it. I also like to see another sign near the entry to the front door. This should also be directed towards the street. This will be your backup in case the neighbor's dog or cat should pull up your street sign and disappear with it (ya never know).

Tip #103: BE PREPARED FOR THAT WINTER STORM

It happens every year to somebody somewhere... a winter storm and suddenly you are without power for days. The most important thing is to preserve heat. Consult with a heating technician about your particular situation. **Ask what your choices are so that your house can have heat should a power failure occur.** They will always quote you some incredibly expensive systems. Most of us can't afford that. **The next step was to find an affordable way to achieve the outcome I wanted.** I went to my plan B to find someone (unlicensed but cheap and knowledgeable) to show me that our entire home hot water system (gas fired) could be kept running as long as the tiny hot water circulation water pump had electrical power. I had a small gasoline power generator that could sit outside and send power to this one breaker (main box breaker off). That really came in handy a few years ago. This old farmhouse was kept warm during that winter ice storm.

Word of caution: Be sure that fumes from any engine cannot re-enter your home.

Tip #104: CHANGE YOUR FRAME OF MIND FROM REACT TO ACT

This applies to all senses of the word. Whether you tend to 'overreact' to emotional issues or perhaps just trying to 'react' to the everyday needs as they develop. I have to admit, I was too much of a 'react' person and once my patient began to develop a steeper progression of symptoms, I found myself deluged with too many tasks that I was not prepared to handle. Let me share with you that when things go south you really should have a plan to handle things that normally get done in a more relaxed time frame. Specifically consider the legal intricacies that must get done when a patient dies. This will differ from state to state, but plan on meeting with your attorney and have him/her prepare a written list of things that you need to do when the time comes. Consider that if your will has to go to probate court, that will add time (as much as six months in some cases) on to the resolution. Have you got enough capital to carry you for six months in a 'down 'economy? Consider that usually a wait time of six months is needed for the legal system to receive any outstanding claims. There are numerous other 'light bulb' type of surprises that you may encounter. Better develop your roadmap now, well in advance of your patient 'going home.' I can't emphasize how important it will be to have your attorney write down what you can expect. Usually this is verbal and my mental retention span for legalese is on the order of a nanosecond... and that's on a good day. To recap again... learn to plan ahead (ACT NOW) instead of being caught with your shirt in the wringer and you just panic (REACT) because you never thought this or that would happen.

Tip #105: ORDER AT LEAST A DOZEN DEATH CERTIFICATIONS

When it's time (after your patient has passed), you want to order at least a dozen original 'death certificates.' You will be surprised how everybody demands an original. Just order twice the number of certificates you think you will need. Our state charges $6 each copy at this writing.

Tip #106: I KEEP A DYNAMITE PILL AT MY PATIENT'S BEDSIDE
(Talk to your doc about this one before you implement it.)

I keep some Dynamite (Nitroglycerin) pills on hand for what ails my patient. I had found that my patient would suffer from occasional problems of breathing, swallowing, and chest pain. All of these would scare him pretty regularly into thinking bad stuff was about to be upon him. I knew from his hospital chest radiographs (aka 'Rays') that he had a non-malignant mediastinal mass in the right side of his thoracic cavity. I also knew that this could press on his esophagus and aggravate the GERD syndrome that is so common with elderly. So I really wasn't too concerned about him having any real cardiac problems. Since the esophagus and other things like that all have valves and motor controls that get a little spastic at times, I would keep a nitroglycerin pill near his bedside. I call these pills his 'dynamite' pills. They do a great job at relaxing sphincter muscles and dilating blood vessels to provide an easier flow at less pressure. While these are great, I started my patient out on a half pill at first and later worked up to a whole pill (remember these are tiny pills too). Of course, I tested one on myself beforehand. With a half pill, I got a lot of facial flushing and a slight headache. I think my patient could eat them like candy if I let him.

Having a pill at bedside for self administration can alleviate a problem your patient may have if you have just run to the grocery. That is always when strange symptoms arise in your patient. The solution is to put only ONE dynamite pill in an easy-open container at your patient's bedside. If you put the whole prescription container near the bedside you might find your patient just took an overdose by accident. Remember, these pills are about the size of a gnat's left foot and holding onto just one can be a challenge at times. This tip will save you muchas worry later.

Tip #107: CARPE DIEM! ("seize the day")

Don't believe any one person all of the time but you can believe all of the people some of the time. Loosely translated it means nobody has a monopoly on brains. Docs are great, but they are human too and have many other patient cases to sort out. Use them, but at the same time *educate* yourself, and if something doesn't seem right or feel right to you, then speak up. Any reputable doc will not mind if you tell them you want to get a second opinion. Actually, that lightens up their burden of liability so they shouldn't mind a bit. If they do mind, get another doc.

To all you wonderful people reading this, I know that you have a computer at home, so just Google (or apple) any questions you have such as "symptoms, causes for chest pain." You will probably be directed to Medline or other articles and blogs. Get your facts together and then have a meaningful discussion with your patient's doc or PA. Question anything you need to question (pertaining to the subject).

One of the more contentious topics that arises concerns the patient insisting that a name brand is best for them while the doc is taking the point of view that the generic is the identical molecule but maybe the binders are different. This often comes up with Coumadin and the generic Warfarin. If you have tried something that has side effects or doesn't work, then tell your doc that. Only until you have tried a generic med and found unwanted side effects will the doc be able to Rx the non-generic med with the words "no substitutes." That will build good communication between you, your patient, and the doc. The better the information flow, the better the outcome. Carpe diem.

Please take some ownership in your burden of responsibility in healing. You make the final decisions. It is so easy to get into the I-will-jump-off-a-cliff-if-you-tell-me-to complex.

I keep finding myself slipping into that same delusion because I so badly want to be the perfect patient and do just what the doctor or hospital says because that is the way I was brought up. Usually, it's a good friend that has to point out the obvious to me before I can engage my brain enough to make my opinion heard.

An example recently was one in which I was on IV for dehydration (don't ask me how but caregivers are bad about not taking care of themselves). In addition, I was told to drink copious amounts of water. After a couple of days, I was getting pretty bloated looking. My legs were swollen to twice their normal size. This didn't make sense to me. Something was so not right with this picture. I asked the nurse to summon a doctor. She said she could not unless I was in a critical state which she said I was not. "I've seen worse" she replied. Later, while talking on the phone, a good friend pointed out my I-will-jump-off-a-cliff-if-someone-of-authority-tells-me-to behavior. I thought about it. I agreed that I was following the same behavior. She suggested that I might be going into fluid overload. Hmmm... made sense to me. I then stopped the IV myself and the little box attached to it started to buzz a warning of a stopped line. In minutes, a doc just happened to stop in. I said, "I think I am going into fluid overload and suggest we discontinue the IV drip." He agreed. I said, "I think we should do an ultrasound to rule out a blood clot in the leg." He agreed and ordered that whereupon the ultrasound revealed a blood clot in my right leg (possibly from a TKA op four months ago, but not sure). Until now, nobody was even thinking in that direction. That was big news to everybody and very important to recovery. Who knew? I was blessed with great docs and great friends during my hospital stay that week. And I had no insurance.

Tip #108: INSTALL A NEW JOHN (aka commode, water commander, or water closet)—Important

I know this sounds a little weird, but it can be spot on for some people. Consider installing a new commode for your aging patient. Many people, especially those with Parkinson's, cancer, and other diseases will have very infrequent bowel movements. Patients that are on pain medicines are very prone to constipation (understatement). All this usually leads to significantly enlarged 'bio-masses' which are capable of clogging up many standard commodes and especially those energy efficient ones that try to flush everything with about an ounce of water. Ask your plumber or department store expert which model to choose that will accommodate the largest mass with the most powerful flush. Some even have power flushes... great, but a bit pricey. You will appreciate this advice after you have had to call a plumber several times to 'freedomize' your clogged toilet... or 'water closet' for shy people. This may sound trivial, but it is no small problem when all your toilets are stopped up and you can't find a plumber on the weekend. A great toilet is something to trade your soul for. Interesting how life changes our perspectives, isn't it?

Tip #109: MAKING A DIFFICULT CATHETERIZATION EASY (For males)

Our anatomy seems to change as we age. For seniors, this changing landscape can lead to many problems such as trying to smoothly insert a catheter. The first thing is to use a suitable lubricant. I personally have never had much luck with "petroleum jelly" products. They begin to dry and get sticky along the catheter, making for difficult insertion. There is a liquid form of it that seems to work just fine for me. It is KY liquid.

For the male, an enlarged prostate gland can present a problem, especially if irritated from numerous failed attempts at inserting a catheter. For the caregiver attempting to catheterize their male patient, try this: slide your 'lubed' catheter while simultaneously rotating it (assuming you are using one of those angled tip jobs) about ten degrees. This will usually do the trick. The next obstacle for many people seems to occur when the catheter is about 75% inserted and it's like hitting a rock wall. It will not budge. What seems to be happening is an involuntary contracting of the muscle layer surrounding the urethra. This area is particularly sensitive and can absolutely block the catheter in a heartbeat.

Here are two approaches: 1) Ask your patient to laugh out loud until you tell him to stop. During this time you will attempt re-insertion by first withdrawing the catheter to the tip... reinserting... and smoothly pushing the catheter all the way in. It is important that you do this with one confident, smooth uninterrupted movement least you telegraph uncertain intentions to the patient's brain which then sends the signal to block the urethra. This is the 'phrenic' nerve stimulation method (it actually causes relaxation of the parasympathetic system). 2) Ask your patient to tell you about something... anything... and while the person is talking perform the re-insertion of the catheter. This is the distraction method. Again, I want to stress that you need to do the full reinsertion. It seems to me that this is almost like a "reset" switch for the patient's brain. Everything is under control now and the train is allowed to pass through the tunnel... or whatever.

If you are still having problems, then remove the catheter and just talk with the patient while observing their breathing and other body language until they seemed relaxed and fully occupied with their conversation and calmly, without saying anything to them, proceed with the re-insertion of the catheter.

There are other methods such as warming the catheter, re-lubricating the catheter, or even using a different person to do the insertion. The mind exerts a sensitive control on this process so don't give up if you fail the first five times.

Never attempt to force a catheter because this could soon lead to some bleeding. It's not a big deal, but it might frighten your patient to see blood coming out of the tunnel. It will congeal on its own. If your patient is on warfarin, Coumadin, or other blood thinners then you need to consult with your doc on "what next" to do.

Tip #110: WARM WEATHER, UTI's, & TOPICAL SKIN INFECTIONS

Summer usually means hotter home temps because your patient has a reduced metabolism and feels more comfortable when the temperature in the house approaches that of a steel mill blast furnace... well, you get the point. This means that those innocuous 'brown' spots on your patients diapers can no longer be overlooked. A house temperature at 80 deg (my house in summer) may feel comfortable to your patient, but bacteria love it. For them, it must be like living on a California beach. E-coli colonies will proliferate at a tenfold rate in their patient's tightie-whities. That inevitably leads to becoming a source of infection for your patient.

What to do? Try this: Either instruct your patient or yourself to use an antiseptic spray or cream and wipe all around the perianal area (yeah... you know where that is... it's the real estate all around your private parts). I like the alcohol gels that you can physically rub around (note: the alcohol may cause a burning sensation for a few minutes as it hydrolyzes with the moisture of the skin). Some people like this because they know it's really working, but others don't like it. There are many products on the market that will work. You might try 3% hydrogen peroxide or some of the Betadiene (iodine) cleaners available from medical supply stores. I have also used Clorox wipes on my patient from time to time with no problem. They contain "hypochlorite" which is not the same as bleach and is milder. Bleach can also be used if you dilute it significantly with water (10:1 ration works for my patient). You can also buy benzalkonium (a bacteria killer) wipes from your local medical supplier. Try different approaches to find what works best for your patient.

Sometimes you will find circular red "sweat" rashes that will continue to get larger on your patients skin. These may be from a bite, sting, or sweat-cultivated-germ-infested hot spot. Here, I personally would not administer an antibiotic orally (but that would be okay). My first choice would be to grind up the antibiotic into a powder, then rub the powder abrasively into the skin. I have found this to be more direct, quicker acting, and more effective than overloading my patient with oral dosages. This method requires the minimum direct exposure to the antibiotic. Overlay this with a light rubbing in of DMSO (next tip) if you have some on hand.

Creams and ointments (like Neosporin) from the local pharmacy are fine also but seem to take a lot longer to work.

Prevention is the best treatment for UTI's—Please instruct your patient to clean their perianal area every time they use the water closet or the "John." Antibiotic sprays are available, but my experience is that my patient can't tell which direction the nozzle is pointing and usually sprays the air or his hand... anything but the surface that needs it. For him, I recommend Clorox wipes, but for a woman with more sensitive skin a betadiene wipe with a wet towelette would be effective. Betadiene does have an iodine color to it, but who is going to be looking down there anyway? Women are more apt to have an easier chance for routine infection because their piping is shorter than that of a male. For the athletic germ, it's just a hop, skip, and a jump and they're in.

Tip #111: THE BIG DMSO SHOW

If I really want to get serious about treating a difficult topical (surface) skin infection, I will apply the antibiotic as described above, rubbing it into the skin, and then apply DMSO gel (available only from a horse supply store or possibly from a farm supply store). The DMSO (dimethylsulphoxide) is a penetrant class of chemical. It will transport the antibiotic into the tissues faster and more efficiently. It might also burn a little depending upon the sensitivity of your skin, but usually not a problem unless you are a whiner. If it is, then wash off and apply copious amounts of baby powder to the area and rub that in for about ten or fifteen minutes while you sing 'lullaby and goodnight' to yourself. Go ahead and pamper yourself.

The horse and livestock industry has been using this product for eons with no problem. They use it for reducing swelling and inflammation. In fact, I have used it for my own needs (leg pain inflammation resulting from spinal stenosis) with great results. I always keep some around the house. The gel is the easiest form to work with, but the liquid works fine also... just a little messier, I think. Oh... some people report having a garlic aftertaste in their mouth once they apply it to anywhere on their body. This is temporary and goes away in a day or two. I am told garlic also keeps vampires away... just another benefit I suppose.

I also know there will always be somebody reading this that will exclaim that these are all bad ideas... maybe they are, but they work for my patient and he has passed 102 years and is still mowing the lawn (in his mind). The proof is in the pudding, as the saying goes.

Tip #112: DOES CRANBERRY JUICE REALLY WORK?

By now everybody has heard of drinking cranberry juice to reduce bacteria in the bladder. Now, after one and a half years of testing, I can verify that it works great. I do not believe you can substitute Cranberry drink, punch, mix, Kool-aid, or whatever for the juice. I have used Ocean Spray brand or Knudson brand (100% unsweetened cranberry juice from concentrate). They come in a 32 oz size and costs about $6-$8. You will find it in the health food section at most Kroger stores. To this volume, I would dilute it four parts water to one part juice for the initial period until the urine infections go away, and then go to a maintenance dilution of nine parts water to one part juice. I use a large plastic pitcher (of 2.25 qts) to which I add one eight ounce glass of juice. I would not use less than this 9:1 ratio. **You must use the concentrate that comes in a glass bottle. Look for it in the health or specialty food section of Kroger's or any other store. If it costs less than $6 per quart bottle, then you probably have the wrong juice.**

Tip #113: LIVE-IN CAREGIVERS: BEFORE YOU MOVE IN DO THIS...

Clean out their attic, garage, and house to accommodate everything you will be bringing. You should have at least 75% of everything already moved in and in its final resting place. Remember, once you become a full time caregiver, you will have about two weeks before depression sets in, and from then on nothing ever seems to get completed. As soon as your patient requires you or someone to be there 24/7, or even 12/7 in some cases, you will enter the world of depression. **Anytime a caregiver can no longer have an unrestricted life he/she defaults to a feeling of being 'trapped' (whether or not they are even aware of it). This quickly forms the fabric of depression.**

Tip #114: ONGOING ASSESSMENT OF YOUR PATIENT'S GENERAL CONDITION—Important.

How many times have I heard a patient say "well, I promise I won't drive anymore" or "I promise I won't climb a ladder" or "I promise I will be careful climbing the stairs if you will just pleeeeezzze let me stay in where I have always been?"

Know this: Your patient has good intentions. Your patient will violate their own rules sooner or later. It is your job to know when to jump in and get proactive before a tragedy occurs.

It's called assuming responsibility. You have NO authority to allow the endangerment of the life of your patient or the lives of innocent bystanders.

Fear this: If you trust your parent's promises you will have to live with those consequences for the rest of your life.

MY MOTHER IS DYING NOW

This is true. This is real time, as I write. Tomorrow, it will be history. I don't know why, but I experienced the strangest urge to express this on-going situation sometimes referred to as 'actively dying.' I know that it was a directive from either my patient's soul or from the Holy Spirit.

I had some feelings of invading someone's privacy... no those were my feelings. In retrospect, I think this was one of the last gifts my mother could leave this world with. I feel that she wanted the world to know that death, as horrible and fearsome as it may seem, doesn't have to be that way. If you truly are a believer, then the transition can be peaceful. She was truly a lamb of God. Her passing may let others know that death is not something to fear and run from, but rather to bring us together so that we may learn to help one another through the struggles of life. How often does one turn a blind eye to an accident victim or mugging because we fear?

What if all the fear in the world left immediately? There would be no reason for wars and killing anymore. Think about it. No fear meaning no more fear of threats of anything. No fear of your neighbor, no fear of living, of dying, and of just being friends.

She showed us that the way to escape fear is through your own salvation with God. I am not the author of this, but the messenger.

MY PATIENT'S GIFT TO THE WORLD

Having said all that, I can now tell you my experience. In fact, I am at my computer, beside my patient as she lies dying. I called Hospice to inform them that I did not want the new hospital bed delivered today because my mother's condition had worsened and I didn't want to disturb her. I told them I had just taken her O_2 stats with my small oximeter and the oxygen level in her fingers was in the range of 71-77. I knew what that meant. If this were a hospital, she would be rushed to the ICU. Her breathing was steady, as she seemed to be using her accessory muscles to breathe. It was time to let God bring her home. I chose not to use oxygen to artificially prolong her life just to support my ego.

During the night, she had shown no appetite or desire to drink. Her hands kind of moved in and out and around, sometimes becoming entwined with her blouse, then untwining, and starting these random movements over again. It was like a dance that her arms were performing... maybe a ritual for Passover is more appropriate. She was no longer indicating any awareness of the temperature as she had so prominently done. In the past she often said she was freezing on a hot day when we were all sweating from just thinking too much.

As I look at her now, she has her eyes shut and there is a peaceful look to her. There are no indications of pain or discomfort. The Hospice nurse says she will be over to check on her. Within minutes, she is there, removes a small morphine pill from our care emergency pack, and carefully places it under the tongue of the patient. "That is to help relax her breathing." She then contacts my patient's doctor and requests an Rx for the liquid form of morphine.

The rest is kinda unclear, but as I stepped out of the room to run to the grocery, I got the call from my respite caregiver, Nila. "Your mother has passed," she said.

"I'll be right there," I replied. Within a few minutes, I am back at home. There are support people from Hospice arriving. I hear the nurse use the term 'actively dying' or maybe it was 'active death' to describe the patient's present status. My mind was racing, trying to collate all this information, but it paused just briefly enough to explore what this new term 'actively dying' felt like. It was new for sure... but felt truthful and predictive... I felt okay with this new word-friend and continued with my collation of the info flow.

The Hospice Chaplain had a bedside final prayer around my patient. We all held hands, save my father, who declined to attend, as she (Chaplin) led the convocation. Then, the call was placed to the funeral home, who dispatched a Chevy suburban. It looked very inconspicuous as it lumbered up the back driveway to the house. I thought it best that they took her away as soon as possible. I think trying to hold onto sad images and experiences in our mind can anchor unnecessary baggage there. By and large, most of us cannot easily accept the reality of death, so during long, open visitations, we placate ourselves with superficial expressions like "well, we can't live forever" or "well, it was just her time to go." But the truth is, we fear what we don't know or understand.

When the 9/11 disaster occurred, I advised my clients to not watch the news because after a while the dynamic fear content would be firmly anchored in the subconscious and trouble them for many years to come.

Indeed there were many clinicians reporting patients developing acute anxiety syndromes and other troublesome behaviors related to that incident. Imagine what our brave soldiers returning home from war are suffering through deep in their subconscious.

> My point is... we should deal with difficult things quickly, learn from them, and not look back. 'Learn the lesson,' but 'don't keep the fear.'

I learned my patient did not suffer, was en route to the Big Castle (no relation to the 'White Castle') in Heaven (told to me by Spirit) so she could rest at last, but be available as a redeemer again and again when called. I learned that death does not have to mean horrible noises and lurches and death rattles; it can come peacefully to the chosen lambs of God. The nurse said my patient probably had her 'death rattle' without our being aware of it.

We said one final goodbye to my mother and the funeral home personnel carried her away. The hospice team is leaving now as another neighbor is arriving to help with making the phone calls to my patient's circle of friends.

Now, I am calling my doctor's office for some kind of Rx to tame these emotions I am feeling. I don't mind some emotions, but when my sister died, it was 'open the floodgates' time and that didn't stop for a long while. I started back with some Cymbalta I had by taking only half a capsule at first. Things like SSRI's (selective serotonin re-uptake inhibitor) and SRI's (serotonin re-uptake inhibitor) need to be taken at reduced dosage when starting, restarting or tapering off in order to avoid unpleasant nausea side effects (which I still got... go figure).

Tomorrow, I will meet with the funeral home. The obituary has to be prepared, and a service place, date, time selected. The next day greets us with cloudy skies and cooler temperatures. The arrangements and contracts are handled. The funeral home will want to have a copy of your power of attorney for the patient (I gave them the wrong document, which stopped the cremation order). Remember, you can't depend on your own wits at a time like this. Next the funeral home wanted our rendition of the obituary. The home submits the obituary to the newspaper. *Advice: Do not make a very long obit.* Mine was about 7 column inches with small picture and for three days cost about $800. Isn't that sad that the newspaper tries to profit off the misfortunes of others? I thought the obits were free. Knock-knock... wake up call for me.

The funeral home shows me some urns for the ashes. They ranged from $565 to $1300 and more. I went to Home Furnishings and got a very nice urn with lid for $12.95. The funeral home will send the paperwork to the capital and receive the official death certificate. I ordered the standard dozen copies. They are $6 each. The grave site had already been prepaid. Don't expect to get any net monetary return off the interest accruements. The original investment of $1047 grew in their account to $2800. The funeral home takes this amount and subtracts the present day funeral cost, which to no surprise comes to within just a few shekels of being $2800, so no money returned there.

The cost of digging the hole for the urn was $510, but included a tent and chairs whether you want them or not. The following day began with a meeting with the church Chaplin to plan the service, such as what songs were to be presented and who might wish to speak on behalf of the patient. Then you will need to procure display boards for pictures and purchase a 'sign-in' ledger for guests (you can get one from Wal-Mart or Staples for about $12), friends of the family volunteered to bring items for the reception. I did not decline that offer ☺.

Of course, rooms for people from out of town need to be addressed. I selected the Marriot-Griffin Gate because they have a buffet. I got a small discount on a block of rooms (normally a block is ten rooms, but they will deal with ya if the economy doesn't seem to have a pulse). This was one of the few 'feel good' experiences a caregiver gets to have. The most outstanding attribute at this location was their willingness to accommodate my changing needs. It was straight out of a movie commercial... whenever I said I need to make a change, I internally braced for them to summon Godzilla to deal with me. Instead, the attendant's reply was simply, "And what else?" Was I dreaming or what? This doesn't happen in real life. A great experience (and no I did not get to stay there either, darn it).

We buried mother four days ago—as for what happens from here, I can only relate my short term experience before the book is published. My wife and I had spent lots of 'close' contact time with the patient so the advent of her death was not sudden in our psyche. In addition, we shared a common bond of a belief in Christianity. We knew she was safe. We knew she was at peace now and, most likely, enjoying watching us try to deal with our other patient.

Of course there are moments when I let myself tear up, it just happens and is a healthy part of the grieving process. My advice for the caregiver is to realize that you are part of your patient's transition to a better world, and you should feel good about that dawg! It is so easy to get our emotions mixed up and feel sad and awful because 'we' lost a companion of long standing when we should be feeling happiness for the patient, who has finally earned their right to be called back to the house of the Lord (or wherever). Remember, this play is not about us, but in celebration of our patient. If 'we' feel bad, it is because we are nursing our egos, which is not really fair is it? That is like playing the sympathy card off of someone else's misfortune. We don't intentionally do that, but that is often the net result. Let your spirits be uplifted for your patient... honor your patient (not you).

How is our other patient doing? I must say he has had his moments of suffering also. This could only be expected after a 68 years of marriage. I can only say he is most incredible in how he has managed to overcome adversity and within four days he is his ol' self again.

What resiliency, considering that he is a non-believer! In fact, just to overcome his grief, he has invited his 'friend' from that nearby town to drive here and we will all be going out to dinner in a few minutes. She's a rotund teacher/fiend who made a 160 mi. roundtrip drive just to honor my patient. What more can I say? You never know what to expect sometimes, eh? 'My, my, apple pie.' (Ya know I am bean held hostage, don't ya?)

CHAPTER 6
IS IT DEMENTIA OR ALZHEIMER'S???

> When my skin sags and my bones get brittle, God is rock-firm and faithful.
>
> Psalms 73:26

This is one of those early on 'speed bumps' that the new caregiver discovers, but doesn't quite know what kind of priority to put on it. I mean who cares? I just have a couple of elderly patients that are slowly losing it. My job is to care for them… feed them and probably some other stuff, but I'm not sure what. Anyway, nothing too difficult I'm sure. Not.

I take myself as a case in point. Well, I'm educated thanks to the help of a generous father, but when I actually took on the role of being a caregiver, I already knew the important facts. I was dealing with dementia. That much I knew. I knew that Alzheimer's was something a lot worse (from what I had heard patients curse, kick, and spit fire at ya) and they had local meetings and support groups for their caregiver's (which I had also been incorrectly told have a high suicide rate). I knew that I was not dealing with Alzheimer's disease. My problem is I can't seem to find much useful information on dementia and how to solve the everyday, at-home problems it presents.

Does this sound familiar? The problem I was having was that somehow my 'smarts' were no longer smart. Actually, you and everyone else will be faced with some facet of this. The difficulty arises from the fact that you are not considering there may be multiple points of view that all hold some validity. In addition, the normal rules for business management are all based on either rational logic or just plain luck. With dementia and Alzheimer's, there is no rational logic and luck is usually not an option.

In my case, I never considered that dementia might present itself in the same manner as Alzheimer's syndrome. In fact, from the point of view of many people, both dementia and Alzheimer's are indistinguishable in the early stages. Many dementia patients are reclassified as Alzheimer's patients as the natural process of aging progresses. The truth is that a number of tests are needed to distinguish simple dementia from Alzheimer's. Hark, can you hear that faint voice… it's… it's saying, "If this were not so, I would have told you." Hmmmm… I wonder who that could have been?

Had I known that, my first 'to-do' list item would have been to call the Alzheimer's foundation and spell out my needs in simple terms. It would have made my transition so much easier. They have trained staff that can field anything you can throw at 'em.

Here is exactly what to say: "Hello, Alzheimer's Association? Okay, please connect me... (any reputable business must be hidden behind at least one connect or press '3'). Hello, I am a new caregiver, and I don't know anything about squat. I really need some help on what to do and when. My patient just has some forgetfulness presently, but I think I need help. I don't even know where to start. Is this something I need to do some planning for? Can you help me?"

I DIDN'T KNOW! That's all ya have to do! E-Z!

My party, however, was just beginning. Like many caregivers, I did not see the connection between Alzheimer's and dementia, and I set out to re-invent the wheel. Why? Lesley Gore would tell you "because it's my party and I'll cry if I want to... and you would cry too if it happened to you." In a strange way that actually sums it up. No knowledge, nowhere to turn, and nothing to do but feel sorry. Fortunately, I discovered that many other caregiver's were running into the same set of obstacles, searching for answers that have already been provided, and feeling down and frustrated just like my wife and I were. If we were computers, we would be flashing an error window that would read "OPERATOR ERROR."

Why aren't there a gazillion books at the bookstore on how to solve these initial 'errors' and flawed thinking? I only found a few (actually four) on the topic, and none of which did much more than provide some 'feel good' portraits of old people or some poems and verse, etc. But I need some help now, and I don't want to read three hundred pages of tiny print until I go legally blind. I said to myself, "Someone should write a more direct and readable book." I must quit having these conversations with myself. Now I am committed to a project that nobody else will probably want to read either. It's just that somehow this higher power kept opening doors for me to do this. Follow the spirit, bro!

Alzheimer's syndrome is the term used to denote a number of behavioral traits that simply cannot be explained by any one condition. The DSM-IV, the latest mental health manual, spews out a bunch of cognitive deficits that must present, such as disturbances in 'executive functioning.' This refers to your ability to organize, plan events, remember shopping lists, etc. Now tell me, how useless is that?

I don't know about you, but I believe I was born with Alzheimer's syndrome. I can never remember a shopping list and have never organized my office. That is always a work in progress. Every few years, I just change offices.

Dementia is the loss of intellectual functioning to the extent that it can interfere with normal social or job functioning.

To a large extent, the symptoms of dementia and Alzheimer's overlap. All Alzheimer's patients have dementia, but not all dementia patients have Alzheimer's syndrome. Alzheimer's syndrome may well be the condition that you, as a caregiver, encounter from day one. Only your doctor can tell (except maybe that dog that does the Bush bean commercials, but he's not tellin').

This brings up another point worthy of noting. **Depending on the company and type of insurance you have, a diagnosis of Alzheimer's can, in some cases, provide benefits that simple dementia would not provide, such as home health care, which is currently being provided in some states.**

As a caregiver, just pretend your patient has Alzheimer's and allow yourself to feel invited to their meetings and support groups. They even have a drop-off sitter's support in many communities. This allows the caregiver to drop off their patient during the day so they can get a brief respite, relax, catch up on their taxes, and fend off other governmental and financial threats, and maybe a friendly foreclosure or two.

In summary, if you have the opportunity, I would recommend having a medical doctor, preferably a geriatric specialist, perform a series of tests to determine if your patient has dementia or Alzheimer's. This knowledge will allow you, possibly, additional patient care benefits and, equally important, it will allow you to plan ahead for the inevitable changes.

Think in terms of home care equipment rental when possible. Mental changes often occur in such a short time span that purchased equipment (such as elevator stairs, etc.) become obsolete before they have had much use.

WHAT PUTS YOU INTO DEPRESSION
&
WHAT YOU CAN DO TO GIT YO BOOTY OUTTA THAT DARK PLACE!
HERE IS WHAT PUTS YOU INTO THE BOX
THE ABU GAHRAIB SYNDROME & MORE

All that pre-thinking and now the time has come. You move in with your parents or patient. At first, things seem lovely because everyone is still reasonably in touch with their faculties.

Bit by bit, things are not going so smoothly. You begin to feel depressed, lifeless, tired all the time, and have no 'want' power to get motivated to do anything. You still have the 'will power' (ability to do something), but the 'want power' (the desire to actually do it) has slowly evaporated. It happens so secretively that you may not note exactly what has changed. You are aware that you don't feel quite the same, but you really can't quite put your finger on it; you become powerless to resist this change that slowly overtakes you bit by bit. You have no choice but to succumb to its pull. Like a magnet, you are drawn deeper and deeper into this numbing state.

Professionally, I have studied a lot about the phenomenon we call depression. I used to lecture that depression took a long time to get into (unless it was a 'shock' transition, such as the death of a loved one). What about the caregiver situation, which certainly does not qualify as a shock stimulus? It's not from grief over the slow demise of our loved ones. It's not from being denied the basic resources for caring. One of the cardinal rules for changing any behavior is that you must have a good understanding of what the behavior is and where it might have been acquired. At this point, your mind is in a fog because you are not entirely convinced that you have experienced any change out of the norm. Usually the best you can do is to relate that perhaps you are feeling 'down' a lot more. This, you chalk up to the weather, your age, the full moon, solar flares, or about anything else you can dream up.

I have talked to many authorities on this and everybody has different 'takes' and points of view. I think most of their theories, sooner or later, converge on three points for expressing what puts the caregiver into depression at double warp light speed.

THREE ESSENTIAL FACTORS WORKING TO PUT US INTO DEPRESSION

(Yes I know there are many more factors, but this is for the average Joe & Jane.)

FACTOR 1: **THE PAST VS PRESENT**

FACTOR 2: **MENTAL/PHYSICAL LIMITATIONS OF THE PATIENT**

FACTOR 3: **MENTAL/PHYSICAL LIMITATIONS OF THE CAREGIVER**

FACTOR 1: Your patient is from a different time and place. His/her sense of core values is built around this. Yours are built around a different value system in as much as you arrived in life at a different time and place. This means there is always going to be room for adversity between the patient and caregiver. The frustration here is that often one is fiercely more financially or politically frugal than the other. Our new age economies are generally poised atop policies that echo "let's spend more." The old line policies after the great crash echoed just the opposite—save, save, save.

The result is you now have your patient chastising you for the way you spend money and make decisions. In addition, the older patient is so far out of touch with real world living costs that everything is a strain on them. Play your best spin, but you can't control their inner programming. I have noticed that even in the most acutely preserved minds of the geriatric group, their process of rationalizing has changed toward the simpler 'deductive' process and less of the 'inductive' process, which requires more brainpower to explore more alternatives and different points of view. This is one of the many reasons a person's behavior slowly changes, because the rationale supporting the new behavior is kinder and simpler (i.e. It lets you have your cake, and eat it too).

FACTOR 2: Your patient will be slowing sliding downhill with regard to their mental attributes. At first, you will not even notice it. Some days will be better than others, but in time your patient may not even recognize you. And worse... they may seem to be disconnecting from the spoken language. Tell them to not go outdoors or not to leave the 'fridge' door open, and they still do. No matter what you do, they will, more and more, refuse to do what you want. Again, you are on a ship without a rudder.

Later, you may find your patient's refusal change from voluntary non-compliance to one of absolute reactionary positioning. For instance, you turn on the shower to give them a bath and they scream because the water is killing them or it's too hot or too cold or they are drowning. They curse at you, tell you that you are hurting them, or tell you to leave their home and more (and those comments are from the better behaved patients). In this case, you have several mechanisms working against you. First, you are fairly powerless to change their reaction in the short term. Secondly, you are being constantly lambasted for being some wicked, hurtful creature that you are not. And thirdly, your own parental authority has just told you to leave the house in no uncertain terms. We can deflect a lot of this hurt by some fancy word reframing (spinning) and other cute games of agreeing with anything they say, but the bottom line is that we are powerless to get done that we need to without being verbally accosted and threatened some times. Fortunately, once the bath is finished and the patient is dry, they may, suddenly, be so happy that they begin praising you.

Physical limitations take innumerable forms. but they all add to frustration simply because handling the patient becomes more complicated. Even if it's just a small limitation, it still adds to the ever growing mound of 'considerations' that must accompany the way you interact with your patient.

FACTOR 3: Unless you have been living with this patient all your life (like a spouse becoming a caregiver for the other), you are going to find another very strong difference. This includes your individual outlooks on religion, morality, sincerity, interaction with others (do you manipulate others, support them or ignore them, etc.), political issues, philosophical issues, and more. You will discover some of the differences small and some huge because while you were living apart (caregiver/parent relationship), you never had to deal with things up close and personal as they are now. They all add up to have a significant effect on your psyche. For me, I am a Christian and dad is an atheist, who loves to argue against Christianity with anyone. That was not a fun issue. The other frustrating issue you might find is how manipulative your patient can be with everyone and yet they might not even be aware of their behavior. Again, this may derive from their changing towards a 'feel good, then do it' type of rationalization. A common issue is that the patient can't understand you are doing anything short of 'free loading' because they are feeling just fine and would still like to drive the car and do the grocery shopping. Conversely, the caregiver sees the patient as unsympathetic, having giving up his job, freedom, and sometimes his marriage to fulfill his promise of providing care for the end years. I mention these examples to help you search the areas of frustration that you may be encountering.

PUTTING IT ALL TOGETHER

> **To deal with frustration, you first have to know from where all the pieces of the pie are coming from. Only then can you take full ownership.**

Ownership bestows upon you the authority to make choices; choices such as whether to hold onto animosity or let it go. I can argue both ways, but it's your choice when you are ready. I get so sick of hearing good-hearted people advising a caregiver to "just let go, forgive and forget everything." Yeah... wait until they get there. Then it's pick and choose to do the best you can, but don't be insincere with each choice you make either. Choose it, think about it, ask yourself if you are really ready to let go, and then act. If your heart isn't buying into something, it just won't work. That will be another growth opportunity for you (aren't you the lucky one?). Be true to yourself. Anyway, we caregivers don't really have the ultimate forgiveness power do we? Yep, God has that and he is keeping an eye on your progress.

What all of these divisions have in common that is so powerful in producing frustrations is that they all involve multitudes and multitudes of situations in which OUR EXPECTATIONS WERE NOT MET. A failure to meet expectations is a self-perpetuating process that sucks the life right out of a caregiver. Being a caregiver is like trying to be at peace with yourself while you are living in Stanley Kubrick's *Clockwork Orange*... more or less.

To get off this train wreck, invoke your 'WANT' power to change it. Become your own spin doctor (you know... turn everything around and make it fun or funny... sort of). My dementia patient (mother) would constantly tell me "I hate you" as I am giving her a bath, so I might break out with a song of "I hate you" done to the theme of South Pacific (PS: I can't sing, but she can't tell either and assumes from my gesturing that I must be really good... now she smiles).

ABU GHRAIB SYNDROME

There is one more significant cause of depression that I have not yet talked about for the simple reason that I still don't know exactly what is forming the underlying platform that supports and gives rise to this depression.

Here is what I do know. Probably the quickest mechanism that will throw you into depression is what I term the 'Abu Ghraib' syndrome. It's the only way I know how to describe the effect of the sudden curtailment of all those slices of freedom you always took for granted. Now they are gone, and your freedom is predicated upon your patients. You can't just get up and take the car to the park or shopping or whatever. Now, everything you do is contingent upon earning the opportunity, whether that comes from a friend that agrees to be a sitter or an aid worker. Your life has changed and will never be exactly the same again. You truly are a prisoner, yet you can never point to any one single event as being that influential.

As I further analyze the underpinning of restricted freedom, I see a corollary with war veterans. Most of them, whether P.O.W.s or not, suffer from some act involving this same mechanism. I don't know if the real underpinning for the fear and hopelessness of restricted freedom involves prepubescent issues developed around core behaviors at childhood, or whether it's a perceived issue reflecting the adult state of mind. I tend to think the real answer lies in the pre-puberty age because the stimuli that are producing such a sudden and powerful impact on the manifestation of depression are so intense.

I CAN'T FACE REALITY SYNDROME

Here is another aspect of the myriad of elements that support depression but is often never mentioned in the literature. This very powerful stimulus has to do with the manner in which we look at life overall (i.e. It's meaning from an existential point of view) and our own specific fears and emotions that relate to our immortality. Loosely translated, I just said "When it's time to go to the big sky ranch are we, deep down, scared spitless, or have we made our peace and look forward to being with God?"

It is tough to psychoanalyze yourself, it's not for amateurs, rather for professionals, like all women, who seem to have an upper hand in intuition and wisdom (unless the issue is about motors, beer, or sports, and then men rock... sorry ladies). Seriously, the real difficulty with self-psychoanalysis lies in the fact that you cannot know now what you will feel as you approach that time to go. You know what you think you're position on death and dying is now, but you are also safely away from that time. Again, this extols the virtue on believing whole-heartedly in God.

What I am leading you to is the realization that very often the patients that we are caring for are also triggering a reality (represented by them) within our minds that death is very imminent and the process of dying may not be a pleasant one. At some level in our subconscious we are reeling from the idea that soon, we too will no longer be in control, mindlessly wandering, wetting in our diapers, or worse... and maybe not even being cared for. We find ourselves talking about this issue more and more, and at times wondering (in jest, I think) if we might pass before our patients do. Knowing what I know now, I think I would like to reach my twilight years in a location that supports euthanasia just to be on the safe side in case nature gets out of control (like with certain types of cancer, ALS, and other burdensome, painful, and poor quality of life diseases). I personally think God would not want a person to suffer needlessly. I don't feel this would be violating God's desire that we not take our own life because the soul is the life and that will not be altered.

This is truly a scary realization, but deserves some serious attention. I suggest you think about it often (but only if you feel you will benefit) until the shock has kind of worn off and your mind just sort of 'accepts' things that are to be. This is a desensitization process that is healthy for healthy caregivers. Some people just can't bear to think about 'future' stuff and they should not try to force themselves. For them, I suggest staying afloat on that river in Egypt (what was the name of it? Help me out... okay, I know, but it was just too silly to say). You know what you can handle.

The almost universal end result is that you will eventually come to terms with the fact that this is a natural part of life. You will be able to see your patients from a different viewpoint... no longer fearful, but with compassion.

Another area that is very important involves pre-tuning yourself to be ready for any unexpected situation, or behavior. This varies with each patient and will be discussed in detail in the chapter on behaviors. Anytime a person (caregiver or patient) feels like they are losing their ability to control issues in the world around them, especially those which interact directly with them, the result is depression. For a caregiver, it's almost unavoidable.

THE MEDICAL AUTOCRACY
—Let 'em die vs. Keep 'em alive

Last, but certainly not least, will be the ever present dichotomy in professional health care standards. They are important to be aware of because they can cause deep frustration in any caregiver that assumes all physicians use the same Hippocratic Oath (which says that all doctors will do their utmost to preserve life). If you make this assumption of commonality among all doctors you might be pushing your loved one down the wrong path.

Let me tell you what I discovered. I am not going to waste time on debating the merits of the two major approaches to geriatric health care ('let 'em die' vs 'keep 'em alive'). In truth, there is a lot of common ground on both sides of that fence. The issue that concerns you is that you must be aware of the implications to your patient from being treated by either one of these doctors. Furthermore, you must recognize that you have the right, and should use the right, to request a second opinion by a doctor of your choice. I often will tell my doctor that I am going to get a second opinion for 'my' benefit. In some cases, I may just go see another doctor without saying anything to my doctor (if time is an issue).

You are under no obligation to report getting a second opinion to your own doctor. I tell the other doctor I am there for a second opinion. A good doctor will not feel uncomfortable with a patient getting another opinion. That is professionalism. Just convey to your doctor that you don't have a strong medical background and need the assurance of having more opinions to allow you to feel more comfortable with what he/she (your doctor) has suggested. I have gone to as many as five different doctors for an opinion before. (This was for me, however, and had to do with a possible neck operation and the majority of opinions were that I didn't need any operation. It's scary to think that the recommendations ranged from needing immediate surgery for neck replacement to having normal arthritis for my age). How many times have you or a friend gone to a doctor and maybe you just didn't feel comfortable with the diagnosis (like you think he/she missed the entire issue)? Or maybe the doctor's Rx for your patient causes a reaction, but you can't convince your doctor to change the meds? Or the doctor just says to your ailing patient, "I wish I am that healthy when I am your age. Take some aspirin and you will feel better."

Here are the two presumptions now being assumed by most doctors dealing with geriatric patients:

THE LIBERAL, LEFT-WINGER DOC (KEEP EM' ALIVE)—Will attempt to find appropriate treatment, home care support, and Rx to keep the patient alive and with 'QUALITY OF LIFE.' For example, my 97 year old mother has diabetes. Doctor #1 says no ice cream, sweets, or basically anything that tastes good should be given to her because in maybe 10 years or so she might develop blindness or numbness in her hands and feet. Left-wing Doctor #2 says, "At her age and with mild diabetes, let her have anything she wants. She will be happier and any extra fat she can add to her thin body would be beneficial."

That was a no-brainer for me. I go with doctor #2, the left-winger, for his liberal stance on quality of life. Yeah, it's ice cream time year-round at this ranch (I guarantee you that even without doc #1's advice, in ten years my 97 year old mother will definitely have numbness in her fingers and toes). Doc #2 offers whatever support we need.

THE CONSERVATIVE RIGHT-WINGER DOC (LET EM' DIE)—Will describe how delicate the patient's physiology is and how difficult it will be to keep dietary restrictions in place in order to maintain the proper level of electrolytes in the body and yadda... yadda... yadda. This is when I asked for outside aid, such as a home health care worker, to stop by the house and periodically take a lab blood sample for a BMP (basic metabolic panel). I need the doctor's agreement to have insurance cover this. The doctor goes over the yadda... yadda... BS... some more about the patient's age... yadda... and then looks right at me and this kid doctor who is half my age says, "I will put my best man on checking into the home health care, but remember we don't do much of that here, so it may take a while... it may take a while." He gives me that secret grin and kinda winks, as if to say, "For the record, I have to say I will do this, but you know I really mean I won't because it doesn't make sense." (At least I hope that is what the wink meant.) Two weeks and two follow-up calls later and the doctor is still saying 'just be patient.' Eventually we did have a sort of cryptic discussion in which he implied that sometimes there is no point in trying to do too much for someone near the end, and this is where the greatest amount of insurance dollars goes when they could be going to other patients with a higher risk/return ratio. That was over a year ago. I fired that doctor soon after this epiphany.

Can ya see how dense I was? THE RIGHT-WINGER DOC was trying to tell me, "My policy is to just let old people die." I never thought that was an option under the Hippocratic Oath. I wasted a lot of precious time before I could see the light. I wasted time that should have been spent saving my patient's life. It's been over a year and my 99 year old patient is healthier than before he ever went to the 'right-winger.' Please understand that I have great respect for the medical commitment of both doctors. I differ on the issue of the type of treatment that is appropriate for a geriatric patient whom I consider to still have some quality time remaining.

The truth is there are a lot of doctors that are 'right-wingers.' And there is a lot of evidence, mainly from a cost standpoint, to show that this is the proper standard of care, and we should pretty much just let nature take its course.

On the other hand, there are 'left-winger' docs foraging for survival also. The left-winger is great when things go pretty much as planned. The drawback to a left-winger liberal is their ferocious need to find the underlying cause of a patient's ailment at all costs, even to a fault. What

I love about them is they will listen and discuss new meds you may have heard about, are often willing to try something new, and pretty much go along with doing extensive blood lab panels to see what is really going on with your patient's health.

The downside is you must keep control. Remember, they are often representing a group of other doctors that have a vested financial interest in the care center, lab, or MRI facility they send you to. They want you to have tests and tests and more tests. Got tests? A lot of this is also necessary from a liability standpoint. Here is a case in point: A few years ago my ex's doctor rushed her to the hospital. During a routine office visit he noticed some surface blood clots on her toes. He was thinking something was causing her to throw clots which were fortunately being lodged in the toes (she never smoked, no drinking, no nothin', just a picture of health). The real concern was that some of them (clots) might migrate back to her 'ticker' and result in a pulmonary embolism. Of course, 'ex' was distraught and panicked. I stayed several days to observe the hospital testing including Doppler's, radiographs, and CTAs; everything was fine.

Her doctor was puzzled. "We still can't seem to find the cause of the clots, but at this point, we can't exclude the GI system either. I am going to order the 'scope' and we will continue working the inside of you until we find the problem. You just don't know, I mean it could be cancer (scare tactic) or something!" He said he would give her a day to think about it.

In the meantime, I just happened to look down at ex's feet. It just so happens that because of the natural way her toes and ligaments are arranged, when she stands her toes 'knuckle up' with the first joints hitting the inside top of her shoes and the tips of the toes were digging into to floor or sole. The clots were in exactly these two locations, and actually, upon closer inspection, the clots were really just what I call blood bruises. I told her, "Forget this, and leave now while you are still alive." In my mind, the movie *Hospital* (George C. Scott, 1971) was now playing, in which Scott loosely says, "We heal nothing, we cure nothing... they (patients) come in alive and leave sicker then when they came in."

I could name many more true stories, but the point is the caregiver must become knowledgeable and assert control. Nobody has all the answers. Respect your doctor, but realize he/she is fallible. Help them be a success by providing well-organized information about your patient. Ultimately, you will have some choices to make that reflect your doctor's wisdom integrated with your ideas of care.

You will be faced with learned members of the medical field making great cases to 'do' or 'not do' treatment options. They are truly wonderfully trained professionals, but they do not have a monopoly on wisdom. We all make stupid mistakes. Don't accept anyone's wisdom until you understand it and feel in agreement. Otherwise, get some additional opinions.

I CAN'T BELIEVE IT—SAY IT AIN'T SO!

As I wrote this chapter, I had just opened the local newspaper. An AP story by Carla K. Johnson jumped out at me. "STUDY: ANTIBIOTICS OVERUSED IN DEMENTIA." The story begins: CHICAGO- A woman dying of Alzheimer's has a fever. Should she be given antibiotics? They raise the issue of "whether the public health issues should ever be considered" continuing to say "Advanced dementia is a terminal illness," says Dr. Susan Mitchell from Harvard affiliated HLI for aging.

Jump back jack! Hello Doc Susan but a simple fact of life is that we all start dying the moment we are born (telomeres on our chromosomes don't last forever, and when they are used up during cellular replication the party's over). Life itself is terminal! Maybe ya want to terminate people a little earlier? Ha. Harvard is affiliated with this nonsense? Does HLI stand for Harvard Life Insurance? Ya think?

DEPRESSION—WHAT CAN GIT YO OTTA THAT DARK PLACE

TAKE CARE OF U—DON'T YOU DARE OVERLOOK THIS!

This sounds so trite you might be tempted to not read it, but here's the downtown on this. I say this as a counselor and marathon wannabe athlete. Your mental state will change with the caregiver role. That's a given. The object here is to minimize adverse changes. Depression will be with you at some level and you may not even be aware of it. Stress will be with you to different degrees. **This raises harmful cortisol, epinephrine, and nor-epinephrine levels, all of which wreck havoc on the body.** Maybe those little aches and pains you previously had have now become full blown issues. Here is what I recommend.

Your body is going to be responding to stress in different ways... physically and mentally. **I want you to see your MD as often as you can afford (yes, I know) and maybe just once or twice a year see a body worker (loosely termed to mean anyone that is KNOWN to have good knowledge of body mechanics and may include massage therapists, rolfers, osteopaths, sports specialists, etc.).** At some point, you will be scrunching up different muscle groups in response to what you are doing and you need professional training to learn a set of exercises you can do at home to relieve trigger points, etc. I want you to exercise outdoors as often as you can.

Explore your local resources for relief aids. Certainly, Hospice is a good choice, but maybe your patient doesn't qualify. I list some other aid organizations in the bibliography at the back of this book.

I know you feel guilty spending $$ on hiring a sitter for your patient, but you should go biking or jogging or exercise whenever time permits. Set a rigid schedule and stick with it, especially when you feel just fine. Please get over the money thing. If you don't, you could be in a race for your own life before you can say "whoa, I want to get off."

Once your mind/body changes enough for you to be clearly certain that things are somehow different with you mentally or physically or when a friend comments on how 'differently' you look such as maybe 'tired' or 'stressed,' you are well on a downhill spiral. By the time you react and seek help, you are operating at a severely reduced capacity and you patient is most likely getting poorer care from you. If you are a runner, biker, or inline skater then you know about the age old adage "by the time you feel thirsty you are already in a state of dehydration."

Remember, it's the exercise that gives your body the refreshing neurotransmitters to ward off this unhealthy decline. Just because you feel good at the moment, doesn't mean you really are. These feelings can be so deceptive because they are very transitory. It is too easy to just do nothing because you feel fine and then, from nowhere, you submerge into a funk that you may not get out of for months or years to come.

Exercise and laugh as often as possible. It's your new medicine. Take it seriously once a day. Side effects of happiness and euphoria are transitory, but not life threatening.

CHAPTER 7
MEDICAL EQUIPMENT AND 'STUFF' FOR THE HOME

> Commit your work to the Lord, And your plans will be established.
>
> Proverbs 16:3

There will be different 'stuff' needed for different patients, but these are things that I would recommend for the 'average' patient. Remember, your patient may only need one or two of these items at the moment, but speaking from experience, I can tell you that can change in a heartbeat (no pun intended). It just takes one rogue embolus to change everything. Get what you can afford and feel is appropriate, but by the same token, do your homework and know just where to get everything else and where you can store items, like clothing and diapers, for efficient use.

1. **ORAL THERMOMETERS WITH LARGE MAGNIFYER OR LCD READOUT AND ONE RECTAL THERMOMETER.**

Some thermometers have a slide over magnifier and others use digital technology. You really must have two of these because when you really need one that is typically when you can't find one and default to a lame argument like "I'll buy one tomorrow." That could be a fatal mistake.

A rectal thermometer does just what its name says. Rectal temperatures may disclose a possible inflammatory or infectious process in the bladder such as a UTI (urinary tract infection) which might not even show up on the oral temperature reading. Yes, you can have a normal oral (mouth) temperature and simultaneously have a raging bladder infection.

I like having at least one digital thermometer 'gun.' It makes temperature checking instantaneous and easy. When it's easy, we will check more often right? Some digitals check for ear membrane temperature and some are designed for oral checking. Ask your pharmacist to help you find which is best for you.

Important temperatures

- 98.6°—A general, average body temperature for normal health, sometimes normal could be 97.6.

- 99.5°—Typically defines a fever for a child or adult.

- 100°—You need to start paying close attention and be looking for some inflammatory issue.

- 101°—This is indicative of some infection going on. It's time to see a doctor ASAP.

- 102°—Phone a doctor for advisement for aspirin or another med to help break the fever. You need to be taking the reins of action now!

- 103-104°—Call 911 now! Place a fan to cool the patient, maybe a rubbing alcohol rubdown for faster core cooling.

- 105°—This is simply not going to be a good day. Know what I mean?

- Note: A rectal temperature will typically be 1-2° higher than the average oral temperature.

2. **BLOOD PRESSURE MACHINE**

Everybody likes to weigh in on this topic and you should understand the pros and cons of this and the type, but in the last sentence I will put it all into perspective for you.

If your patient is sick, or maybe just headed a little south, you undoubtedly have seen various aid workers hovering around with their stethoscopes and 'cuff' taking blood pressure (BP) readings. You feverishly try to understand what is going on. You ask one person what the BP was and maybe several more people. Pretty soon, you realize a lot of the readings are quite a bit different from each one. That can be pretty scary... like is this ship out of control?

The first thing I want you to know is that there are two common types of BP machines used in the office setting. One is the aneroid barometer type and the other is the mercury type, consisting of a simple bourdon tube with mercury and scale markings. This is called a mercury sphygmomanometer or a MS type. The MS type is the gold standard because there is nothing to go wrong and nothing to calibrate.

The aneroid type has a sealed air bladder and spring tensions that get really out of whack if a person were to accidentally drop it on the floor. Of course, they would report their error immediately and get a new aneroid, along with a good behavior star. Not going to happen, is it?

So now we look at the mechanics of taking the actual measurement of the BP by listening to the 'echoes' of resurging blood flow. I will just bypass this discussion because if you talk to ten people you will get ten different techniques. Maybe they are all similar or close to each other, but we are not playing horseshoes here either.

The true scene is you have a lot of people getting mixed results with their BP equipment. I have personally asked a well-known cardiologist to give me the blood pressure himself on my 99 year old patient. When he left the room, I asked his nurse to re-check that pressure with her aneroid BP tester. The difference between the nurse's and the cardiologist's measurements were 30 mmHg!!!

If an error of that magnitude appears to be acceptable, then what's the point? Here's the skinny: The doctors aren't trying to fine tune anything. They want supportive info that says when the patient checked in under his care, that the patient was stable at the time, or whatever. So relax, it's just a yardstick that is designed to catch someone's attention really quickly if certain lows, highs, or abnormal rhythms are encountered. For an old patient, I generally get uneasy if the lower BP figure goes below say 50 mmHg, but I also know my patient's history. For someone else, this might take on a different meaning entirely.

A GENERALIZED DANGER ZONE FOR YOUR PATIENT'S BP

- SYSTOLIC (UPPER READING)—OVER 160 mm Hg OR LESS THAN 80mm Hg

- DIASTOLIC (LOWER READING)—OVER 80mm Hg OR LESS THAN 50 mm Hg

The above danger zones will represent different potentials for danger depending on the individual. For example: A patient with vascular disease (sclerosis) may get along just fine with a diastolic as low as 40 mmHg.

These zones are just general guidelines. See a trained professional if you have any concerns.

For the new caregiver, go out and buy a digital BP machine. Consumers union can probably give you the best advice for that. Otherwise, trust your heart. Now here is the hooker: **Don't try to compare your BP readings with the readings at the doctor's office. They won't be the same for no less than a dozen reasons.** What you are looking for is to make a long term record of your patient's BP changes with YOUR equipment. You need to be looking for patterns of change. You might need to alert you doctor that there has been a continual pattern of increasing BP after beginning a new medication for lowering it, for example. It's all about changes in the BP readings... not accuracy. Don't pay any attention to what your doctor or the nurse records (unless put down some scary figures).

The exception to this statement is if they all produce a BP in one of the 'danger zones.' Then, *it's time to ask questions* such as, "Should I be concerned with that lower BP reading of 40?" or "Should I be doing anything differently in handling the patient with a BP reading of 40?"

Danger zones mean you should get actively involved because very often a nurse or doctor may forget to mention special considerations in handling the patient. An example would be if the patient has orthostatic hypertension. If his BP is in a danger zone, it becomes very important to instruct the patient to not get up quickly (like to answer the phone) because they may faint and injure themselves.

3. **IDENTIFICATION BRACELET**

These can be purchased from a number of places. Try you local medical supply outlet first so you can 'try before you buy.' The bracelet should have the patient's name, address, phone number, and medical alerts (if any). They usually run about $25, but are well worth it should your patient decide to take a walk 'back home.' I use that term because you will often hear the patient saying "I want to go home now" when in fact they are already in their home.

4. **A 911 ALERT LANYARD**

Most of these devices work by having the patient press a button which transmits a signal to a receiver located somewhere in your house.

The receiver is connected to another device that will then dial a number depending on the system you have and how you have it programmed. About 99% of these device manufacturers make you think that no matter where you are, if you get into trouble, just press the red button and 911 will be at your beck and call. I see lot of misrepresentations in this field. 99% of these devices are limited to distances strictly within the house and in some case within the same floor level or room level if your walls are framed with the trendy metal studding.

None of them will work when you are at the grocery. I only know of one company that makes a device that will actually let you be doing gardening work outside and still transmit a signal over 600 feet to the transmitter inside your house. This company is 'First Alert' and it is a onetime purchase whereas most other devices soak you for about $300-$400 a year in rental or monitoring fees or whatever.

The only drawback is that these devices are about the size of a cell phone. If you go to sleep with one and roll over you have just pressed the 911 button and you will get results. What I like about these is once you press the 911 button you will be able to have a two way voice conversation with the 911 dispatcher to better communicate your needs and rule out an 'accidental' call.

Whatever device you choose, you should actually test it out. The 911 operator is used to this. Say, "This is the CG for Mary Jones. We are testing a new alert device. Can you hear my voice clearly?"

Most likely the operator will say, "Yes, I can hear you and I show that you are at address XXXX, is that correct?"

You affirm the information and the test is done. Remember that, sooner or later, your patient will outgrow the device, i.e. they will not have a clue what to do with it. Then, you can make your device a gift to the patient's advocate at your local church or a similar organization.

5. **NON-SPILL DRINKING CONTAINERS**

There are several varieties of these. I use the type that has no separate handle but the body is shaped to comfortably fit the hand. There is a mechanism that prevents inadvertent spills. The patient sucks liquid through a straw. They are sold at Kroger's and other fine stores.

There are other types available and we use something different for giving the patient purees, soups, etc. that may not pass through the small pinholes in all of these baby containers. For this application, we use a latex nipple type which we have modified. Remove the nipple, invert it for better access, trim the opening to the desired size, re-invert, and re-connect. Now you have a nipple with at least a ¼ opening for thick purees.

6. BED PROTECTORS

These are green rectangular pads that you put under a sheet (usually two pads) and center about the middle of the bed. The idea is to protect the expensive mattress from being contaminated should the patient have an 'accident' at night. Sometimes, I will place one on top of a sheet as an additional measure of protection or if the patient develops a bed sore. At Kroger, they go by the name 'Underpads' and a pack of eighteen cost about $6. They are 23" X 36."

Remember, the green plastic side faces down with the soft white side facing upwards toward the patient. This, of course, is the absorbent side.

7. AMPLE SUPPLY OF DIAPERS

There are many types and brands of diapers. Find one that is comfortable for your patient and has the maximum absorbency. Some types have buttons, others have a Velcro strap, and there are many more types. I use the simple pull up type. I find I get a good buy at Kroger's on Depends. You should figure on spending less than $1 on a good diaper (a 40 ct box of Depends with extra absorbency runs about $22 or approximately 55¢ each).

If you use the pull up type as I suggested, the best way to quickly remove these is to take a pair of scissors and make a cut on each hip side.

SPEED CHANGING—If you bunch up the side, you can cut clear through each diaper side with one scissor clip. This frees up the diaper to be pulled out from between the legs and in one continuous movement you can deposit it into the stink bag that you previously hung on the bed post. Plop it into the bag, tie it up, and that heifer/bull smells better already. Now, grab both pant legs and pull them off the patient at once. Put on the new diaper, return the pants, and then turn patient 180 degrees so you can pull up the diaper. I keep my hands on opposite sides of my patient and pull up the diaper, quickly going around it for final adjustment. Then pull up the sweat pants and you're done.

I think at some point in the future this will be done by highly trained aid workers who will prowl the neighborhoods. When they come to the address of one of their patients, they will run in and it's like a Valvoline quick change. There will be a NAFTA worker on the floor checking fluid levels (urine), another checking her feet who yells out "blah... blah... bay three, feet are worn," and finally, there will be a third worker checking for false teeth... "hup, hup... three glasses of salad oil sir/madam, would you like your ego topped off with another glass?" Then, there will be a techie that will say your warranties are out and you could expire soon. Would you like an engine rebuild?

I think when my time comes and I am wearing diapers, I want something radically different. Maybe I will be the first to start diaper changing as a sport. I will volunteer to be the first. There could be time trials and pit crews... so much to look forward to.

8. AMPLE SUPPLY OF LATEX GLOVES

You may want to try both the powdered and unpowdered. I know it sounds like the powdered ones are a no-brainer choice, but actually I despise them. The powder is hard to wash off and so is the odor that goes with it. I am sure there are some brands in which this is not the case... try and see what suits you.

9. AMPLE SUPPLY OF SMALL PLASTIC BAGS

Don't just have a roll of plastic bags sitting on the shelf, but rather have maybe a 100 of them already pulled off the roll, opened, and then crinkle stuffed back into the storage box. The reason is simple. Your patient may have a limited ability to stand and behave in a manner you want, so you will not have time to fumble with trying to get a bag open before your patient walks away or falls down. I like the used Kroger bags, or sometimes I buy a roll of 4 gal. bags (scented) from Wal-Mart and pre-open them for standby. A 100 ct roll is only $3-4.

10. AMPLE SUPPLY OF PANTS, TOPS, AND SOCKS FOR THE PATIENT

Remember, you will most likely be changing the patient's pants several times a day because of overflow wetness from the diaper. The number of changes will depend on your patient's degree of incontinence. I would recommend a warm material that is soft and with or without a drawstring. Men's sweats are available year round at Wal-Mart. These fit either men or women. I would avoid the color grey unless you want the smallest of dampness to shine. Grey shows wetness to a fault (but sometimes that is good depending on how you are managing the situation). Expect to pay about $5 per pair.

With most aging patient's, you will find that because their metabolism has slowed and their body fat may be significantly reduced, they will experience feelings of 'chill' even on a summer day when you and I might be sweating.

For socks, if your patient is incontinent, I recommend you buy the kind that only comes two or three inches above the heel of the foot. These are generally advertised for the diabetic. I find these at Wal-Mart very reasonably priced. The point here is that as your patient ages and their systems begin to not work so well, fluid buildup becomes common. A tight fitting sock will compound this problem by making blood flow return more difficult and fluid begins to build up in the ankles. The exception to this is where perhaps your doctor sees a need for compression stockings to facilitate circulation.

Tops can be button-up or pull-over, but always keep in mind ease of changing. I use both the button-up and pull-over varieties, but my personal favorite is the pull-over because of the ease of application.

11. AMPLE SUPPLY OF FLUSHABLE WIPES

These are pre-moistened wipes that are ideal for bodily clean up issues. The flushable kinds are not supposed to clog up your toilet, but I try to aim them for the trash can just to be on the safe side. Kroger sells a plastic box of these for less than $2, and refill packages of the wipes can be bought separately.

12. SUPPLY OF CLEANING AND DISINFECTANTS

I always use either 50% bleach for cleaning or Lestoil. You can use a more dilute bleach solution if you are sensitive to it, but that means you must also allow more contact time for the same 'germ kill ratio.'

Lestoil has a strong pine oil scent which some people might find objectionable, but I like it. Lestoil is often mistaken for being the same as Pine Sol. This is not the case. Lestoil has different cleaning chemicals in it that make it good for floors and laundry. I also like to use copious amounts of "Windex" or an equivalent for some applications.

13. PULSE OXIMETER

(The following is just my opinion. I am not a medical doctor, so I cannot cast this stuff in stone... that gets done when you waited too long to react, ☺)

Pulse oximeters can be pricey, but mine cost $68 from internet (from portablenebs.com/tripleoximeter.htm) delivered by mail to my front door. Most hospital supply houses sell them from about $200-$400 and often require a prescription to even buy one.

Not really a 'must have,' but I like to recommend them. Any nurse, in almost any hospital, is just too eager to whip out this little gizmo. About the size of a book of matches, it has a small infrared LED and receiver. Put your finger into the box, a light shines on your finger, and viola... you will get an instantaneous oxygen saturation level in your peripheral blood and pulse rate. Besides looking very 'haute couture,' it will really give you some good info.

Anytime your patient begins to complain about not feeling well, check their 'O_2 sat' levels. Assuming you have taken the level when the patient was feeling well, you have something to compare it to. If not, here is a guideline:

O_2 is less than 88

This is not good and I advise calling a doctor. This is close to being critical (around 85 or less). It's time to make some calls, talk to a doctor, call 911 (your choice).

A reduced O_2 sat may be the result of a pulmonary (lung) infection, fluid leaking into the lungs, and other bad stuff. Be sure to check more than one finger to get a better average number.

O_2 is 70-80

Your patient will soon be going into 'active death.'

O₂ is 90 or greater

Good news! The higher the number, the better. Just remember that your readings are for that moment in time, and can change on a dime. I have seen chain smokers with one foot in the grave still have O$_2$ sats of over 95%! How? I don't know, but they live on a precarious balance that could shift to serious problems in a heartbeat.

14. A STANDBY O₂ CYLINDER WITH REGULATOR AND/OR CPAP BREATHING MACHINE (nice, but pricey)

Depending on how ill your patient is, this would be a worthwhile addition. These are pricey, but so is life.

I won't call this an alternative, but it comes pretty close. If you just happen to qualify for a CPAP (continuous positive airway pressure) machine for treating sleep apnea (snoring more or less) by your insurance company, you will find this device, complete with muzzle, very helpful. It establishes a positive airway pressure in your lungs. Even though the O$_2$ level is the same as in the room air, the higher pressure effectively does a better job of tissue saturation (in my opinion). I have one and I love it.

If you choose to use one, I would recommend the ResMed Escape II for the simple reason that it is by far the quietest I have ever tested. The backpressure engineering is superior. Is noise control important? Not if you are single.

Also, if you ever break a rib, this machine will be your sweetheart for sure. Believe it or not, it's not just the patient who falls from time to time. In either case, the excruciating pain of a broken rib can be made bearable with a CPAP machine. I certainly am not a cardiologist, but I would think that the CPAP forced ventilation would help to reduce cardiac loading and assist in maintaining a more normal sinus rhythm. Anyway it worked for me when I had a few broken ribs from my inline skating.

MEDICATIONS THAT I COMMONLY USE
Available as non-Rx

Please note that most of these medicines have warnings about not taking them for more than a few days without conferring with your doctor. Medicines that cause a lot of loss of fluids, such as the Pepto Bismol and

Milk of Magnesia, could lead to electrolyte disorders and bad things. I always look at the risk/benefit ratio (before tearing off that scary label).

Pepto Bismol—This is for an upset stomach. The patient likes the pretty, pink color of this med. I always administer orally from a table spoon. All the patient has to do is swallow, which in this case, is even an autonomic response when done correctly.

Milk of Magnesia—This is for constipation. I use it for the more difficult cases. The downside is you never know just exactly when the patient will open the flood gates or how wide will the gates open. I give a couple of ounces to my patient, and usually in a few hours there is a result... and a few hours later another result... eventually ending.

Mira Lax—This is for constipation. It is a relatively new chemical (simply a high mol. wt. polyethylene glycol) that seems to have no side effects and is really more of a stool softener. Since I have been using this, I rarely have to resort to the ol' standby Milk of Magnesia. I use a daily maintenance dose of about one third capful. Initially, I would give a full capful in a divided dose for the first two or three days, then back off until I am at one third capful for single dosing. This is my patient's permanent maintenance level and I administer once daily.

Bicarbonate tabs—This works great for stomach problems, but I have a new patient reluctance because she doesn't want to drink so much water for a stomach that already feels bloated. I can understand that. Otherwise, I would give one tablet in about two ounces of water.

Kroger baby aspirin (81mg)—These should be given once per day and the earlier you start (as in N-O-W) the wiser you will be. This is a good preemptive strike against any blood clots forming. Think of a missile that travels until it meets a new gang cloister, say the bloods... yo dawg, it could happen. NSAIDS (non-steroidal anti-inflammatory drugs) will not work here because they lack this tiny little chemical in aspirin which ultimately becomes a Prostaglandin A2 inhibitor in the blood stream. Use too much aspirin over a long period of time, and you cause some body tissues to ulcerate and start bleeding. This would be about 500 mg/day.

Aleve—This is a handy NSAID for conquering headaches, body aches, and just old-fashioned aches. It is not uncommon for my patient to sleep in the wrong position and wake up with 'horrible back pain' or occasional neck pain. While other wise souls in the family are ready to call 911, thinking my patient must have fallen and has a sacral fracture, I slip her two Aleve for this level of pain and, in about 30 minutes, things are getting better, and by dinner time she has forgotten all about the pain.

The point here is that the caregiver is often out-voted, but sometimes needs to make the final call.

I always listen to others input, but since I had seen similar pain situations with this patient, I felt there was a high likelihood this was ligament related and not a broken sacrum. Caution: this belongs to the class of NSAIDs. These can cause acute kidney failure (which is usually reversible) if over administered or if the patient already has a kidney problem.

Of course, I have a slew of other Rx and non-Rx meds that I didn't even bother to mention because I rarely use them. Some were gifts from Hospice such as nitro for a weak ticker and steroids when the patient wants something different. Before long, you too, will have a med warehouse in your kitchen.

Ben Blyton

THE REAL NITTY GRITTY ON MRSA AND OTHER GERMS

They are everywhere and they are here to stay. Sooner or later, it will be germ warfare time with your patient. That can have a lot of different meanings to a lot of different people.

I have good backgrounds in microbiology (I owned a vet lab), chemistry, physiology, and so much more it would make ya puke, so I can give you some straight talk that nobody else will. For instance, I know from doing culture studies that antibiotics are most effective when given as a high 'loading dose' and then tapering off for the next two days. Anything beyond that, and the culture plates would eventually show mutant colonies that were resistant to the antibiotic. So what is the first thing the nurse or doctor tells ya to do? You guessed it! "Take these antibiotics for the full 10 days."

Not too long ago one of the medical advisory boards (sorry, can't recall which or when) said that antibiotics should only be given for three days with a higher concentration given the first day. Furthermore, they claimed that anything taken beyond the third day had little, if any, curative effect. That recommendation never became popular because the drug companies were going to lose a lot of $$ if you were to quit eating pills like French fries. The sad thing is that the healthcare professionals who insist you take the full course enchilada for ten days, don't really have any clue why they tell you that other than it's what the drug companies have told them... and the parroting is passed on to nurse to caregiver to patient.

I took over the caregiver role of my parents when my dad became critically ill with cardiomyopathy. He was not expected to live. He was released to Hospice care (they take ya when they figure you only have three to six months or less to live). His condition worsened. I decided to take control because, for some reason, the meds that the cardiologist was prescribing were doing more damage than good.

To make a long story short, for over two years he has been robust and healthy. He even mows the grass on the riding mower when the weather is decent. He is just over 102 now. Germ control is recognized for what it is and he rarely gets an infection (but he carries a small one in the bladder all the time... nature's way of saying "hello, you are not alone anymore").

I wish I had a nickel for every time I heard a health care worker talk about how critical germ control is and almost at the expense of everything else. Yes, it CAN be, if you have a depleted immune system for example.

Or maybe you are on steroids or some medication that is affecting your normal immune response. Most patients I have come into contact with are the garden variety that are just aging and everything physiologic is slowly diminishing.

It is true that new types or variations of germs are constantly jostling for the best position in the starting gate. This is because of our constant attempts to kill them with extended terms of treatment beyond three days. Of course they are going to mutate, but the drug and tobacco companies rule.

MRSA—Methicillin-Resistant Staphylococcus Aureus

This seems to becoming more prevalent. In your daily inspection of your patient, always look for new skin areas with generalized swelling and redness. You may never see the typical white pustule of white blood cells. If you see a semi-firm red area that continues to grow (sometimes like a boil), contact your doctor or nurse immediately for advisement. This nasty little germ is a variant of the more common Staphylococcus aureus. MRSA is more difficult to eradicate. There are many sources for this critter, so don't waste your time looking for them. Some people have even been found to be natural 'carriers,' which means the surface of their skin may contain populations of MRSA, but they don't become infected because their skin's immune system keeps it in check. The irony is that some people go to extreme measures to clean everything in the house to a literal germ-free state and a visitor could walk in the door, shake your patient's hand or give them a hug, or sneeze, and guess what?...infected! It really does happen more often than you think.

Sometimes contact with other people is the greater health threat. I knew a massage therapist who claimed she was a carrier of MRSA, but that the hospital said it wasn't significant enough to be a threat to the clients. Who would know? Can you imagine someone rubbing those germs all over you and into your skin? I knew a hospital worker who said the hospital she worked at (hint: a major hospital in Lexington) said the hepatitis C she had would not be a threat to anyone. Who knows where she might go in the hospital?

> **The point I want to make is to keep your life in perspective. If you get a germ attack, then deal with it. Worry about the most common germ threats. The most important thing to worry about is whether your patient has developed a pathway that will let germs inside. Germs sitting on top of the skin are not likely going inside.**

Germs sitting on top of skin that has been repeatedly scratched or is reddened from the action of urine contact for too long will receive their invitations to come inside where it's nice and warm. Over scrubbing the skin, thinking that more is better, could kill ya if you cause abrasions of the epithelial cells and open the doors to direct contamination by a germ source (like the patient with feces under their fingernails scratching their skin). Your priority is to keep the doors of your body's skin closed to outsiders. Remember that the skin has a natural defense with its thin coating of natural oil which has antimicrobial properties. Sometimes using too much alcohol gel cleaners can erode this barrier and cause drying and cracking of the top layer of cells. This is not safe, but we are drawn to the fantasy of alcohol gels because they just sound 'so right.' Use them, but in perspective.

There are only a couple of common germ threats: Staphylococcus E. and E-coli. Staph E. is ubiquitous; it's everywhere, but most commonly found covering the skin. Unless your immune system is weakened, don't worry about it.

Think about it, do you ever see dogs getting sick from their favorite pastime of licking their privates? No, they just get happier. We hear about the rare E-coli OH57 serotype variant and we overreact to all germs. E-Coli comes from fecal contamination. Again, when you are dealing with patients with dementia, you can expect anything. Often one of my patients would 'dig' fecal balls out of her rear side. Sometimes, she would carry them around like cookies, and sometimes she would touch about everything in the house, contaminating the house. In fact, E-coli is not a big threat either, unless you give it a way to enter the skin (or try to bake those brownies in the oven).

Apply some soap and water, and gently wash away. The threat is gone. The mistake so many people make is that they furiously scrub their hands or skin with a washcloth or brush. The harder I scrub, the cleaner, right? Allow me to give you this classic example of germ threat: When I first began caring for my dad, I had to learn to catheterize him. Everyone from the Hospice nurses to the medical supply store that sold these long plastic catheters all made it clear that the catheter is to be used once and discarded. This is to prevent infection. What was puzzling to me was why would his urologist keep telling me not to check for infection... just do the catheterization. He also said that the bladder does contain a normal amount of bacterial flora, and the catheters would keep this in check by fully emptying the bladder each time. IF that is the case, then it doesn't really matter about how clean the catheter is right?

I typically use the same catheter on my dad for about four months and then discard for a new one. I just rinse each time and dry it with a hand towel. The sellers are the real gangsters on this and I can't understand why the visiting RN's didn't seem to get it either. They were intent on seeing that I discarded the catheter each time while they actually overlooked the very real fact that the patient's diapers were coated with the latest bowel movement. Too often the medical techs only know to do what they are told (reminds me of the Emperor's new clothes).

Marketers make big money by scaring the pants off us about germs. I heard a commercial a while back extolling the 'fact' that the average oral (mouth) cavity carries over 100,000 different kinds of germs. At the time, I had my own lab and I put that to the test. I was only able to culture about 6 distinctive kinds of germs. SIX... as in 6. I have no idea where the other 99,994 germs were? Maybe if one considers variants of variants etc... nah, that's just nonsense. But that claim just sounds truthful, doesn't it? I mean germs are soooo small and none of them know each other and so they are probably all different. So who would know? Ask a doctor and he will probably agree... until you ask him upon what precisely he would base his belief on. **Don't believe everything you hear or read about germs. Use your common sense.** Maybe you want to be scared; then believe what you need.

THE MOST IMPORTANT THING I WANT YOU TO REMEMBER ABOUT GERMS IS...

Your body needs the protection of an undisturbed skin cell layer. Don't tear it up by rough scrubbing. A normal non-antibacterial soap does fine. Occasionally take Windex or a similar product and wipe doorknobs and refrigerator handles. Keep some Lestoil or something similar around for wet mopping floor areas. (Note: Lestoil and Pine sol are significantly different, even though they smell the same.)

I know sometimes with sick patients that are drooling all over everything, it is easy to overreact to dish and utensil cleanliness because we can see drool or food particles clinging everywhere. Read my lips now... clean your stuff if you want to be neat but NOT because you think you are eliminating a viable germ threat that could make you or anyone else sick if they ate off that plate or spoon or whatever. Germs from your patient (generally your parent) are not able to do any damage because they go straight into your digestive system where they are destroyed. (How do ya think dogs and cats can eat road kill, smack their chompers, look for more, and always feel great?) Alright, you say what if the germs were botulism? I say your patient would have wings by now. What if they had a virus? Again, they probably would be very ill before this. I agree that spit doesn't seem appetizing when it is in the form of drool, but does seem appetizing when in the form of a kiss. Is that freaky or whaaat?

I mention all this about food and dishes because some people I have known will spend all their time on meticulously cleaning every eating utensil and no longer have time to do more important sanitizing like the door knobs that the visitor with the runny nose just handled, or the table top and glasses that blocked the sneeze of the well-wisher out visiting all the church's sick congregation. Spend your time wisely.

To help control general sanitation in the kitchen and other areas, I have a throw away plastic liner in each trash can (I don't like the stainless steel flip top cans personally). For the big kitchen trash can, I use the plastic kind with a 'flip up' lid when you depress the foot pedal. Unfortunately, the manufacturer doesn't seem to have any bags properly designed to accommodate the can and not constantly fall into the can as you push more and more garbage into it. The solution is simple... I use the white bags with the two strap handles. Fold these over the outside of the can and use a 6-10" tie-down strap (stretchy thing) and connect across the backside of the trashcan between the two handles. The other thing I do is to remove (unsnap) the lid each time and when replacing a new liner I just snap the lid down on top of the liner itself. This gives added support, and most of all, it keeps debris out of the hinging mechanism that can be a respite for germs.

SOME MEDICAL EMERGENCIES

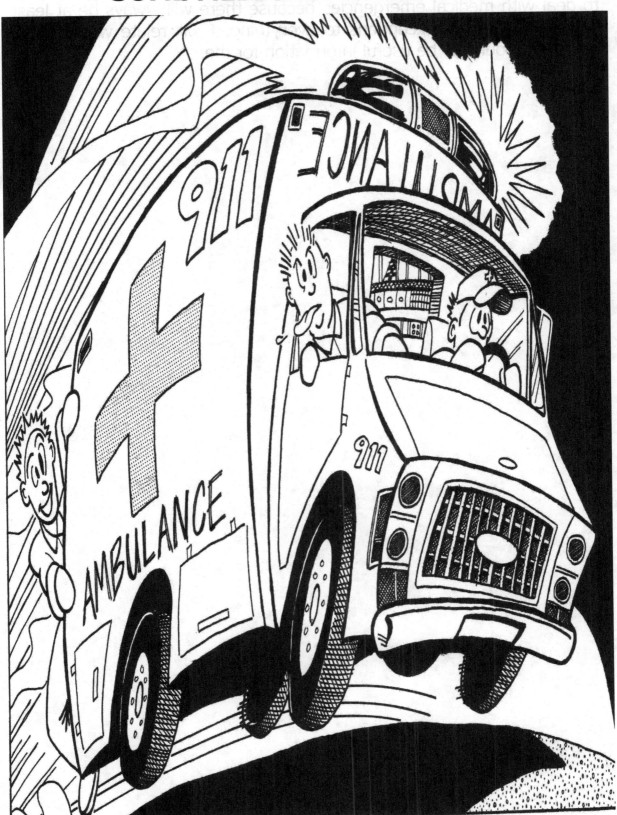

I am not a medical doctor, therefore, I cannot proffer advice on how to deal with medical emergencies because there will always be at least a baker's dozen of exceptions to everything. I will relate what I have personally found to be useful information for me.

DIZZINESS

If this doesn't pass within a few minutes of lying down, I would call 911 and let someone else rule out cardiovascular events. There could be many causes here.

If the dizziness does pass within a few minutes, then I would schedule a heart workup with a cardiologist as soon as possible. Typically, this will be gradual onset cardiomyopathy, but is frequently complicated by a transient embolism or even dehydration.

When I think 'dizziness,' I think either heart or meds. Here is important stuff about meds. Your doctor may be the greatest in the world, but he is not always right. This is usually in regards to medicine because some of the standard heart medications work well for some people, but might almost kill others. If your patient keeps getting worse and the doctor's office keeps telling you, "It's pretty normal for patients to feel worse on this medicine before they begin to feel better," then monitor your patient like a hawk. Check vital signs several times a day with whatever equipment you have. If the patient keeps spiraling downward, then YOU call the cardiologist and say you would like to back off on the dosage and then try a different medication. Remember, unless you make the call, the doctor can only assume your patient is doing great on his meds.

Also, make sure you discuss with your patient's doctor if it is okay to give them a daily aspirin (81 mg ONLY). If the patient is on another blood thinner, you would not want to add aspirin. Do not assume that if 81 mg a day is good for preventing blood clots, then an adult aspirin (325mg) given daily would be even better. The problem here is that too much aspirin can often be the source of internal bleeds when given over a long time. Again, this depends on many factors.

Another common type of dizziness occurs from what is called 'orthostatic hypertension.' This is a condition in which your body's sensors can't always adjust quickly enough for increased blood flow needs after you stand up. This delay means there is insufficient blood flow to the brain and you feel dizzy. This problem can usually be safely resolved if the patient is trained to get up 'slowly,' thereby giving the blood a chance to circulate. This is usually not an emergency if the situation is self-resolving.

Weather barometric pressure changes can also cause dizziness, but again, this is not an emergency and will resolve in a day or two as the weather changes.

CHEST PAINS

211

Chest pains are always a cause for concern because there is truly no way of knowing for sure what is causing them. The primary concern is whether the patient is about to have a heart attack or maybe is in the process of having one. I can only speak in generalities, signs, and symptoms regarding a heart attack.

MIDLINE CHEST PAIN AREA

Not usually a threat—it usually presents as a fairly sharp pain directly in a vertical line with the sternum (that little plate-like thingy where your ribs seem to stop and below it everything is soft, which most people erroneously call the stomach). This is called angina pain which is caused by a deficiency of getting enough oxygen to the muscles. It is often preceded by eating, stress, or exercise. While most people, understandably, get more anxiety from this experience, it is non-life threatening as long as it's transient angina, of course. Remember, the normal heart is physically positioned to the left of this midline and that's one pain location that should alert you to make a 911 call. Suspect GERD as a source and try Prilosec (a proton inhibitor) or a Dynamite pill prescribed by your doc.

OTHER POSSIBLE HEART PAIN AREAS

Consider a threat—it usually presents along the neck, shoulder, or arm areas. Pain may present in any or combinations of these areas. Call 911 if in question. At the very least, I personally would give my patient one adult aspirin (325mg). Please note that I did not say to give an Aleve or ibuprofen or any of many available NSAIDs. Aspirin will inhibit clot formation because it functions as a prostaglandin A2 inhibitor. The other meds don't work that way. Often, coronary events present with a sensation of pressure around the heart area. Ask your patient what they feel.

SIGNS OF A POSSIBLE APPROACHING HEART ATTACK

Consider a threat—everybody has their own list of 'sure fire' signs and omens, but here are some that seem to be reasonably consistent.

BEHAVIOR CHANGES

Consider a threat—your patient may suddenly begin to express his/her feelings and emotions differently, more directly, with more fear, anxiety, possibly even anger, and confusion. It is not uncommon for the patient to complain that, "Something is wrong with me. I don't know what it is. I just don't trust what's going on. I don't understand why I feel this way?" Here, I would suspect that the patient may be going into tachycardia (rapid heartbeat). This feeling of 'impending doom' may be experienced from a few minutes before or up to 48 hours before a 'cardiac event.' It signals a definite need for professional evaluation, and even then, there are 'false negative' results, so continue to watch your patient much more carefully in the next few days.

CHANGES IN SKIN TONE

Consider a threat—look carefully at the pallor of face. Is it a bluish-grey? That's not good. Check their oxygen levels with your pulse oximeter. Anything below 90% is a concern. Anything at 88% or less and you need to start dialing 911.

Look at the hands, fingers, and feet for bluish color. (Sometimes a patient with thin skin will have a natural bluish color because of the proximity of small capillary beds closer to the surface causing the reflected/refracted natural light make the skin to appear bluish.)

SIGNIFICANT HEART RATE SWINGS

Consider a threat—if the patient's heart rate drops to less than 50 bpm (going into bradycardia) or climbs above about 125 bpm (going into tachycardia), you should consult a doctor ASAP.

ACUTE STOMACH PAINS

Hopefully this will just be gas buildup, usually relieved by rolling the patient slowly from side to side to allow passage of the gas. Sometimes, it helps to bend the knees and move the legs closer to the patient's trunk. *However, the real problem you need to consider is a constricted or twisted colon.* If you feel the abdominal area and it feels very painful and hard, then you need to call 911. A patient with a constricted colon needs urgent evaluation! If you are not sure, dial 911.

BREATHING DIFFICULTY

Sometimes this comes on very gradually and the patient isn't sure when the problem began, then suddenly, he/she can no longer compensate and begins gasping for air. Sometimes audible lung sounds and a wet cough are a clue. These may be signs of congestive heart failure in which fluid begins to back up into the lungs. As precious lung space is deprived, so is the body's ability to perfuse the blood with enough oxygen. For smokers, this is an even greater threat because, for one thing, you are dealing with a reduced overall gas permeability of lung tissues because less is available.

This may warrant a 911 call depending on your evaluation. Expect the hospital to administer furosimide or an equivalent to help the body dump its overload of fluid from the lungs. They may also administer morphine for pain. Be sure to let them know if you are allergic to anything. Of course, other things could be done also to speed up the removal of large volumes of fluid. Please note your patient's normal breathing pattern. Sometimes, and I can name a few examples, an outside caregiver, nurse, or whomever will just not be alert to breathing sounds and often plead, "It's just his/her normal breathing." Don't buy that unless you have made your own mental notes on how their normal breathing sounds. You always have the option of insisting that a RN or doctor puts the ol' stethoscope on and auscultates (listens) for lung sounds.

CONSTIPATION

I know this is one topic you just don't want to know about, but sooner or later you will, literally, have to become immersed in it. Most reference books won't touch this delicate issue, which is a shame because everyone seems to get in to deep... well you know, sooner or later. Most stages of aging proceed through different degrees of constipation. The initial phase may respond to something as simple as exercise. Then the patient moves toward reduced bowel motility and here the caregiver must have some idea of what kinds of constipation medications to give their patient. Eventually the bowel becomes atonic and has little ability to perform natural peristalsis (the squeezing motion of bowel muscles). Here is where things get a little more difficult because you (or someone) may have to deal with bowel impaction problems that have to be resolved by physical palpitation and extraction of the feces.

Constipation can have a number of causes which include: side effects

217

from meds, diet, no exercise, and dependence on constipation medicine itself. Now, to treat this topic properly, I would need to get into a lot of technical stuff and even discuss the conditions and graphs which define constipation. It doesn't take a rocket scientist to know when you are constipated. No sir, no charts and graphs needed, just give me that ol' time common sense. In short, 'nothin' happening' is all ya need to know.

EXAMPLES OF SOME TYPES OF CONSTIPATION MEDS I COMMONLY USE

MILK OF MAGNESIA—Laxative—Works in 1-6 hours. It works by absorbing water into the intestines and enhancing peristalsis. Good for periodic use.

METAMUCIL, CITROCEL, ETC.—These work by cellulose absorbing water. Bulk forming to stimulate peristalsis. A couple of large glasses of water are recommended when taking this, which might be difficult for an elderly patient or even a young patient for that matter. I haven't seen much success in my personal efforts with this. There is also some possibility of making the constipation worse in cases where this tends to just "ball up" but I cannot confirm those rumors.

SODIUM DOCUSATE—A stool softener/laxative—Works in 1-3 days.

It works by making fatty oils miscible, which helps keep the stool in a softened state. It is available in standard gel caps or in liquid form. It seems to work well, but has bitter taste to deal with.

***MIRALAX—A stool softener/laxative—Works in 1-3 days.

It uses high molecular wt. 'polyethylene glycol 3350' that helps to absorb water. I have just been using this for about 6 months on my 97 year old patient and so far she has not had any further episodes of acute constipation. The stool becomes soft, but not runny or hard. I cannot taste this medicine and it dissolves easily in milk or Gatorade (great in Gatorade). I know the instructions say to only use it for a week, but I think that refers to the full dosage of two capfuls per day. I have my patient on no more than ½ a capful per day and have had no noticeable problems.

I think this med might just be the single greatest treatment for constipation to ever come down the tracks, but again I have only had firsthand experience of about 6 months. I am continuing this regimen with the patient.

SENNA—A stimulant laxative—Works in 1-3 days. This is derived from natural vegetable glycosides.

ALL BRAN CEREAL—(Kellogg)—Take 1/3 cup per day. Works in 2-3 days. (This is one of my favorites on cereal with honey)

ENEMA—Place the patient in a laying down position on top of a pad protector. With the patient in the fetal position, insert the long nozzle of the enema applicator (it is recommend that you cover it with some type of gel for easier insertion) into the rectum. Then, you squeeze the bottle until all the fluid has emptied. Allow patient to straighten out and wait 15-30 minutes. The patient, hopefully, will expel the fecal mass before being jettisoned into the next room.

For containment, I personally might have the patient standing in the bath tub in a bent over position. Insert, squeeze, and wait. This method is not quite as effective as the lying down method, but is a whole lot easier to deal with if it does work.

For long term care and treatment of constipation, please consult your doctor for the best and most appropriate system.

For me, as a caregiver to parents over the age of 97, I use a combination of the sodium docusate, senna, and Mira Lax for them. I try to give some in the morning and the other in the evening. I do this because it works for my patients, albeit one responds better than the other. I also know my doctor prefers not to use them every day because these, and most all constipation meds, will weaken the body's natural ability for GI track movement. I understand the position from a liability standpoint, but when the patient doesn't have any motility left then it's time to do whatever works. I know I will still be dealing with constipation issues. I also use, on an infrequent basis, the Milk of Magnesia when I think my patient is beginning to become blocked again.

Remember that your patient may have difficulty in swallowing pills and that you have some options. Some pills can be obtained in liquid form. For non-liquid pills, and liquid pills for that matter, I use a tablespoon of applesauce and embed the pills in that. This seems to make for a smoother transport down the throat.

Also, I may pre-dissolve the pills in hot water and add a sweetener. This works fine with the exception of the sodium docusate, which is so bitter you might bite your tongue trying to swallow that.

HOW TO DEAL WITH CONSTIPATION EMERGENCY

There will be a time when your patient appears to have steadily increasing abdominal pain. You can lay the patient on their back and place your hand over their left abdominal area. Feel for hardened and/or irregular areas, confirming hardened, packed stool. Of course if the patient is obese, this palpitation may not reveal anything. So you try the enema. It doesn't work. You try another enema, and it doesn't work. Your patient is desperate, and it's late at night on the weekend (of course). What do you do?

You call a home health care provider to send out a nurse, but they tell you it will be several hours before a nurse can arrive. The situation is desperate. What do you do? You could call 911, but chances are, your patient will be parked in the admissions waiting room for hours while other patients with more serious problems are addressed.

Okay, I think you can see where I am headed with this. Let me relate what I have learned. Remember, I am not a medical doctor, but I didn't want my patient to die of pain waiting for one either. So from the standpoint of liability, I speak about the theoretical patient (which in these cases was actually my patient).

I quickly gather up the prearranged supplies recommended to be in the household, specifically, I grab a box of 'tissue wipes' (I want the kind that is flushable), a tube of Kroger's lubricating gel or KY gel, and a pair of latex rubber gloves.

The concept is to put on the gloves, lubricate one digit (finger) with the gel, and to insert into the patient's rectum quickly, feeling around the fecal mass testing to see where the weaker or most easily accessible spot on the mass is. By removing the easiest to get to pieces you quickly gain access to more and more of the larger and more solid portions. If your patient is standing in the bathtub, you can either throw these pieces into to tub, a nearby container, or even the toilet. Time is the enemy here, because this will be traumatic to the patient (as well as to the caregiver).

Amid the complaints of pain, you must remain focused and committed to removing as much as you can, as quickly as you can. You won't have time to try and be neat and tidy... just 'Git R Done.'

Unless your patient has a predisposed condition that precludes digital removal of packed feces, there should be no complications. The walls of the colon are rather elastic and strong. You might accidentally engage a small polyp that may produce an uneventful bleed, but other than that, you and the patient will have a successful outcome.

Let me emphasize that what will determine the successful outcome will be your firm commitment; no wavering once you start. Can you imagine what the patient would think if you gingerly inserted your gloved index finger only to be frightened back out every time they gave a call of pain? In very short order, you will stop this amateur stuff some way or another. What you will do is focus on firmly restraining the patient, while working decisively and as quickly as you can. Remember to use plenty of lube gel on your gloved finger. I found I could put one arm around the patient for restraint while I used the other for doing the procedure.

I don't know how painful this really is and I don't care to find out but, I just know that pain levels in geriatric patients can often be distorted significantly. I have heard my mother scream about how the shower I wash her with was just 'killing' her even though I am careful to continuously check the temperature of the water against my wrist. Or in some cases, the opposite might be true.

I use the wipes to quickly clean up around the anus and other areas so I can get the patient out of that environment and to lie down for a while. It is not be uncommon for pain to create a vasovagal (circulatory) response, causing the patient to become very weak, dizzy, or both for a short while. In the rare case of a black out, just lay the patient down and, within a minute, they will be starting their own recovery. At the same time, you could be grabbing the phone in case you needed to call 911. I have not had this happen to any patient of mine, but I have experienced it with myself after getting a severe muscle cramp from over-exercising. The pain started the vasovagal response and, in short order, I went out... but then, I was back in touch without any further problems. This is the body's way of telling us to chill out, relax, and go with the flow.

CHAPTER 8
COMMON TYPES OF BEHAVIORS EXHIBITED DURING DEMENTIA

> Jesus said, "Come to me all you who are weary
> and burdened, and I will give you rest.
>
> Matthew 11:28

I am sure to hear from a lot of people that I didn't mention this or that behavior that they just 'know' is more common. Ok... you are right, and thanks for pointing that out. I will reference your correction in my next book. Here are some behaviors which you may come across.

Note: The following behaviors are not in any particular sequence, nor relevancy to frequency of occurrence.

THE GERIATRIC MIND

I don't know when all aging minds begin to revert to deductive reasoning and away from the highly inductive form, but here is what to expect. **Your patient, relying on deductive reasoning, will absolutely not be able to see things the way that you do.** For example, my patient was given an award in the form of a parchment (unframed). I thought it would be nice to frame it. He didn't. In fact, he swore that someone must have stolen his parchment award and he had no idea who might have given him a new framed award. He was sure he had two awards now, one framed and one unframed. In short, your patient will make conclusions that will absolutely puzzle you.

Once you understand how deductive reasoning works, you really will be able to overlook some of the extreme frustrations that arise.

Another strike against you being on even turf with your patient is that his/her needs, desires, and intentions are different from yours. I often would get very frustrated with how my patient would not seem to listen to my direct questions. How could he not be interested in what I was saying? It took a while and my wife's wisdom to help me realize that a patient may have an entirely different view of what is worth being interested in. **Your patient may not have any interest in what you are saying. Believe it, let it go, and move on.** That is why they sometimes behave the way they do. It is just a fact. Accept that and deal with life on their terms. Let this final dress rehearsal be all theirs.

Be prepared for changes in your patient's rhetoric. Sometimes it is just 'colorful,' but often it downgrades into real gutter talk. Each person is different and some caregiver's describe some pretty degrading situations. The old adage about 'the devil made him do it' may actually have a ring of truth in it.

I don't understand why my patient asks about my nephew who just got a DUI. I queried, "why do you keep asking about him?" He replied that it's because he cares about the misfortune of others. What I can tell you is that he takes great delight in telling all his friends about his in-laws or outlaws and how it worries him constantly. This elicits immediate *rescues* of compassion from anyone who listens.

In other words, he really delights in manipulating others, using them for his ego. But is this a strategically orchestrated behavior or does he in fact believe his own lies? While he is the only one who really knows the truth (and he's not talking), I can relate the following experience:

After my mother died, he immediately took up with a very, very rotund woman (about 300 +pounds) and seemed to relish in her companionship. When she would call at night he would say "thanks for calling hun... is everything alright with you?" After she hung up I could hear him saying "shit... shit." He often refers to her as "the fat lady." Puzzled, I asked him one day "Do you think M_____ is attractive." He replied, "No, she is ugly and fat." Another example of manipulation benefiting his needs? Is my patient aware of the issues of civility here? Does he even know what he is doing is wrong? Is he a passive-aggressive addict? (although this is not a strict definition of PAPD)

Elderly patients are often in a state of delusion themselves. Let them enjoy their last rodeo but with supervision. Speak kindly.

THE EMPORER'S NEW CLOTHES: INDUCTIVE REASONING

There is an important behavior deficit that I am finding to be more widespread than I previously thought.

This has to do with the way in which the geriatric or senior person processes information input from the world around them. There is a definite flaw here, and I see it most often in elders who seem to be the most 'intact' mentally. At first I thought it was just my patient, but then I began to see this in his senior biographer and many of their senior friends.

This is an important concept because it will most likely produce a constant division between what you think is right and what the senior thinks is right.

In a one paragraph summary it can be said that **seniors begin to see their views as objective reality and will defend them as such.** Their views may present as individual positions they have established, positions backed by misconstrued facts from news sources or associates, or even positions based on their emotional 'feel good' palate (i.e. If it feels good, it must be right... reminiscent of Woodstock I guess, but I wasn't there either. I don't think).

To better understand the behavior beget by simple deductive reasoning, let me give you a couple of typical examples. This first example was briefly referenced at the beginning of "The Geriatric Mind."

My patient had just received some kind of award, a Kentucky Admiral award I believe. It just lay on his desk waiting for the next victim to come calling. Then he would casually remark about how, despite not needing or asking for this, it was seen fit that he should have it. I thought it would be nice to frame it. The next day I had it framed and then carefully placed it back on his desk. After his mid, mid, morning nap he awoke and realized his unframed award was gone. He carefully looked up and down the new frame job on his old award. He made no connection. He asked, "Who brought this new framed award and where did my old award go to." I tried to explain that this is the only award forgetting my lesson in deductive reasoning for the geriatric patient. "Well, then there are two awards because this is not the award I had yesterday!"

Another example: Last night was forecast to be really cold, about 5 degrees. I have a giant outdoor thermometer for my patient to see the temperature with. However, somewhere around the 30 deg freezing range, the dial froze up. The next morning, the temp was actually 4 degrees outside. The first thing my patient said to me that morning was "Well, I guess it didn't get as cold as they said it was going to be" referring to the outside thermometer half covered with frost. I replied, "Could it be that our outside thermometer is frozen, ya think?" Again he just wasn't able to easily see multiple outcomes for one observation. It's either his way or the highway, if ya get my drift.

What you need to know is that this deficit in unbiased analytical reasoning will always put you at odds with the patient. There will always be conflict. Conflict strengthens our faith.

It is a win/win situation for the patient. You cannot reprogram their minds or attempt any rational discussion aimed at changing their point of view. All you can do is damage control. Yo, dawg, just suck it up and do what yo gotta do for the care of your patient.

The longer you care for a patient, the more difficult caring becomes until you finally arrive at the happy state of Aha (I get this lesson). Just do what has to be done in your best way and know you will be blessed for your good deeds soon.

In another example, my patient called a member of the board at the University where he had taught. He said, "I think I deserve that annual award (given by the university to a deserving faculty). I also think I should be financially compensated for all the mileage for the years and years of driving to class to teach" (it's true; I'm not making this up). My concern was that if he got the award then someone else probably more deserving was not going to get the award. He finally pulled enough strings to get the award (but no free cash). Visitors would often ask how he came to be nominated. Later he told me (as though he were trying out his version of explanation) "I guess someone stopped by to visit and just saw my plaque from Lee Todd (the president of UK) and were impressed enough to mention it to someone else who decided to bring the idea of presenting me with the doctorate of letters before the board of directors." Hello patient... can you say "lame?" I did get some laughter out of that.

I just could not hold back any longer. I said, "Don't you remember? You begged D__ to bring the matter before the board and you even asked if the board could perhaps reimburse you with some cash for all your trips to teach at UK. It's just politics... no one just happened to see your other plaque and thought what a great soul you must be. You just pirated that award to the expense of someone probably more deserving of it." He did not deny this at all and said, "It's all politics anyway." But is he just parroting me or does he understand that he was the principal part of the award charade? Does he maybe believe his own lies?

As a caregiver you will be often presented with the most outlandish behavior by your patient. This will wear on you for sure. Just know what to expect and let your patient dream for their own imaginarium. When you can't take it anymore there is always Lortab (Just kidding).

You cannot offer constructive criticism to your patient. It won't work. The last bit of understanding I can give you will help you avoid this geriatric pitfall. Many of us caregivers, at one time or another, mistakenly thought that a good way to correct a behavior problem is to point out the error of the patient's way and let them gleefully discover a new life lesson. (Now hit the smart button) You realize now that dog won't hunt. The geriatric mind rationalizes differently than yours and secondly, having missed your learning point, they will react in just the opposite way you had intended and probably with strong words.

1. THE GRANDIOSE BEHAVIOR THEME—"I AM SO GREAT"

This can drive the caregiver nuts pretty quickly. The patient, like any 3 yr old, wants to express his feelings of worth in hope of reciprocal praise and affection. If the patient served in the military you might hear a lot of war stories, or if they traveled a lot, you will hear embellished versions never before told. The patient wants to tell everyone all they can. They may even insist you call a news conference. This can be pretty gut-wrenching for both the caregiver and the innocent visitor who just stopped by for a brief visit and now has to swallow their own puke just to keep a good image. It's surprising to me how this behavior seems to be fairly common, especially from retired military service members.

From a patient's standpoint, they are actually giving themselves some good 'talk' therapy. As long as the listener will pretend to be interested, the patient will see this as one of the healthiest things they could do, just short of eating more ice cream and cookies.

For the caregiver... just recognize this as a natural part of the aging process (of a three year old) and deal with it.

2. YOU ARE HURTING ME! LEAVE ME ALONE! I HATE YOU!

This will happen every time your 3 yr old (going on 90) patient encounters something they would rather not do. It always happens when I try to give mother a shower bath. I am always careful to test the water temperature on my wrist first and wait a minute to be sure it stays the same. The moment the water touches her, I get screamed at, cussed at, and told to "leave me alone." My first experience kinda shook me up until some friends in similar situations told me just ignore it. "It is the 3 year old kid coming out in them." After that, bathing was so much easier (for me anyway). I noted that after the bath was done and I was drying my mother with a towel, she would praise me for the bath. That was when I knew everything was alright again.

Not all geriatric patients complain this way. My 99 year old dad has a Hospice girl that gives him a bath 3 times a week. He never complains and they both seem to enjoy calling each other 'honey-poo' and 'sugar pie' names. He can't seem to get enough! (Ha ha! Is that sick or what? Just joking, and, of course, you recognize that as the classic "Feldinghaus regressive syndrome" being acted out-just joking.)

3. SOMEONE HAS STOLEN ALL MY VALUABLES!

I have heard this behavior from a great many people. There is no need to try and talk your patient out of their belief. Spin this one. Maybe say, "Yes, I have already reported this to the police and they're on the lookout."

When you find where the patient misplaced the item your spin is: "Why look here, the thief put it back over here for some reason."

Often, the patient may claim that their car has been stolen (even though they no longer have one). Your spin might be: "I sent the car out for a tune-up. You never know when you may need it."

In the spin department, be careful not to overdo it. For example, don't feed a fictitious story about secret agents or spies tracking your patient's every move.

4. HALLUCINATIONS (ALL TYPES)

These are often caused by various meds, but can also be the result of small infarcts that may damage small areas of the brain. Sometimes your patient may say, "Who are those people in my room?" or "Where is the room I have been staying in? Someone has put me in another room." More frightening are the hallucinations that involve scary things or maybe animals coming through the wall towards them.

Support and console your patient and spin when you can. Make them feel safer. Then note if these events keep happening, and if so, confer with the doctor on the patient's meds.

5. INFATUATIONS—IN LOVE—LET ME BUY YOU THINGS—I WANT TO DONATE MY MONEY—ETC.

These descriptions are all manifestations arising from the same underpinnings. When the patient is ill, or just medicated in some cases, their cognitive abilities are affected. What they perceive as reality is, in fact, not reality, but a distortion of their transferred needs and desires. Most of the human race is short on feeling enough love and caring compassion. Who doesn't like a friendly hug?

The scary problem is that the patient may really feel in love and want to marry the nurse or aid worker or at the very least donate a large chunk of their assets to them. If you don't already have POA, you could be in for some bad news later. A patient who has been through trauma and a week or two hospital stay may well have fallen in love with a nurse a fifth their age. Again, it is like the tale of the tiger with a splinter in his paw... you do remember that one?

Once these deep feelings of bonding have been triggered, they are intense and controlling. You must find out exactly what the source is before you can spin and desensitize them. Now, the caveat is once you do get the patient to acknowledge and give up their fantasy, you are now looking at dealing with a new case of depression your patient has just acquired. Dealing with that means you must find something equally as meaningful for them to focus their attention on. This may mean designing a scrap book with all their achievements, writing letters to grandkids, cousins, or people that have a meaningful relationship with the patient.

6. THE MISCOMMUNICATION—IMPORTANT!

One thing that most all caregiver will overlook is their difference in age, cultural roots, growing up environment, etc. The nitty-gritty here is that communication is not necessarily the same anymore for the caregiver, young aid volunteer, and the patient.

An example of this occurred when a young aid volunteer visited my 99 year old patient. When she left, she said, "I love you." That's just common vernacular for the 'now' generation. Not so for the old-timer from yesteryear. My patient really thought she was confessing her love for him. I had to explain the communication gap so he could let go of that anxiety-producing issue.

Another type of miscommunication occurs from the patient's incorrect interpretations of the world around him. For example, when my patient was in the hospital, he had to be maintained on a catheter, which meant that nurses were daily checking for signs of edema or infection and cleaning his genital area. The implied communication to my patient was, "I think the nurses liked playing with my penis." This was his quote. This has become his new erotic toy that he verbally touts to the Hospice workers that come to bath or administer to him. Give him a minute, and he's talking about his genitals to them. Sick... sicko, but laughable.

Probably one of the most common types of miscommunication involves the kinesthetic sub modality of 'touch.' I am only talking about the aid worker or church visitor who kindly wants to hold dad's hand while listening to him. The transference issues from the patient can be very strong and often sexually deviated. I needed to make several calls to aid workers, etc. to NOT hold hands with the patient. Again, another call for you to have POA should the need arise.

7. THE NUDIST

The patient may just forget to put their clothes back on after going to the toilet or may just not want to wear them for whatever reason. They may walk around indoors or even outdoors, and unless someone encounters them... they may never know they are wearing the 'Emperor's new clothes.'

Upon confrontation, spin with light-hearted humor and a smile. Never scold or embarrass the patient. Another aspect of this behavior is the emergence of an embedded tendency toward sexual promiscuity or increased libido needs. Sometimes the behavior will take nothing more than the form of what I call 'erotic rhetoric.' The patient may take erotic satisfaction from talking to a nurse, bathing attendant, church visitor, or literally anyone about some aspect of his/her genitalia or hidden desires that the patient just can't seem to understand and inquires if maybe his guest might have some thoughts along that line. To an outside observer, the patient's efforts to remain unnoticed are incredibly lame because they usually forget to whom they have played out there neediness to and they end up telling everyone again and again.

For instance, the patient may comment, "I think nurses enjoy touching my penis. I don't know why that is, do you?" This is usually because the nurse had to catheterize or disinfect the patient, but that's all it takes to flip that other brain switch. There is no way to stop this behavior that I know of. If you call their hand, the patient will look like a deer in headlights, innocent. Then they proceed, over the next few weeks, to ask every guest if their caregiver's assessment was really correct about their erotic dialoguing, and then it starts all over again. Sometime you may need to contact frequent visitors and remind them not to hold hands or stay more than a brief time. I find it really amazing to what extent the patient will go for 'erotic relief.' They may make repeated phone calls to people half their age, who they only vaguely know, asking for a 'visit' and all the while thinking their behavior has been completely disguised and no one is the wiser. It's sad and pathetic, but true. Even the visitors would laugh about this behavior if it were not so sad.

There are many ways for the patient to be manipulative with guests and, sometimes, they in turn could be manipulative with the patient, but in a different way usually. In any case, the point I make is that you need to be on top of this behavior so some inappropriate advance to the

wrong person doesn't gets a chance to happen. (Unless you've got deep pockets!)

8. THE SUNDOWNER

There exists, among a large population of geriatric patients, a type of behavior (actually a collection of different behaviors which is why this is termed a 'syndrome') that differs markedly between day and night, quite literally. There are numerous theories that have been thrown at this syndrome to explain it, but as of now, nobody really knows. Suffice it to say then that this syndrome may include the following hallmarks in behavior: confusion, anxiety, restlessness, anger, crying, and mood swings to name just a few. What you need to understand is that the onslaught of these behaviors may come about rather quickly and catch the caregiver totally off guard. I am talking days and weeks instead of months and years in some cases. The other point is that with some experimentation with meds or environment, some patients have gotten relief. It is generally thought that the syndrome is somehow related to serotonin levels in the body and that is affected by natural sunlight availability. Some patients respond to use of bulbs, tubes, etc. that emit a spectrum that closely resembles that of natural light (but don't be fooled by stores that sell light bulbs painted blue and call them daylight bulbs. You will need to do some internet searching to find the real McCoy.)

The reason a lot of nursing homes are closed for visitation late in the evenings is because of the sundowner effect. Their patients may start walking around aimlessly, sometimes having a 'zombie-like' appearance, which may be disconcerting for family members or newbies to the scene.

It is also worth noting that this syndrome does not necessarily have prerequisites such as dementia or Alzheimer's. Some caregivers have used potassium supplements, haldol, clonopin, Tylenol PM, and other meds to try to control this wandering behavior. The latter tend to be for anti-anxiety, but also have side effects for some patients.

9. MANTRAS

They come in all shapes and sizes, but represent any ordered sequence of numbers, even sounds that can be repeated over and over.

This is another interesting, albeit annoying behavior. It involves the involuntary elicitation of tones, noises, gestures, words, numbers, and statements. I have seen most of these behaviors in the geriatric group. My mother often would count numbers over and over and then shift to a gurgatative noise that she could make with each breath, almost like the sound of someone suffocating (try relaxing to that sometime). Then, at other times, she would just walk around the house and drive her cane into the wooden floors as hard as she could (I think this was to wake any dead spirits in the house. It woke mine every time.)

Mantras are an enigma. They can come and go at random. They can seem quite impenetrable for a while and then suddenly, without any warning, they may disappear. Nobody really knows if there is one single cause for this behavior or whether it is a culmination of syndromes and just plain ol' tired synapses or what. Accept it and make peace with it, but don't try to change it.

10.   REFUSAL TO COOPERATE

This is another 'difficult' behavior to deal with. My patient will try to complain and protest about anything that a 3 year old child would. So, let's see, that would be refusing to take a bath/shower, refusing to eat what you put out, refusing to be taken out to the doctor's office for a checkup, and well, you get the picture. Only the patient knows what they are objecting to and they probably don't remember, so they keep objecting. The caregiver can do the spin-doctor thing and call the trip to the doctor's office 'an outing,' 'a trip that all retires are required to make,' etc.

The objection to food usually means the patient wants something with some taste added. This is usually something sweet. Remember, the geriatric patient will often lose the sense of smell first and that means their ability to detect flavor will often be compromised as well. One of my parents has no sense of smell so most all food is flavorless. People with olfactory (smell) impairment generally have no problem detecting the basic tastes such as sweet, sour, bitter, and salty. Applesauce is great to add to your patient's food to 'sweeten it up.' Other items I use include cottage cheese, bananas, and maybe a cookie broken up over the food.

11. THE EGOTIST

Their swords are double edged. On the one side is incessant lamenting usually about how they are not being treated fairly, they are denied the familiarities of life as they once knew it. Understandably, they feel maligned and short changed from their perspective. There is the constant implication that everything is the caregiver's fault. Even though you, the caregiver, know this is not the case, you cannot avoid some of the impact of this train wreck on your psyche, especially when a visitor from church stops by to see how your parents are doing and all they hear is this 'woe is me' stuff coming from them.

The other side of this sword displays the 'it's all about me' attitude. In this case, the patient is always disregarding other people's feelings and needs in order to put theirs first. If visitors stop by, they want to commandeer the speaker's post at any cost. I have even seen my patient push my mother aside and tell her to "get out of here" so he could continue spinning his tales to the young home health care lady. I know he doesn't really understand that he is even exhibiting this inappropriate behavior and if called on it he will always be quick to counter with some lame excuse.

The point is this or any behavior can be exceptionally cruel and demeaning to the spouse and other family members at times. Be aware and keep this behavior in check in a manner fitting your situation.

Have some rescue options ready such as "It's time for my patient's nap now." Remember the old sage, "Nobody likes a braggart?" Well, with this behavior, the patient remembers that as "*everybody* likes a braggart." I guess my dear old patient is just a couple of fries short of a full plate, and that's not bad at 102 years of age.

12. THE WIDOW MAKER

Boom... Boom... Boom... Boom... It goes on at all times of the day or night. To some caregivers and spouses, it is one of the most aggravating behavioral quirks. It is like the ancient form of communication wherein one Indian tribe would signal another by various sequences of drum sounds. In this case, the patient has no drum, but uses their cane or walker instead. For a long time, I wondered why my mother would make this noise as she walked the halls of our antebellum farmhouse. A slow, steady beat is produced by 'thumping' the walker or cane squarely down onto our wooden floors (already stripped bare of any carpets or other trip hazards). My patient does this all through the night sometimes. Even the dark of night does not betray the widow maker her appointed rounds. When she uses the four-footed walker, my wife and I feel the vibration throughout the framework of the house. I call this the 'widow maker' behavior because this constant banging could drive any spouse off into the sunset ne'er to return. Nobody knows why the dementia patient chooses to make this noise, but I have had several people say it almost drove them crazy, especially since there was no way to stop it short of locking up all canes and walkers. I think this behavior must be akin to bat radar as they listen for the return echoes, but I'll have to ask Batman and Robin.

Now, at last, there is a solution! After many sleepless nights from the bat radar, I engineered a solution. The idea is to isolate the hard surface of the cane foot or the walker feet (4) from the floor. Simply put, go to Home Depot or Lowe's and buy the appropriated number of rubber cup chair leg protectors (I used the 1 and ¼ inch diameter size). These must slip very loosely over the existing hard rubber pads on the cane/walker feet. Now, here's the difficult part (say what?). I purchased some foam rubber weatherizing material. It was about 1 ½ inch square and about 2' long. Cut off four pieces about 1 and ½ inches long. Purchase some contact cement. Now, simply coat the cane feet, each end of the foam rubber pieces, and the bottom of the chair cups (be careful not to get the cement on the sides of the cup). Air-dry until tack free. Stick the foam rubber pieces on each foot (only one piece per foot... I know you already knew that, but your friend may not have). Then push the chair cups over the foam rubber and compress all the way down (just to seat the cups). Now you have a free floating cushion. But you are not done yet. The last step is easy. Find some flat insulation pipe wrap. Cut out circles just about ¼" smaller than the outside diameter of the chair cups. Coat each surface with contact cement again, fasten to the contact cement and, shades of Gotham City, you now have the first stealth cane (well almost).

For a short cut, just eliminate the foam chair cups and glue over the rubber cane feet a good quality 'black' foam that you can buy at most professional air conditioning stores. This is the insulation wrap used to wrap pipes going to your AC unit or possibly your neighbor's unit. It comes in a roll (foam tape by VAPCO, cat N:FT-1 ⅛" x 2" black). If you use the wrong material here, it won't work. So many people have thanked me for this easy tip!

13. THE KLEPTO

Yeah, the name itself gives this behavior away. Your patient may take literally anything and hide it somewhere. We have seen parts from the food processor disappear or glasses, plates, 911 pendants, and even a plate of food hidden back in the dark recesses of a closet shelf. They may take their own things and hide them only to claim the next day that somebody must have stolen them. You don't want your patient accusing guests or your relief sitter. I don't know if 'klepers' are even aware of what they are doing, or if they take things as part of some ritual since they used to be responsible for keeping a neat, secure and orderly house.

I remember the first time that Hospice arrived with walkers, a toilet, O_2 cylinders, an O_2 generator, and a few more things. A week after that, I noticed these items disappearing, only to discover that the other patient had hidden them in the next room to maintain a neat and orderly house which she had done for so long. The only problem is that sometimes false teeth, a purse or wallet left unattended, or some document left out are hidden because it's all fair game to the 'kleper.' Where it will end up is anybody's guess. The 'Kleper' can be especially frustrating because they did it, won't remember doing it, and will deny doing it. There's no recourse for you but to bite your tongue, double ouch. Even if you find an item right in front of your patient, their claim will be, "I guess the thief must have put that back." Smile and fully agree with your patient.

14. THE WHITE SOCK 'EFFECT'

I just noticed the other day that my 102 year old patient was looking for his white socks (one of the first things I had thrown away). He claimed he might need to dress up from time to time and wanted white socks. I said, "You're kidding me right?" He replied, "Oh no, a lot of people at my club are wearing white socks." I told him that went out of style decades ago but never really convinced him of that. He feels out of fashion now. I began to observe more geriatric people also were wearing white socks. Then... horror of horrors... I happened to be up watching the Letterman

Show on television and guess what? Yep... here he comes on stage wearing a dark suit and white socks. Yikes!

I think the color is so symbolic, ya know? Think about it... white... purity. We are pure when we come into this world (white diapers and later jeans and white socks)... then we go through the black stage (socks and underwear)... and finally at the end of the cycle we revert back to white socks and diapers. Ultimately, the last vestige is a white sheet. I am trackin' Letterman's days for sure.

You must realize that your patient's view of reality and yours will conflict most of the time... don't try to reach common ground. There is none. Just smile.

HOW TO TALK TO YOUR DOCTOR

How many times do you leave your doctor appointment feeling that you never really had a chance to explain a lot of important stuff? You felt that the doctor wasn't interested in what you had to say, didn't you? Okay, there is equal blame to go around, but we just want to communicate our side of the story and hope that the doctor knows what to do with the rest. Remember the Boy Scout's marching creed, (and maybe Girl Scout's too?) "Be Prepared."

USING THE FORM BELOW, and BEFORE you visit your doctor, you should TYPE out the <u>patient form sheet</u> and store it in your computer:

"Your single greatest concern about the patient is" → PRIMARY PRESENTING COMPLAINT

"Your other concerns about the patient are" → OTHER COMPLAINTS

"Your patient's symptoms supporting your concerns are" → WHAT I KNOW & OBSERVE

"What you think may be causing the problem is" → WHAT I THINK I KNOW

Your format might look like this sample. Make 2 COPIES, one for you to keep.

A DOCTOR APPROVED PATIENT FORM SHEET

PATIENT'S NAME: _____ AGE: _____

TODAY'S DATE: _____

MEDICATIONS THE PATIENT IS CURRENTLY ON:
_____

PRIMARY PRESENTING COMPLAINT:
_____

OTHER COMPLAINTS: _____

WHAT I KNOW & OBSERVE: Example: I CAN SEE BLOOD IN THE PATIENT'S URINE JAR SAMPLE, NO CLOTS OBSERVED, BRIGHT RED COLOR

WHAT I THINK I KNOW: Example: I THINK THE PATIENT IS BECOMING INTOLLERANT OF A MEDICATION THAT IS CAUSING THIS AND SEEMS TO HAVE A FEVER AT TIMES.

MY QUESTIONS ARE: Example: CAN YOU SUGGEST DIFFERENT MEDS TO TRY? DOES THIS MEAN INFECTION? WHAT DO I NEED TO WORRY ABOUT THE MOST RIGHT NOW? WOULD BLOOD TESTS BE IN ORDER NOW?

SYMPTOMS ARE WORSE WHEN: Example: ABOUT 4 HOURS AFTER TAKING MEDS

SYMPTOMS ARE EASIER WHEN: Example: UPON MORNING URINATION BEFORE MEDS GIVEN

Begin with the most important concerns in case you run out of time allotted for your visit. Remember that the average doctor visit is limited to about 15 minutes. Of that, you will have no more than about 5 minutes of 'air time' with him/her.

By using the patient form, or something similar, you will have the respect of your doctor because you are showing professionalism and consideration by not wasting his time with 'chit-chat.' Give the patient form to your doctor the moment he/she walks in and NOT after he talks and the two of you chit-chat a while about the weather and your aches and pains. **If possible, ask the scheduler to put the copy into your folder BEFORE your visit. Your doc will have a chance to view it without you distracting him/her.**

Please keep focused on the reason you are there. YOU DO NOT TALK about the weather, YOU DO NOT TALK ABOUT family, YOU DO NOT TALK ABOUT sports, YOU DO NOT TALK ABOUT HOW YOU ARE FEELING... Nyet! DO NOT DISTURB the doctor while he reads the information. When he has finished, then he/she is fair game. Ask away as you use your copy as a guide. Leave a copy with your doctor and you put the other copy in your personal folder. A lot of times, a doctor may pull a patient's folder at the end of the day and review something that he/she found puzzling. With your fact sheet in hand, no mistakes will be made, and that is peace of mind for both you and the doctor.

On the rare occasion that the doctor exhibits 'aversive' behavior in some way, such as setting aside the patient form you have just handed him/her, you need to raise a red flag (in your mind). This may indicate that the doctor wants to maintain unquestioned control, or has a different philosophical approach to geriatric patients, or may feel unsure about how to answer your questions. Just remember, this is a 'red flag' response and you need to look at your inner strengths and patient commitments. If you are a strongly committed caregiver, then you will need to consider switching doctors and becoming more medically literate on your own to help make decisions.

What I have found within the medical community is that there are at least two basic doctor philosophies on caring for geriatric patients. These are:

1. THEY ARE GOING TO DIE ANYWAY ATTITUDE

2. IT DOESN'T HAVE TO BE THEIR TIME TO DIE YET ATTITUDE

Proponents of the first group feel that, at some point, medical intervention just begets more medical intervention and the patient is the one that has to suffer. Just let nature take its course.

Proponents of the second group feel that as long as the patient shows continued favorable responses to reasonable treatment, then by all means, continue to treat them. By reasonable treatment you would exclude suggesting, perhaps, a heart transplant for a 90 year old patient showing normal, left-sided cardiomyopathy. The trauma of the op would kill the patient... not good, not reasonable. I personally feel that all reasonable efforts that give relief to the patient should continue. I think God and prayer can truly work miracles if we just ask.

If your doctor is a proponent of 'they are going to die anyway,' you need to be sharpening your pencil, turning on your computer, and Googling until the cows come home. You can learn a lot. Often meds cause side effects making a patient feel worse after a doctor visit. That doctor may not agree with changing meds. At this point, I would visit one or two pharmacists and get their opinions. If they have ideas that sound reasonable, try another doctor for a second opinion. If that isn't possible, look at the literature information available and make your own decision on the medications. This is when you need God on your side... believe me.

I have saved my dad's life on at least three separate occasions because I just didn't believe he was getting good advice. Often because of the great numbers of patients, a doctor has to take a 'one size fits all' approach with meds and therapies. For the patient that can't tolerate one of the meds, he/she may begin to spiral downward in health. To make matters worse, there are some meds (such as for the heart), that actually do make a patient worse as a normal sequence before the body adapts and accepts the medicine. I remember telling the cardiologist office that my dad was getting worse and please check with the doctor and let me know what to do. The call I got back was, "This is normal for that drug, so just keep on taking it and eventually things will get better... it just takes some time."

I made my own decision, backed off to half dosage for two days, then backed off to quarter dosage for two days, then threw the meds away. Dad continued to steadily improve. I always call upon three outside resources when I make independent decisions: A) A drug reference guide book (available at most pharmacies), B) A pharmacist, and C) God.

There are times when the caregiver must get involved and apply their most educated guess.

If you want to know more about how to relate to your doctor, I recommend this **300pg**. book, *The Intelligent Patient's Guide To The Doctor-Patient Relationship*, Barbara M. Korsch, M.D., Caroline Harding, Oxford University Press, 1997, ISBN#0195102649. (Then make an appointment with me to discuss your intense fear of communication failure and other underlying anxiety syndromes.)

Ben Blyton

ALTERNATIVE THERAPIES

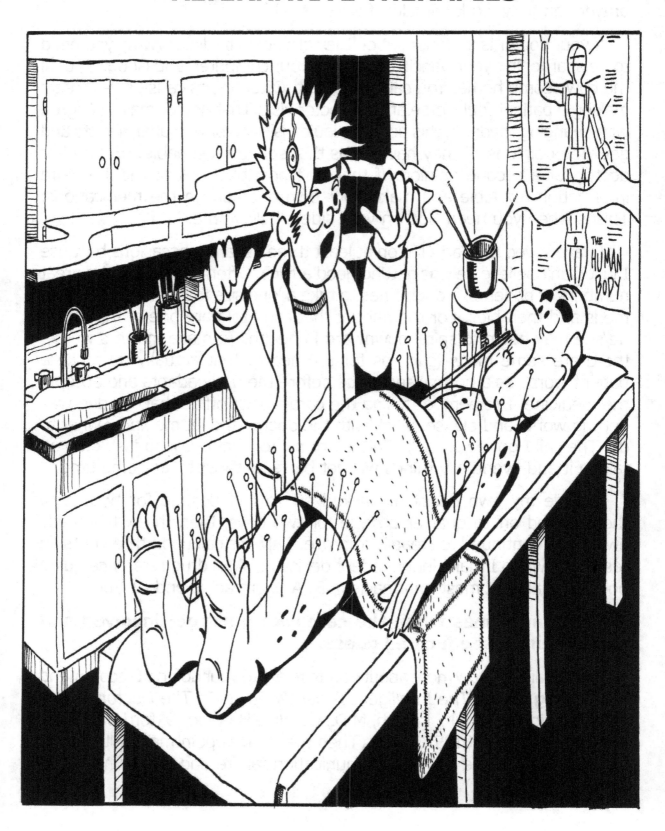

I could write volumes on this topic as my education outside of the University of Kentucky has been steeped in this arena. My education includes (from various schools) naturopathic physician (ND), hypnotherapy instructor (NGH),Transpersonal Hypnotherapist certified by N.A.T.H, certified cranio-sacral therapist (Upledger Institute), Reiki master (Usui Lineage), and some private training in acupuncture. In non-alternative therapy, I have a Master's and Bachelor's degrees from the University of Kentucky. Both are in the sciences. I had a fifteen year private practice in counseling and clinical hypnotherapy. I was active in volunteering services to community aid centers.

I'm sorry to dump that at your feet, but I felt it was necessary for you to understand that I do understand alternative therapies, *I do get it*, and I have lobbied in support of it. In 1998, I was the first person in this state to get a licensure bill for hypnotherapy into the state occupations committee (where it eventually died). I personally drafted this bill (with the help of the LRC). I am sure I some of my colleagues in the alternative fields of therapy may be upset for presenting my position... sorry.

I am often asked if alternative therapies really work. Understandably, a caregiver at their wits end and knee deep in alligators, wants desperately to believe that a cure awaits them somewhere.

The good news is there can be that cure. Alternative therapies do work. The bad news is not knowing where, from whom, and in which field of endeavor it lies.

Here are some universal mistakes consumers make when choosing an alternative therapy.

1. Assuming all practitioners within a field have the same training

2. Assuming all practitioners in a field have the same ability

3. Assuming all the advertising about a field is the truth and applies to them

4. Shopping for the lowest rates

I am always amazed at how we (mainly a guy thing) will spend hours investigating the best quality DVD player, I-pod, or whatever, but when it comes to treating our health, we just look for the cheapest rate. I guess it's really a control thing, but an interesting phenomena, yes?

There are many determining factors that figure into whether an alternative therapy might be appropriate or not. Some we have control over (e.g. choice of therapist) and some for which we have no control over (e.g. genetic markers).

To optimize your chances of success, you must do your homework. You must understand the theory upon which the different therapies work (easy, you can do it). You must decide if you can 'buy into' the theory because some therapists swear by some outrageous claims. Ask the therapist for just one session with your client, just to see if he/she is responsive to that particular therapy. After you have had time to discuss this with your patient, you can schedule more sessions if appropriate. Remember, a health care practitioner has a business to run and needs you to buy into the logic of having many sessions. In truth, there really is logic here, but I have seen it carried too far also. You do what you choose. There are times when you need to cut your losses and pull out. If you terminate early, you may lose money that may have been prepaid for more sessions, and at the very least you will be given the standard 'quitter's soliloquy' that puts the treatment failure on your not having completed the full x number of days or years of treatment. Of course, if you do complete the full treatment program, any treatment failure will again be shifted onto you with, "Now remember, Ms. Jones, at the very beginning I made no promises because everyone is different."

I recommend a trial session or two because a lot of therapies for chronic conditions will involve many, many sessions. Some fields, like hypnotherapy, may only involve a few. Some therapists swear that the old mercury amalgams used to fill teeth are the source of all ills. I have known patients to have all their teeth with mercury fillings removed (at no small fee) only to find nothing changed. The flip side is where you visit 'feel good' therapists that do physical manipulations, massage, meditation, hypnotherapy, etc. all of which are be designed to make anyone feel better than when they walked into the office. Everyone loves a massage, but that doesn't mean that massage therapy will be curative for the patient. If the patient benefits, then go for it!

The two most important determinants for success that I have found are: 1) the patient's natural ability to access the subconscious aspect of the brain/mind. This is where the autonomic nervous system is accessed and the body's entire HPA (hypothalamus/pituitary/adrenal) system can be influenced. 2) The native skill and ability of the particular therapist. Some therapists can be intellectually brilliant, but have trouble tying their shoes. With other therapists, you can almost feel that special, indescribable energy literally exuding from their very presence and you can feel changes occurring in your body as they work. This is part of the 'mind' connection that is so essential, but can hardly be put into words.

The good news is that no matter what field of alternative therapy you choose, if you have done your homework and selected a therapist known for his/her skills, your patient will benefit in some way. It may not be a cure, but some benefits, sprinkled with some hope and a prayer, can be pretty powerful medicine in its own right.

As a general rule (although most therapists will not reveal this and may deny it), therapy works best for ages less than 70 years old. As a therapist, I rarely would even agree to work with anyone over the age of 70. The exceptions are the fields that deal with meditation, gentle osteopathic, muscle manipulations, or acupuncture. These are fields in which the outcome is not as dependent upon focusing the brain to do a task (e.g. hypnotherapy, thought field therapy, neurolinguistic processing or programming, shamanic journeying, etc.).

A good subject is one whom can make the proper mind/body connection. A good subject using hypnotherapy can, for example, facilitate the recovery from recent neurological dysfunctioning (such as from a stroke) or anxiety disorders, fears, phobias, psychosomatic breathing disorders, and many more areas including the popular smoking cessation and weight loss areas.

A note of caution: You may hear rumors of this or that person getting great success from that inexpensive stage show hypnotist. This is not the norm, and is one of the quickest ways to throw money away that I can think of. For the 5% (that is one person out of twenty) that it does work for, the effect is usually limited to a short time period. The reason is because the kind of therapy used by the stage performer and the private office practitioner are based on completely different principals. This concept is very difficult to explain to the price conscious, bargain shopper that all of us have become. We, me included, don't always know when to turn off that internal switch. Considering all of the 'top line' practitioners that

I have known, none has advertised at a bargain rate. Ya git what yer a payin' fer! If you want cheap, ya git cheap.

Some other pointers include looking at the practitioner's wall diplomas to see where they received training. For hypnotherapy, look for N.A.T.H (National Assn. of Transpersonal Hypnotherapy) by Allen and Dee Chips. Another reference would be the N.G.H (National Guild of Hypnotists). While this may be the largest professional organization in the world, it in no manner should imply it's the best organization. I will always side with transpersonal hypnotherapy for effectiveness.

For Reiki, I like the Usui lineage but that is really insignificant because it is the teacher that makes the therapy successful.

For Cranio-sacral(CS) therapy I recommend the Upledger Institute because I am familiar with it and know the rigors of getting certified through it. At the time I got my certification, there were only four certified CS therapists in the entire state of KENTUCKY. There should be six or eight by now.

Remember- many states do not require licensure on some therapies so anybody can legally become a practitioner with no training in those areas. They can print up their own certifications!

> **It is the individual therapist that is the greatest determining factor for success. The most brilliant, most educated are all found wanting beside the "gifted" therapist.**

Not everybody can be a good subject. So maybe it's not your therapist but you. A client that does not take alternative therapy seriously will most likely not be a good subject.

Take this knowledge and your wisdom, get a cup of coffee, and think some more before doing anything long-term and never in lieu of mainstream medicine, but always as an adjunct to it. Rephrasing: Don't buy a milk cow until you know she's a workin' fur ye on all teats.

RESEARCH INTO BRAIN DISORDERS

The Sanders-Brown Center on Aging in Kentucky has a huge leg forward on cutting edge advancements into the understanding of brain disorders.

I have heard so many positive things about this center. If they can't help you directly with what you need, they can certainly point you in the right direction. When you call, speak slowly and try to be as articulate as possible as to what kind of assistance you need. The switchboard is not manned by MD's, ya know.

They also have any number of ongoing research projects that you can get involved with. Most, but not all, are dealing with Alzheimer's disease. Since dementia often seems to be part of Alzheimer's, I thought it only appropriate to include this research. Here are some programs they currently list:

SOME RESEARCH PARTICIPATION OPPORTUNITIES

(Participation may require a cerebral donation)

Passive Immunization against Toxic beta-amyloid in Alzheimer's disease: Phase 3 Program for Bapineuzumab (AAB-oo1) in Alzheimer's disease.

In simple terms, they give you a shot of mouse antibodies that are trained to attack beta-amyloid deposits. They claim to be having good success with this.

My assessment: I like the idea of monoclonal antibody attacks, plus it saves you from having to go to the local flea market and grabbing a few rabbits to make your pab with. (Using a monoclonal cell line is like the Cadillac model for repeatable results.)

Naturally occurring antibodies (IVIg) against Alzheimer's disease.

Researchers have identified natural antibodies that attack Alzheimer's disease in human blood. The idea is that we all carry (or should carry) these immunoglobulins in our blood as natural Alzheimer's attackers. (I assume they attack the beta-amyloid, but they did not specify what they attack)

My assessment: Interesting, but I need more information

The Concert Study on Mitochondrial Enhancement

The Concert study is a Phase 3 Clinical trial evaluating a new drug on patients with mild to moderate Alzheimer's currently on donepezil.

The drug acts on mitochondria (the brain's batteries) to enhance brain function. Improvements up to eighteen months have been demonstrated.

My assessment: I like the concept, but I would want to ask questions about the rate of decline in brain function after the eighteen month period (i.e. Does it level out or drop like a rock, ☺).

S-Connect Phase 3 study of a medical food to improve cognition

Some pretty clever people at MIT have developed some food with just the right ingredients (use Souvenaid with Fortasyn Connect) to help the body naturally (sort of) increase synapse formation (so you can be smarter). You must be over the age of fifty with mild to moderate Alzheimer's.

My assessment: I am all for snackin' so I would be first in line for this study. I would want to be assured the food tastes good. (seriously, my only question is how does this differ from the action of prescription SSRI's)

In summary, the Saunders-Brown Center always has cutting edge research in motion. Someone there can answer whatever question you have (you just have to find that person, ☺). They also have great resources (including this book) on many topics of interest relating to your caregiving.

In case U B a philanthropist, consider giving them a private grant. We all will benefit from it.

CHAPTER 9
HUMOROUS TIMES & JUNK

Be constantly renewed in the spirit of your
mind[having a fresh mental and spiritual attitude].

Ephesians 4:23

"Amid all the storm clouds, God has always sprinkled in a few with
beautiful silver linings that I will treasure forever."

Ben Blyton

RANDOM PONDERINGS

WHY IS IT?????????????????

Why is it... that there is such a huge disconnect between knowing what needs to be done AND doing it? If you are reading this, then clearly you have above average intellect yet I can accurately predict that sooner or later you too will be wearing the dunce hat. I forewarn you to save you from the pitfalls that lie ahead for the unprepared.

Why is it... that my geriatric patient who cannot hear will make a mad dash to answer the phone just to parrot "what? I am sorry I can't hear you, I'm over 100 years old."

Why is it... that everything our patient does is blameless? I say this with tongue in cheek of course but it nonetheless is frustrating that no matter how audacious their behavior others will be quick to leap to their defense with "they can't help it... it's not their fault." I guess, in a way, I look forward to this part in my old age also. I will act pretty indigent and indignant I'm sure. I could do what I want, say what I want, and maybe just act outrageous sometimes to see how others will handle it. Hmmmm... WHEN YOU ARE OLD YOU CAN DO NOTHING WRONG.

Why is it... that the old adage of "getting wiser with age" was nothing more than a cruel myth?

Why is it... that the adage of calling old age the "golden years" was nothing more than another cruel myth? It should be the "rust years."

Why is it... that exposed fecal artifacts don't seem to register any input to the geriatric brain? I tried to tell my patients "if it's brown, it's probably not a Hershey, so get rid of it" or "that's not a chocolate cookie you are carrying in your hand." It just doesn't seem to have meaning to them anymore. I guess the O.J. Simpson corollary instruction would be **"If it's brown, you must put it down."**

Why is it... that a geriatric person seems to lose perspective of good social and people graces? Male patients seem to think nothing of ignoring their friends when it suits them. Ignoring their caregiver's advice or instructions is a sport for them. Lying and making sexual innuendos to the nurse is a pastime game (which seems a little like the dog that chases a car... what's it going to do if it catches it?).

Their motto seems to be: Narcissism Rules! Fear me, yeah dawg!

(You may need to turn down the volume on that sentence.)

Perhaps geriatric behaviors are the *field of dreams* for evolutionary psychologists.

Why is it... that my patient is constantly trying to give everybody else credit for things that only my wife and I were responsible for. This includes everything from upkeep of the house, cooking meals, daily medical care and house/grounds maintenance and paying bills.

"A caregiver's efforts are never recognized in his own home." Sound similar to "a prophet is never recognized in his own town?"

For example, a friend of his stops by and brings him a half dozenWwhite Castle burgers. By feeding time my wife has spent a couple of hours cooking with fresh herbs and veggies, etc. He rarely says thanks, or heaven forbid, "good meal!" But put some White Castle on his plate and he tells my wife "that was a good meal." I am not sure what his message is there, but it's one we could do without.

I just finished mowing all the grass and trimming the hedges when a friend stopped by. She said, "Your yard looks great." I strained to listen to hear my patient say something complementary about how my wife and I had worked so hard to accomplish that. He said "well, we got a little rain the other day and *that* made the yard look better."

If you feel unappreciated and even despised at times take solace in knowing that the greatest caregiver of all was hated, despised, and tortured and even put to death that HIS patients might have a chance for eternal life.

I get lots of advice to "just let it go"... "it's his age ya know"... "he doesn't really know what he is saying so ignore it." One thing you will learn is that it is easy to give advice, but when suddenly the tables are turned, it's a whole different matter. **Learning to let go of ego-based frustrations is one of the lessons we are presented on our journey of caregiving.**

Often my parent will ask a question seemingly knowing that before I can get the answer out of my mouth he will turn his back on me and walk away. How degrading is that? Just let go? I am trying... reallly hard. Ya see? I really am in the trenches with you and I know a small amount of your pain and I respect the beauty of your soul.

As a caregiver, I have met angels and saints whom have shown me the way. Not now, but one day these friends and I shall reunite when the final trumpet calls and there shall be a place with your name too.

If you feel frustrations in your caregiving role take solace in knowing you are not alone.

The other day my patient asked me, "Do you think I should renew my subscription to the newspaper?" (so rhetorical it was nauseating). I replied, "I don't think I care about renewing it." To which he replies, "Well good, then I will renew it." Whaaaaat? Next, I just had to ask him, "Would you like the maple syrup edition? It's no extra cost ya know and the newspaper pages arrive with maple syrup sticking them all together so that is one less job for you to do at breakfast." He really didn't get it but just kind of smiled and nodded. Ahh... caregiving is like such a box of assorted chocolates, isn't it?

Laugh at the experience and learn from the journey.

Why is it... that geriatric patients even bother to spend thousands on hearing aids and then never wear them? My patient said he has spent about $5K on them for him and his wife. I also bought them a lanyard type of amplifier from Radio Shack that makes the placement of a headset so much easier than those microscopic hearing aids. But will they use any of this stuff... naw. They just like to tune their caregivers out. That is unfortunate because these devices really could facilitate communication. Now I have to endure my patient telling these outrageous lies to his Hospice girls like, "I am so lonely... there is nobody to talk with here." Ha... he's such an alpha dawg.

Why is it... that geriatric patients never seem to remember what you or any family member tells them, but they will remember things a stranger says? For example, I don't know how many times my patient has asked the question of why probate court had to be involved in his late wife's estate. I now realize that it is pointless to answer that any more. For him it must come from either a stranger or preferably a physician. He automatically discounts the knowledge from family. Nurses he considers slightly above family, but definitely inferior to a physician. With one big exception... an attractive nurse. Her words become pure prophesy without challenge. Geriatric patients often have enhanced libidos. Don't assume they are too old to create surprises for the caregiver and a few headaches too (hide any tools that can be used to sign a document).

Be vigilant about new friends your patient may acquire. There are more than a few people that will take advantage of your patient's weakness if given a chance.

Why is it... that my 102 year old geriatric patient is still blessed with incredible faculties of memory and speech yet cannot articulate anything sensible? I mean this human computer can recall both his SSN and that of his spouse? That is 18 digits! He listens to tapes for the blind on some of the most technical, social, and political issues confronting civilization. His mind is like a giant sponge, always soaking up knowledge. Then tell me why when he greets someone at the door bearing some homemade goodie all he can think of to say is "Well, meals on wheels?" I have seen instances in which a neighbor would bring something over, go back for something she forgot and yep... you guessed it... the tape plays again and again "well, meals on wheels!" I thought he would at least regurgitate something from Chaucer.

Along the same line, I couldn't help but notice that when visitors stop by his dialogue becomes even more predictable. "It's going to be a hot one today"... "What's the price of gas today?" It's sad to see a great mind struggle for something meaningful to say. Or maybe this patient enjoys seeing us struggle with a reply to such premeditated, rhetorical nonsense? I just gotta laugh as the possibilities.

As a caregiver strive to learn multiple points of view. Only when you can see more than one point of view can there be lighthearted humor.

With that great mind, why does he insist on forgetting everything I have told him? No matter whether it's about his bank account or news about his grandson, he will be quick to tell any and all that he is just kept in the dark... nobody will tell him anything, oh woe. I heard him doing this spin to the hospice volunteer... before she left he had her exploring his mole... no I'm not going there. Hmmm... maybe I can buy a fake mole for myself.

Why is it... that visitors always think your patient is such an angel and you are... well... sumpthin?

Why is it... that others always tell me what a 'sharp' mind my patient has? Where is it? Ha, sometimes he is his own worst enemy. I have been telling him to knock off bragging so much to Hospice about how well he is. He has been with Hospice for about two years. My patient brags to a fault. The other day he was telling the Hospice doc how well he was, "I will be mowing the grass when the weather gets a little warmer... I cut down a tree today with my handsaw..." Finally the Hospice doc got a chance to speak. She explained that the reason she was there was that they might have to take him off the Hospice care program. He no longer fits the criteria of a patient who is presumed to have only six months or less to live or was still in need of special care. Gotcha!

The Hospice nurse commented that my patient had gone from weighing 128 lbs to 178 lbs and perhaps he should watch the amount of sugar he consumes. My patient normally drinks three or four chocolate drinks per day, two bowls of chocolate ice cream with cookies, two waffles with lots of syrup and sleeps 95% of the day. "Well, I just don't understand that," he commented sharply. "I guess it must be the waffles... maybe I could eat one less waffle and add maybe half a banana?" (one waffle has only 5 gms of sugar) Where is that sharp mind??

Why is it... that my patient recalls all his medical information and disposition with seemingly great detail but yet he is pretty much 100% wrong. Well, ha, at least he does it with great conviction. Trust me, this inaccurate info is the info your Hospice team will believe also.

Why is it... my patient will never take ownership of anything gone wrong? If you were to catch him with his hand in the cookie jar he would be the first to say, "It's not my hand... I can tell you for a fact it's not." One real example is the case of his house slipper mysteriously being contaminated with fecal chocolate. When we finally tracked down where this aroma was coming from his reply was, "I don't know anything about that... it's not mine."

Why is it... that even trained people like Hospice aides, and the world for that matter, will always believe the oldest or feeblest person in the room?

PATIENT HUMOR

"HAPPINESS INCREASES WITH AGE, POLL FINDS"

A Gallup poll shows that according to the survey results of 240,000 Americans in ages from 18 to 85 there was a trend towards increasing happiness with age after passing the age of fifty.

The person behind this interesting study was a professor from the University of Warwick.

Unless a patient has slipped into deep dementia, I have not seen anything like the results of this survey. I just thought this news article was so laughable it deserves mention. Ask your patient if they are a happy camper.

PS: I tried to contact Dr. Andrew Oswald of the University of Warwick by email. I got an automated reply that said they were experiencing high volumes of email. I bet.

TIMELY ADVICE 'THE AMERICAN GERIATRICS SOCIETY'

In the KMA (Kentucky Medical Assn.) newsletter for Kentucky's physicians: "Tips for safe driving—consider not driving at night, in heavy traffic, and snow or rain or on unfamiliar roads." I am not sure whether this article in the KMA is to educate our doctors (I hope not) or for the doctors to get more grant money to generate more of these insights (this article was chock full of other revelations of similar nature. I just thought this might be kind of humorous to the caregiver... I don't know why, because the stuff is so top shelf, ya know? Arrrghhhh! Maybe this is part of the 'dumbing down of America' plot? Now that makes sense.

Look around you and see where you can find humor. Finding humor means you are still able to see a balanced perspective in life.

HUMOR FROM MY PATIENT

Scene: 99 year old father soundly asleep on his bed. 96 year old mother walks up to bed, shakes him awake saying, "Wake up, wake up."

As my bleary-eyed father is struggling to wake up, his wife says, "Now go to sleep, go to sleep," turns around and walks to her bedroom.

Scene: 97 year old mother with acute dementia sits beside her husband and tries to tell him something, but the verbiage comes out distorted, unrecognizable, like a baby that has not yet learned to speak. 99 year old father makes a light-hearted play on words by verbally gargling something entirely meaningless back to her. Incredibly she responds with the very coherent statement, "I didn't say that!." Hmmmm... go figure.

Scene: 97 year old mother pleads with 99 year old father (just released from hospital for heart problems and prone to hallucinations from his meds) to sleep in the twin bed beside her bed. I placed the porta-potty between their beds. Later, I get a call from a neighbor saying father just phoned and said he wanted "out of here." I explained it was nothing and that he was having more hallucinations about being a prisoner or something. A minute later the 911 dispatched EMT van pulls up to the door and six linebackers wearing 'EMT' on their jackets jump out and run towards the house. I open the door and they explain they got a call from a man that said he was trapped. Uh-oh, I thought as I could now hear father weakly calling, "Get me outta here."

We all ran upstairs to the bedroom and there was my father in his birthday suit sitting in his porta-potty, stuck, and unable to get out. The scene was like a quarterback huddle at the Super Bowl (maybe that's how it got that name?). I explained that he was not being held prisoner and everything was a misunderstanding. We all had a good laugh and the EMT team returned to base.

Scene: 99 year old father answers the tezlephone. It is his secret woman 'friend' from another town 80 miles away. Thinking he is by himself, he continues to chat-chat-chat. Unbeknownst to him, dear mother is just slowly and quietly walking around as she always does. She comes up behind him where he is blocking the path just in time to hear my father say "Well, good bye, hun," before hanging up the phone.

I am upstairs with the downstairs monitor turned on. I hear mother say, "Giff, who is hun?"

I thought I would laugh myself to death... well you know. Definitely 'busted'!!

Scene: 99 year old father in acute constipation pain. "Help me, do something!" he yelled out.

I tried the enema, it didn't work. I put on exam gloves and tried to digitally extract the stuff. I knew I was too timid to be effective, but didn't know what to do. "I can't get it out," I said.

Dad replies, "Well go get one of the neighbors to get it out."

I laughed to myself, wondering where his subconscious need to persecute his neighbors was coming from. Eventually I had to call a nurse, who arrived in about an hour. She put on the glove, added lubricant, and without hesitation just went in and dug it out. That was when I realized you can't be timid in a constipation rescue attempt. It's a horrible job, but somebody has to do it.

Scene: 97 year old mother somehow finds the kitchen door unlocked. Sometime later, my wife goes to the kitchen to prepare the next meal. There, seated properly at the table, is my mother timidly eating what appears to be a large saucer of yogurt and saltine crackers. Closer inspection had my wife and I bursting with laughter. The 'yogurt' actually came from a large jar of hand cream my wife uses after doing the dishes. Mother had unscrewed the cap and poured the contents into her saucer, added some saltines, and with some imagination she might have been day trippin' to the Riviera. Clever gal, huh?

Scene: 99 year old father eating his morning waffles from the toaster. "I think there is something wrong with the toaster. I could only get one out (he is presently eating it), but the other one seems to be stuck."

I looked down at his plate and exclaimed, "Dad! You are eating a raw sausage patty. It's still red in middle." I couldn't help laughing to myself because I knew what was in the toaster. Sure enough, it was the matching pair. This sausage patty just got so hot, it fell apart in the toaster and died in a pool of fat. No wonder it wouldn't come out, it was dead. I will always fondly treasure that moment of humor he left me with... priceless. Ha ha ha!

Scene: 99 year old father, cogitating on the state of the world, says, "Our cousin X doesn't even have a job!"

I reply, "Oh, you mean X that works as a caregiver for both of his parents?"

"Yeah, that's the one. And he doesn't even have a job. Well, maybe I should say he's not employed." Finally noticing my face turning deep red with rage for the huge disrespect for this caregiver who happens to be my cousin, he continues, "Well, that is not to say that as a caregiver he doesn't do any work."

X's patient has had Parkinson's for the last 20 years. I have nothing but the utmost respect for him and his mother, who suffers from painful ailments herself as they take on the struggle to deal with the issues of life. I couldn't help but to silently laugh at the huge crevasse between our worlds.

I think this is probably one of the classic examples of the incredible awareness differences between the caregiver and parent. I thought it was funny in retrospect, but also worthy of making a point. Neither of us sees the world as it is, but rather as we are, and we are oft found wanting. Our Lord feeds our soul with lessons (but sometimes my wife says I have been eating too many lessons! Joking with ya!)

PRESS THE 'EASY BUTTON' PLEASE

Scene: 99 yr old father relaying some new information about me that I had never heard about before. This pertains to when I was adopted as a baby.

I guess my parents had not seen me before but evidently had completed the paperwork agreements, etc.

"The nurse brought you out for us to see and you had the ugliest black birthmark on your face... you mother was unnerved (sic) and didn't know what to do. I asked the nurse if there was anything that could be done and she said she would see. She took you away and returned in about FIVE (5) MINUTES! The birthmark was gone! But you seemed to have healed okay because there is absolutely no indication of the mark or any scar now. Oh, it was really bad too, like the one I have on my back (he refers to a Lichens Planus non-malignant growth)."

I laughed to myself the rest of the night. I didn't have the heart to tell him that was impossible, save for an act of God. Some birthmarks can't be removed but they all require some sort of surgery for removal none of which can be done in five minutes and without leaving a scar. I think the nurses probably had given me some chocolate to quiet me... which produced the birth mark.

Scene: 'Pass those buffalo wings, governor'

With the kind help from the Governor's office, I had arranged to

have my patient have his 100th birthday celebrated at the Governor's mansion. When the director of the mansion queried as to what food might my patient want... maybe escargot, or shrimp, maybe calamari? I said probably any of those, but I will ask him.

A moment later and feeling a little sheepish I said, "He wants

Buffalo hot wings."

"Did I understand that you said 'Buffalo hot wings'?"

Well he got his wings served in the finest silver settings. His guests, whom had traveled from all over the state, were all somewhat surprised at the menu. I thought that this was so funny, yet from my patients perspective it was totally natural... just like the white socks he was wearing.

Scene: Congratulations on 101st from Coach Calipari

The new basketball coach had just signed on with the University of Kentucky. For my patient's 101st birthday, I invited Calipari whom had a scheduling conflict. I explained that my patient was such a fan of basketball that some people even called him 'Dr. Basketball.' I was using that name in a complimentary manner.

The next week, arriving in the mail was an autographed book by

Calipari addressed to "Dr. Basketball." My patient took it all in stride and said, "well I guess the word has gotten out around my colleagues at the University of what a big fan I am so one thing must have led to another."

I had to laugh since I actually had told him I spoke with Calipari's office and he was sending a book. He choose to create his version. As a caregiver you will often encounter situations in which your patient changes his/her view of reality to fit their needs. Enjoy it. As it turned out my patient had a birthday dinner at the Cedar Post Country Restaurant in Georgetown with former coach Joe B. Hall (which is another story, ☺)

Scene: In good health

My dad's new nurse had just arrived. She queried him, "When did you last have a bowel movement?" Without missing a beat my 102 year old dad replied, "just now when I started thinking about you coming."

Scene: "Who are those people?"

My dad's relatives had arrived. Some of them had stopped by last year and so it was great to see them again. Dad was the uncle of the young eighty eight year old man in attendance. Well, they talked and talked and everybody talked and talked and there was still plenty more to not talk about. When our guests finally left my 102 year old dad turned to me and with a cold poker face said, "Who were those people?" I said, "are you serious... you really don't know?" He replied, "No." I could hardly stop laughing.

Scene: The Barber Shop

I was taking my dad to the barber shop. With a slow and careful

drawl he ventured, "You know, I haven't had to pay for a haircut in four years," he said proudly. I replied, "Well, you won't be paying for this one either." He sort of glowed with an air of victory.

THE GOD EXPERIENCE

So often, people ask me, "How can you believe in something that is just not there?" That is quite understandable, but ultimately irrelevant. When you believe in God, you experience a feeling right? That feeling is an emotion. An emotion is a real-time event. It's like saying, "I feel stress," which is nothing more than the possibility to engage an action potential. If I say, "I am feeling a lot of strain," then the description of stress has now morphed into something that involves motion (I guess the smart boys would use a term like kinetic effect) whether it is electrical (from contracting muscle fibers) or chemical (like your pH shifting to heartburn city) or a combination of the two (like nerve synaptic action discharges) that really stir up the body chemistry.

My point is we already graciously accept some things we can't see (e.g. stress and love), but which we all take for granted and logic has trained us that nobody will criticize us and we can remain popular.

Then what happens when I interject the "God" experience? The moment you really accept Him, is the moment you can feel something (the opposite of stress, I believe). You can't be in middle of the road because it's feels safer. Have you ever spoken to a tightrope walker or trapeze aerialist? I have. Do you think their mind is saying something like, "I think I can make the catch?" NO, and a thousand times no! Their mindset has been retrained to say, "I WILL easily make the catch" or "I HAVE perfect balance and my feet are one with the rope." They have no hesitation and no second thoughts or questioning.

My question to people at large is, "Why are we so resistant to committing to feel the presence of the Lord?" I think the answer is clear and rather simple. We are creatures of God that need to love and be loved. We fear things that might interfere with this goal. If science says God did not create man, and the bible says he did, then I would be unpopular and unloved to believe otherwise.

Let me tell you something. I am not a saved again fish or member of some religious cult. But I do believe in God. I do believe in the resurrection (I can't explain it, but I don't need to either). I believe I was chosen to write this book and, in some way, help people to turn their thinking around... maybe their lives.

You might be thinking why I even bothered to mention religion in the first place. True, it is a very controversial subject, church and state are mandated to keep their distances, and if the subject of religion has any effect on this book, it will most likely be negative because there are so many non-believers. But that's okay with me. When the publisher asked me if I expected to make money on the book I replied, "I don't expect to make, but rather to accept a loss. I'm okay with that. This book is a mission that I really never intended to undertake, but God just kept opening the doors and I will continue to walk through any door he opens for me."

The real answer to why this subject is so relevant is because strength and healing comes through God. Of course, modern science has meds to fight infections, etc., and tools to repair broken bones and all that stuff, but when push comes to shove, it's God that makes the tough decisions. It is He who heals.

Let me share with you what I can only term the miracle of God's work. No, this is not going to be about someone walking on water, but about something that I experienced while in the recovery room at a hospital. In 2008, shortly after becoming a caregiver, I had spinal surgery to decompress nerves from spinal stenosis. Afterwards, as I lay in my recovery room, I was kept lightly sedated for pain control. By the following day, I was fully lucid and feeling the pain (no pain, no gain?), so on the second day I decided to try an experiment. I had noticed that every time I closed my eyes, even if for just a second of time, I got a dark image of what appeared to be a tangle of nerves, bunched up and crippled looking. Sometimes, I could visually scan up and down these nerve bundles. I wondered if this was what my literary hero from Hopkinsville, Kentucky was able to do in real life? I am speaking, of course, about Edgar Cayce for whom an entire foundation (The Association for Research and Enlightenment, ARE) was established at Virginia Beach. Documents showed that Edgar Cayce could go into another, possibly hypnotic, state of mind to actually see and diagnose ailments on patients several hundred miles away. What equally impressed me about Cayce was that he read the bible completely through one time for each year of his life.

Then, the idea came to me that I could apply my favorite mantra for healing. My request to God was going to be this: "Let the golden light of Christ's consciousness surround and heal these bunched up nerves." Now, as a counselor and hypnotherapist, I know about the power of positive thinking, and I know about a great deal of unusual behaviors that the brain can project. In other words, I was not going to be fooled very easily. I asked that the light of Christ's consciousness be spread over the nerves to completely heal everything right now. Well, was I surprised to see a slowly progressing band of multicolored light (like a rainbow) spreading around this group of nerves with no conscious help from me. To test consciousness, I allowed myself to completely open my eyes precisely upon my own volition. Effortlessly, I opened and closed my eyes several times. If this were a dream, it would most likely have ended now because of the interplay of consciousness (opening and closing eyes). When I closed my eyes again the healing pattern continued unabated. Ah ha! I thought. This is simply the effect of the medication to enhance what I am mentally projecting. Plausible. Then I applied the train wreck test. "Lord let the progression of this healing band of light stop now."

This was now MY instruction (but, of course, not what I really wanted). I opened my eyes at will to insure that I was still entirely cognizant. When I closed my eyes, I could see the healing band of light steadily continuing to a symmetrical closure, at which time I somehow knew the job had been done. To this day, I have reflected on that experience, each time treasuring it more. You see, I had asked God to heal the problem area. He knew what was best for me, just as he does for you. That is why the healing continued when my superficial desire was for it to stop. He knows what's in your heart.

God works for me in so many ways. There was a time I used to comment about how 'coincidental' some occurrence was, or that I was in the right place at the right time. I know you have experienced that too. Ever tried to do the mathematical probabilities on any of these coincidences? It would astound you. The odds are more likely you will get struck by lightning on a clear day. I still haven't figured out why street lights (usually on interstate roads) will almost invariably blink out when my car is within two light poles distance. Rarely, will more than one occurrence present itself during any single drive. I can't will it to work; I can't consciously create the effect no matter what I do. It just happens when I totally disconnect my intention for controlling it (that's why I can never prove that I do it). I don't understand it, but I can see it happen and others traveling with me have witnessed it. I pulled into a service station once and at that very moment all the pumps shut down along with the lights. Coincidence? Now consider that for the last year and a half (since my Mother passed) I see the same number sets everywhere. I see the numbers 11:11. They jump out at me everywhere. Maybe some of you have had the same experience? I sometimes think it is the Holy Spirit letting me know that my path is being lit and to be forever mindful of His presence.

True, I could have framed the interpretation differently, but this is what I mean by letting God have control of your life. Don't deny him, but affirm him! Incidentally, I had no idea what to title this chapter heading and as I looked down at the bottom of the page there it was, standing alone, "THE GOD EXPERIENCE." I did not consciously type it there.

My Epiphany

Last, but not least, I want to share the 'epiphany' I had recently. I was changing my mother's diaper, which was full of unpleasant smelling urine. No sooner had I got them off, then she opened the floodgates on me! I mean it was running down her legs all over the fresh sweats I had just put on her, and this was the second time that day this happened. I was frustrated, angry (especially since I just listened to my other patient complain about having to spend a nickel to rent her a hospital bed to prevent her from falling out and breaking a hip or worse), and I felt defeated. It was then, as I was taking a wet wipe and cleaning her legs and drying them with a paper towel, that I felt the humbling presence of Him.

The parallel was so appropriate. I thought of Jesus washing the feet of his disciples, and here I was washing the feet of my mother. I remember Jesus having to give up his life before he could be given life to return with our gift of salvation. I too had felt that I had given up my life (as I knew it), but I was given life again through His grace. As caregivers, we too can be healed by our stripes. I felt blessed with this opportunity to wash my mother's feet. As I tucked her into bed again, I thanked her. She passed away two weeks later.

THE GOOD HUMOR BONE

"Having a good sense of humor is almost mandatory for survival as a caregiver"—make yourself laugh if you have to!

Blond Guy Joke

A blind guy on a bar stool shouts to the bartender, "Wanna hear a blond joke?"

In a hushed voice, the guy next to him says, "Before you tell that joke, you should know something. Our bartender is blond, the bouncer is blond. I'm a 6' tall, 200 lb black belt. The guy sitting next to me is 6' 2," weighs 225, and he's a rugby player. The fella to your right is 6'5" pushing 300 and he's a wrestler. Each one of us is blond! Think about it, Mister. You still wanna tell that joke?"

The blind guy says, "Nah, not if I'm gonna have to explain it five times."

Blond Girl Joke

A blond wants to buy a microwave. So she goes in and asks the sales clerk, "How much for that microwave?"

The sales clerk replies, "We don't sell microwaves to blonds."

The next day she dyes her hair red, goes in and asks the same question. The sales clerk answers, "We don't sell microwaves to blonds."

The next day she dyes her hair brown and goes and asks the same question. The sales clerk replies the same way.

The blond asks how he knows she's a blond.

The clerk says, "That isn't a microwave, it's a TV."

Café Joke

A guy sits down in a café and asks for the hot chili.

The waitress says, "The guy next to you got the last bowl."

He looks over and sees that the guy has finished his meal, but the chili bowl is still full.

He says, "Are you going to eat that?"

The other guy says, "No. Help yourself."

He takes it and starts to eat it. When he gets about half way down, his fork hits something. He looks down, sees a dead mouse in it, and he pukes the chili back into the bowl.

The other guy says, "That's about as far as I got, too."

Reflections

Isn't it a bit unnerving that doctors call what they do "practice?"

Where do forest rangers go to "get away from it all?"

Why don't they make cat-flavored dog food?

Why do they report power outages on TV?

Love

A guy and girl were making out. All of a sudden the girl stops and says to the guy, "I think I just swallowed your gum"

He replies, "No, I was just clearing my throat."

The Highway

A cowboy was walking across the beach by the ocean when he stumbled upon a small vase. He picked up the vase and shook it, and out popped a genie.

The genie said, "I am not really lost, but I will grant you one wish for your troubles."

The cowboy thought about it for a moment and said, "I would like a highway built from Wyoming to Hawaii so I can ride my horse to Hawaii."

The genie thought and replied, "That would take years and lots of dirt and pavement, is there anything else you might want?"

The cowboy thought and said, "Yes, I want to understand women."

Then the genie frowned and sighed, "Would that be a two or four lane highway?"

A Naughty Joke (Okay, the devil made me do it, but it is so funny)

It was the finals in a poetry contest. The two finalists were a Yale graduate and a redneck. The final contest was for them to write a poem in 2 minutes containing a word given to them by the judges.

The word was "TIMBUKTU."

The Yale graduate was the first to give his poem:

"Slowly across the desert sand, trekked a lonely caravan.

Men on camels two by two, Destination Timbuktu."

The audience went wild. They thought the redneck would never stand a chance against the YALE GRADUATE.

Nevertheless, the redneck stood up and gave his poem:

"Me and Tim a-hunting went, met three whores in a pop-up tent.

They were three and we were two, so I bucked one and Timbuktu."

The redneck won hands down.

The Talking Clock

While showing off his new apartment to friends, a college student led the way into the den.

"What are the big brass gong and hammer for?" one of his friends asked.

"That is the talking clock," the man replied.

"How's it work?" the friend asked.

"Watch," he said. He proceeded to give the gong an ear shattering pound with the hammer.

Suddenly, someone screamed from the other side of the wall, "KNOCK IT OFF, YOU IDIOT! It's two o'clock in the morning!"

The Contract

They say marriage is a contract. No, it's not. Contracts come with warrantees. When something goes wrong, you can take it back to the manufacturer. If your husband starts acting up, you can't take him back to his mama's house. "I don't know; he just stopped working. He's just lying around making a funny noise."

-Wanda Sykes-Hall

Q & A

Q: Why did the tomato start blushing?

A: Because it saw the salad dressing!

Q: What do you call a bunch of rabbits walking backwards?

A: A receding 'hare' line.

Q: Why didn't the skeleton cross the road?

A: Because it didn't have the guts!

Q: What do a tornado and a redneck divorce have in common?

A: Somebody's gonna lose a trailer!

Q: Why can't a blond make Kool-Aide?

A: She can't figure out how to put the 2 quarts of water into that little package.

Another Blond Joke

A neighbor is outside gardening and the blond next door comes out to check her mail.

A few minutes later she comes out and checks her mailbox again.

This continues for ½ hour until finally the neighbor walks over to the blond and asks if she's expecting a package.

"No," say the blond. "My computer keeps telling me I have mail!"

Another Blond Joke (I really am not making fun of blonds; my wife is a blond. They're just great jokes!)

A woman walks into the doctor's office and says, "Doc I hurt all over!"

The doctor says, "That's impossible."

"No really! Just look when I touch my arm, ouch! It hurts. When I touch my leg, ouch! It hurts. When I touch my chest, ouch! It really hurts!"

The doc just shakes his head and says, "You're a natural blond aren't you?"

The woman smiles and says, "Why yes I am. How did you know?"

The doctor replies, "Because your finger is broken."

Boll Weevils

Two boll weevils grew up in South Carolina. One went to Hollywood and became a famous actor. The other stayed behind in the cotton fields and never amounted to much. The second one, naturally, became known as the lesser of two weevils.

The Funeral Procession

A woman was leaving a 7-11 with her morning coffee when she noticed a most unusual funeral procession. A long black hearse was followed by a second long black hearse. Behind the second hearse was a solitary woman walking a pit bull on a leash. Behind her were 200 women walking single file. The woman couldn't stand her curiosity.

She respectfully approached the woman walking the dog and said, "I am so sorry for your loss and I know now is a bad time to disturb you, but I've never seen a funeral like this. Whose funeral is it?"

The woman replied, "Well, the first hearse is for my husband."

"What happened to him?"

The woman replies, "My dog attacked and killed him."

She inquired further, "Well who is in the second hearse?"

The woman replies, "My mother-in-law. The dog turned on her."

A poignant and thoughtful moment of silence passes between the two women.

"Could I borrow that dog?"

"Get in line."

The Nobel Prize

A man is driving down a country road when he sees a farmer standing in the middle of a huge field of grass. The farmer is just standing there, doing nothing, looking at nothing.

"Ah, excuse me mister, but what are you doing?" he asks.

The farmer replies, "I'm trying to win a Nobel Prize."

"How?" asks the man, puzzled.

"Well, I heard they give it to people who are out-standing in their field."

For Mathematicians

One of the world's most clever mathematicians was arrested by the police in an airport for smuggling a bomb in his carry-on luggage.

The math guy says, "You don't understand... It's to make the plane safer!"

One of the officers asked, "How could it possibly make the plane safer?"

The math guy said, "You see, the chances that a bomb is aboard the plane are extremely small. But the chance of two bombs being on the plane would be practically impossible!"

Another Naughty Joke

A man meets a woman in a bar. They talk, they connect, and they end up leaving together.

They get back to her place where her bedroom is completely packed with teddy bears; hundreds of bears of different sizes on shelves all the way down to the floor.

The man thinks to himself, "How cute and warm her heart must be," but says nothing.

After a night of passion as they are lying together in the afterglow, the man rolls over and asks, smiling, "Well, how was it?"

The woman says, "You can have any prize from the bottom shelf."

Blonds Strike Back!

What's the real reason a brunette keeps her figure?

No one else wants it.

What do you call a brunette in a room full of blonds?

Invisible.

What's a brunette's mating call?

"Has the blond left yet?"

What do brunettes miss most about a great party?

The Invitation.

What do you call a good looking man with a brunette?

A hostage.

Thoughts by George Carlin

How is it possible to have a civil war?

If one synchronized swimmer drowns, do the rest drown too?

If you ate pasta and antipasta, would you still be hungry?

If you try to fail, and succeed, which have you done?

More Q & A

Q: What did Spock see when he looked in the toilet??

A: The Captain's log.

Q: What do you call cheese that isn't yours?

A: NACHO CHEESE!

Q: There are 2 flies in the kitchen, which one is the cowboy?

A: The one on the range.

Q: What did the fish say when he ran into the wall?

A: Dam

Q: Why did the golfer wear two pairs of pants?

A: In case he got a hole in one.

Golf Jokes

Bill returned home from a day of golf looking terrible. His wife asked, "What happened to you?"

Bill replied, "It was terrible. Charlie and I were on the fifth hole, it's a beautiful day, all of a sudden, and Charlie dropped dead from a heart attack!"

His wife said, "Oh no! That is terrible!"

"I'll say, all day long it was 'hit the ball and drag Charlie'!"

Jim and Jack were on the 14th hole, ready to tee off, when a funeral procession drove down the adjoining road. Seeing the hearse, Jim stopped, took off his hat, and placed his hand over his heart.

"Wow!" said Jack, "I never knew you had so much respect for the dead."

"I ought to," said Jim, "I was married to her for forty years!"

Wife Has Car Trouble

My wife came home yesterday and said, "Honey, the car won't start, but I know what the problem is."

I asked her what the problem was and she told me there was water in the carburetor. I thought for a moment then said, "You know, don't take this the wrong way, but you don't know the carburetor from the accelerator."

"No, there's definitely water in the carburetor," she insisted.

"Ok honey, that's fine, I'll just go take a look. Where is it?"

"In the lake"

Sherlock Holmes

Holmes and Watson had gone to bed and were lying there looking up at the sky. Holmes said, "Watson, look up. What do you see?"

"Well, I see thousands of stars."

"And what does that mean to you?"

"Well, I guess it means we'll have another nice day tomorrow. What does it mean to you, Holmes?"

"To me, it means someone has stolen our tent."

Imagine That

A guy goes into a bar. He's sitting on the stool and hears, "You look great!" But there's nobody near him. Again he hears, "No, you really look terrific."

"Hey," the guy calls to the bartender, "What's with the nuts?"

"Oh," the bartender answers, "They're complimentary."

Sports Jokes

Q: Why do the Dallas Cowboys Players have T.G.I.F scribbled on their cleats??

A: 'Toes go in first'

Q: Why are they replacing the turf in Dodger Stadium with cardboard?

A: The Dodgers look better on paper.

A Detroit Redwings fan, a St. Louis Blues fan, a Colorado Avalanche fan, and a Dallas Stars fan climbed to the top of Mt. Everest. They looked over the edge in awe.

Then the Redwings fan shouts, "This is for the Wings!" and jumps off the cliff.

Well, the St. Louis fan, not wanting to be outdone, shouts, "This is for the Blues!" and jumps to his death.

Seeing the trend, the Stars fan looks around for a moment. Then he walks behind the Avalanche fan, gives him a big shove and yells, "This is for hockey fans everywhere!"

It's A Gas!

A business woman explains to her doctor that she was always breaking wind. At board meetings, during interviews, dinners, everywhere... it was impossible to control.

"But at least I am fortunate in two respects," she tells the doctor. "They neither smell nor make a noise. In fact, you'll be surprised to know I've let two go since I've been talking to you."

The doctor reaches for his pad, scribbled an Rx and hands it to her.

"What's this?" she asks, reading the Rx, "Nasal Drops?"

"Yes," replies the doctor. "First we'll fix your nose, and then we'll have a go at your hearing!"

The 911 Call

A couple of hunters were out in the woods, when one of them was accidentally wounded by his own gun. The other hunter grabbed his cell and called 911.

"What is the nature of your call" the operator says.

"My partner has just been shot!"

"Now listen very carefully and do exactly as I say. First, I need to know if he is dead yet"

"Just a minute"... silence for a moment and the sound of a gunshot. Returning, the hunter says, "He is now, what do I do next?"

The Robber (I heard this from my barber)

There was a long line of customers at the bank when a gunman walked in and robbed it. The gunman turns around as he's leaving and asks a man, "Did you see me rob this bank?"

The frightened man says, "Yes, Sir."

Bang! The gunman shoots him right in the head.

The gunman turns to the next man and says, "Did you see me rob this bank?"

The man says, "No sir, I didn't see a thing, but my wife standing over there in the red coat saw it all!"

The First Case of Dementia (from the same barber)

Many years ago there were two dinosaurs sitting on top of this mountain. Between clashes of thunder and lightning mixed with the hard rain and rising waters, they make out the outline of the "Ark" with all its boarded cargo going by. The first dino looks at the second with a look of total exasperation and says, "darn... was that for today?" (So now you know what really caused the extinction of the dinos)

The BP Oil Spill of The Century – How it was really stopped!!

After repeated failures to stop the leak finally a headline appeared one morning. "Louisiana governor stops the BP oil leak... totally." A newsman queried, "Just how did you achieve this feat?"

In true Cajun style the governor drawls, "Weelll... we just put a wedding band around it and it quit putting out!

Ya can't beat those Cajuns for coming up with a solution to 'bout anything.

For Politicians—It's how many?

President Bush was in a cabinet meeting when someone mentioned that 3 Brazilian citizens were killed in the latest drug war.

"OMG! How awful! That's just terrible! Quick, draft up a letter condemning this outrage!"

Bush turns aside and whispers to his aide, "Just how many are in a Brazillion?"

The Coded Message

Osama Bin Laden himself decided to send George W. Bush a letter in his own handwriting to let the President know he was still in the game. Bush opened the letter and it appeared to contain a single line of coded message: 370HSSV-0773H

Bush was baffled, so he e-mailed it to Condi Rice. Condi and her aides had no clue either, so they sent it to the FBI. No one could solve it at the FBI so it went to the CIA, then to the NSA. With no clue as to its meaning they eventually asked Britain's MI-6 for help. Within a minute MI-6 cabled the White House with this reply, "Tell the President he's holding the message upside down."

How Much Is A Billion?

A billion is a difficult number to comprehend:

A billion seconds ago, it was 1959.

A billion minutes ago, Jesus was alive.

A billion hours ago, our ancestors were living in the Stone Age.

And...

A billion dollars ago, was only 8 hours and 20 minutes at the rate Washington spends.

Rules of Washington

Don't lie, cheat, or steal... unnecessarily.

An honest answer can get you into a lot of trouble.

The facts, while interesting, are irrelevant.

Chicken Little only has to be right once.

"No" is only an interim response.

You can't kill a bad idea.

If at first you don't succeed, destroy all the evidence that you ever tried.

The truth is a variable.

A promise is not a guarantee.

If you can't counter the argument, leave the meeting.

Things Found Only in America

Only in America...

...can a pizza get to your house faster than an ambulance.

...are there handicap parking places in front of a skating rink.

...drugstores make the sick walk to the back of the store to get their prescriptions while healthy people can buy cigarettes up front....do people order double cheese burgers, large fries, and a diet Coke.

...do banks leave both doors to the vault open and then chain the pens to the counters.

...do we leave cars worth thousands of dollars in the driveway and put our useless junk in the garage.

...do we buy hot dogs in packages of ten and buns in packages of eight.

...do they have drive-up ATM machines with Braille lettering.

Religious Humor

A man walked into the ladies department of Macy's and shyly said to the saleslady, "I'd like to buy a bra for my wife."

"What type of bra?" asked the clerk.

"Is there more than one type?"

"Look around," said the sales lady. He saw a sea of all types.

He was relieved when the lady said, "Actually there are only four basic types to choose from: The Catholic, The Salvation Army, The Presbyterian, and the Baptist types. Which one would you prefer?"

Befuddled, the man asked about the differences between them.

The saleslady responds, "The Catholic type supports the masses,

the Salvation Army type lifts the fallen, the Presbyterian type keeps them staunch and upright, and the Baptist type makes mountains out of molehills."

Typos from Church Bulletins

Ladies, don't forget the rummage sale. It's a chance to get rid of those things not worth keeping, and don't forget to bring your husbands.

The peacemaking meeting scheduled for today has been canceled due to a conflict.

The sermon this morning: "Jesus Walks on the Water."

The sermon tonight: "Searching For Jesus"

Next Thursday there will be tryouts for the choir. They need all the help they can get.

Barbara remains in the hospital and needs blood donors for more transfusions. She is also having trouble sleeping and requests tapes of Pastor Jack's sermons.

Our youth basketball team is back in action Wednesday at 8 pm. Come out and watch us kill Christ the King.

Don't let worry kill you off—let the Church help.

A bean supper will be held on Tuesday evening in the church hall. Music will follow.

Church Sign

Honk if you love Jesus,

Text while driving if you want to meet Him.

RANDOM THOUGHTS FOR THE DAY

1. I think part of a best friend's job should be to immediately clear your computer history if you die.

2. Nothing sucks more than that moment during an argument when you realize you're wrong.

3. I totally take back all those times I didn't want to nap when I was younger.

4. There is great need for a sarcasm font.

5. How the hell are you supposed to fold a fitted sheet?

6. Was learning cursive really necessary?

7. MapQuest really needs to start their directions on #5. I'm pretty sure I know how to get out of my neighborhood.

8. Obituaries would be a lot more interesting if they told you how the person died.

9. I can't remember the last time I wasn't at least kind of tired.

10. Bad decisions make good stories.

11. You never know when it will strike, but there comes a moment at work when you know that you just aren't going to do anything productive for the rest of the day.

12. Can we all just agree to ignore whatever comes after Blue Ray? I don't want to have to restart my collection... again.

13. I'm always slightly terrified when I exit out of Word and it asks me if I want to save any changes to my ten-page research paper that I swear I did not make any changes to.

14. "Do not machine wash or tumble dry" means I will never wash this—EVER!!!

15. I hate when I just miss a call by the last ring (Hello? Hello? Damn it!), but when I immediately call back, it rings nine times and goes to voicemail. What'd you do after I didn't answer? Drop the phone and run away?

16. I hate leaving my house confident and looking good and then not seeing anyone of importance the entire day. What a waste.

17. I keep some people's phone numbers in my phone just so I know not to answer when they call.

18. My 4-year old son asked me in the car the other day, "Mom, what would happen if you ran over a ninja?" How the hell do I respond to that?

19. I think the freezer deserves a light as well.

20. I disagree with Kay Jewelers. I would bet on any given Friday or Saturday night more kisses begin with Miller Lites than Kay.

21. And finally, have you ever wondered if that dollar bill you're holding has ever been in a strippers butt crack? You are now!

QUOTES

I haven't always been a quote person, but there are times when I need quotes to give me firm ground to stand upon. Many of these quotes I can directly relate to from my caregiving experiences. Some are just for fun. Some are for reading to the patient. Some help us see another point of view. Savor those that feed your soul.

Winning isn't everything—but wanting to win is
-Vince Lombardi

In great attempts, it is glorious to fail.
-Vince Lombardi

Perfection is not attainable. But if we chase perfection, we can catch excellence.
-Vince Lombardi

The purpose of human life is to serve and to show compassion and the will to help others.
-Vince Lombardi

Wisdom outweighs any wealth.
-Sophocles, Antigone

One word frees us of all the weight and pain of life: That word is love.
-Sophocles, Oedipus at Colonus

The world is full of willing people, some willing to work, the rest willing to let them.
-Robert Frost

The woods are lovely, dark, and deep,
But I have promises to keep,
And miles to go before I sleep,
And miles to go before I sleep.
-Robert Frost

It has been said that man is a rational animal. All my life I have been searching for evidence which could support this.
-Bertrand Russell

Most folks are about as happy as they make up their minds to be.
-Abraham Lincoln

You cannot escape the responsibility of tomorrow by evading it today.
-Abraham Lincoln

The important thing was to love rather than to be loved.
-W. Somerset Maugham, 'Of Human Bondage', 1915

Good advice is something a man gives when he is too old to set a bad example.
-Francois de La Rochefoucauld

If we had no faults of our own, we would not take so much pleasure in noticing those of others.
-Francois de La Rochefoucauld

It is often merely for an excuse that we say things are impossible.
-Francois de La Rochefoucauld

Many people despise wealth, but few know how to give it away.
-Francois de La Rochefoucauld

No persons are more frequently wrong, than those who will not admit they are wrong.
-Francois De La Rochefoucauld

The glory of great men should always be measured by the means they have used to acquire it.
-Francois de La Rochefoucauld

Even if you're on the right track, you'll get run over if you just sit there.
-Will Rogers

An onion can make people cry, but there has never been a vegetable invented to make them laugh.
-Will Rogers

Our constitution protects aliens, drunks, and U.S. Senators.
-Will Rogers

The best doctor in the world is the veterinarian. He can't ask his patients what is the matter—he's got to just know.
-Will Rogers

There ought to be one day—just one—when there is open season on Senators.
-Will Rogers

The income tax has made more liars out of the American people than golf has.
-Will Rogers

It's a job that's never started that takes the longest to finish.
-J. R. R. Tolkien

Little by little, one travels far.
-J. R. R. Tolkien

Determine never to be idle... It is wonderful how much may be done if we are always doing.
-Thomas Jefferson

Every citizen should be a soldier. This was the case with the Greeks and Romans, and must be that of every Free State.
-Thomas Jefferson

Honesty is the first chapter of the book of wisdom.
-Thomas Jefferson

Never trouble another for what you can do for yourself.
-Thomas Jefferson

The man who reads nothing at all is better educated than the man who reads nothing but newspapers.
-Thomas Jefferson

Walking is the best possible exercise. Habituate yourself to walk very far.
-Thomas Jefferson

I believe that banking institutions are more dangerous to our liberties than standing armies. If the American people ever allow private banks to control the issue of their currency, first by inflation, then by deflation, the banks and corporations that will grow up around [the banks] will deprive the people of all property until their children wake-up homeless on the continent their fathers conquered. The issuing power should be taken from the banks and restored to the people, to whom it properly belongs.
-Thomas Jefferson, (Attributed)

Health is worth more than learning.
-Thomas Jefferson

Always forgive your enemies; nothing annoys them so much.
-Oscar Wilde

I think that God in creating Man somewhat overestimated his ability.
-Oscar Wilde

If you want to tell people the truth, make them laugh, otherwise they'll kill you.
-Oscar Wilde

Man is least himself when he talks in his own person. Give him a mask, and he will tell you the truth.
-Oscar Wilde

Morality, like art, means drawing a line someplace.
-Oscar Wilde

Most people are other people. Their thoughts are someone else's opinions, their lives a mimicry, their passions a quotation.
-Oscar Wilde

One can survive everything, nowadays, except death, and live down everything except a good reputation.
-Oscar Wilde

A countryman between two lawyers is like a fish between two cats.
-Benjamin Franklin

A slip of the foot you may soon recover, but a slip of the tongue you may never get over.
-Benjamin Franklin

Beware of the young doctor and the old barber.
-Benjamin Franklin

Do not anticipate trouble, or worry about what may never happen. Keep in the sunlight.
-Benjamin Franklin

God heals, and the doctor takes the fees.
-Benjamin Franklin

Having been poor is no shame, but being ashamed of it, is.
-Benjamin Franklin

He that lives upon hope will die fasting.
-Benjamin Franklin

He that would live in peace and at ease must not speak all he knows nor judge all he sees.
-Benjamin Franklin

There is nothing new under the sun but there are lots of old things we don't know.
-Ambrose Bierce

Cogito cogito ergo cogito sum (I think that I think, therefore I think that I am.)
-Ambrose Bierce

A hospital is no place to be sick.
-Samuel Goldwyn

Health is not valued till sickness comes. Be not slow to visit the sick
-Dr. Thomas Fuller

A wise man should consider that health is the greatest of human blessings, and learn how by his own thought to derive benefit from his illnesses.
-Hippocrates, Regimen in Health

It's no longer a question of staying healthy. It's a question of finding a sickness you like.
Jackie Mason

Now there are more overweight people in America than average-weight people. So overweight people are now average. Which means you've met your New Year's resolution.
-Jay Leno

You can either hold yourself up to the unrealistic standards of others, or ignore them and concentrate on being happy with yourself as you are.
-Jeph Jacques

Be careful about reading health books. You may die of a misprint.
-Mark Twain

A vigorous five-mile walk will do more good for an unhappy but otherwise healthy adult than all the medicine and psychology in the world.
-Paul Dudley White

Health consists of having the same diseases as one's neighbors.
-Quentin Crisp

Health nuts are going to feel stupid someday, lying in hospitals dying of nothing.
-Redd Foxx

No one is where he is by accident, and chance plays no part in God's plan.
-A Course in Miracles

There is no such thing as an idle thought. All thought creates form on some level. Every thought leads to either love or fear.
-A Course in Miracles

If you knew who walks beside you on this path that you have chosen, fear would be impossible.
-A Course in Miracles

When you have learned how to decide with God, all decisions become as easy and as right as breathing.
-A Course in Miracles

Women like silent men. They think they're listening.
-Marcel Achard

If it's free, it's advice, if you pay for it, it's counseling; if you can use either one, it's a miracle.
-Jack Adams

If your actions inspire others to dream more, learn more, do more, you are a leader.
-John Quincy Adams

Remember there's no such thing as a small act of kindness.
-Scott Adams

There is no pain so great as the memory of joy in present grief.
-Aeschylus

Dreams are free, so free your dreams.
-Astrid Alauda

Be brave enough to live life creatively. The creative is the place where no one else has ever been. You have to leave the city of your comfort and go into the wilderness of your intuition. You can't get there by bus, only by hard work and risk and by not quite knowing what you are doing. What you'll discover will be wonderful. What you'll discover will be yourself.
-Alan Alda

Quit worrying about your health. It'll go away.
-Robert Orben

Make your own recovery the first priority in your life.
-Robin Norwood

If I could drop dead right now, I'd be the happiest man alive.
-Samuel Goldwyn

Death is more universal than life; everyone dies but not everyone lives.
-A. Sachs

We do not die because we have to die; we die because one day, and not so long ago, our consciousness was forced to deem it necessary.
-Antonin Artaud

Be open to your dreams, people. Embrace that distant shore. Because our mortal journey is over all too soon.
-David Assael

Death is nothing to us, since when we are, death has not come, and when death has come, we are not.
-Epicurus

If you live to be one hundred, you've got it made. Very few people die past that age.
-George Burns

When you lose someone you love, you die too, and you wait around for your body to catch up.
-John Scalzi

For three days after death hair and fingernails continue to grow but phone calls taper off.
-Johnny Carson

I read part of it all the way through.
-Samuel Goldwyn

When someone does something good, applaud! You will make two people happy.
-Samuel Goldwyn

I've done the calculation and your chances of winning the lottery are identical whether you play or not.
-Fran Lebowitz

Life is something that happens when you can't get to sleep.
-Fran Lebowitz

My favorite animal is steak.
-Fran Lebowitz

The opposite of talking isn't listening. The opposite of talking is waiting.
-Fran Lebowitz

Do what you can, with what you have, where you are.
-Theodore Roosevelt

When they call the roll in the Senate, the Senators do not know whether to answer 'Present' or 'Not guilty.'
-Theodore Roosevelt

When you play, play hard; when you work, don't play at all.
-Theodore Roosevelt

Whenever you are asked if you can do a job, tell 'em, 'Certainly I can!'
Then get busy and find out how to do it.
-Theodore Roosevelt

Far and away the best prize that life offers is the chance to work hard at
work worth doing.
-Theodore Roosevelt

In truth, there was only one Christian, and he died on the cross.
-Friedrich Nietzsche

No price is too high to pay for the privilege of owning yourself.
-Friedrich Nietzsche

I believe that all government is evil, and that trying to improve it is largely
a waste of time
-H. L. Mencken

It is even harder for the average ape to believe that he has descended
from man.
-H. L. Mencken

It is inaccurate to say that I hate everything. I am strongly in favor of
common sense, common honesty, and common decency. This makes me
forever ineligible for public office.
-H. L. Mencken

It is the dull man who is always sure, and the sure man who is always
dull.
-H. L. Mencken

Eighty percent of success is showing up.
-Woody Allen

As the poet said, 'Only God can make a tree'—probably because it's so
hard to figure out how to get the bark on.
-Woody Allen

I can't listen to that much Wagner. I start getting the urge to conquer Poland.
-Woody Allen

I don't want to achieve immortality through my work... I want to achieve it through not dying.
-Woody Allen

I took a speed reading course and read 'War and Peace' in twenty minutes. It involves Russia.
-Woody Allen

I was thrown out of college for cheating on the metaphysics exam; I looked into the soul of the boy sitting next to me.
-Woody Allen

If only God would give me some clear sign! Like making a large deposit in my name in a Swiss bank.
-Woody Allen

Interestingly, according to modern astronomers, space is finite. This is a very comforting thought—particularly for people who can never remember where they have left things.
-Woody Allen

It seemed the world was divided into good and bad people. The good ones slept better... while the bad ones seemed to enjoy the waking hours much more.
-Woody Allen

Life is full of misery, loneliness, and suffering—and it's all over much too soon.
-Woody Allen

On the plus side, death is one of the few things that can be done just as easily lying down.
-Woody Allen

How to make God laugh: Tell him your future plans.
-Woody Allen

I am thankful for laughter except when milk comes out my nose.
-Woody Allen

If you're not failing every now and again, it's a sign you're not doing anything very innovative.
-Woody Allen

Erotica is using a feather, pornography is using the whole chicken.
-Isabel Allende

The bad news is time flies. The good news is you're the pilot.
-Michael Altshuler

Be of service. Whether you make yourself available to a friend or co-worker, or you make time every month to do volunteer work, there is nothing that harvests more of a feeling of empowerment than being of service to someone in need.
-Gillian Anderson

Focus on the journey, not the destination. Joy is found not in finishing an activity but in doing it.
-Greg Anderson

Only one thing has to change for us to know happiness in our lives: where we focus our attention.
-Greg Anderson

When we are motivated by goals that have deep meaning, by dreams that need completion, by pure love that needs expressing, then we truly live life.
-Greg Anderson

We learn the inner secret of happiness when we learn to direct our inner drives, our interest and our attention to something outside ourselves.
-Ethel Perry Andrus

Everything in the universe has rhythm. Everything dances.
-Maya Angelou

I believe talent is like electricity. We don't understand electricity. We use it.
-Maya Angelou

I believe the most important single thing, beyond discipline and creativity is daring to dare.
-Maya Angelou

I've learned that every day you should reach out and touch someone. People love a warm hug, or just a friendly pat on the back.
-Maya Angelou

I've learned that making a 'living' is not the same thing as making a 'life.'
-Maya Angelou

I've learned that people will forget what you said, people will forget what you did, but people will never forget how you made them feel.
-Maya Angelou

I've learned that you can tell a lot about a person by the way he/she handles these three things: a rainy day, lost luggage, and tangled Christmas tree lights.
-Maya Angelou

There is no greater agony than bearing an untold story inside you.
-Maya Angelou

Life is not about getting through the storms, but about dancing in the rain.

-Bunny Armstrong

I take nothing for granted. I now have only good days, or great days.
-Lance Armstrong

The portal of healing and creativity always takes us into the realm of the spirit.
-Angeles Arrien

Everyone has an invisible sign hanging from their neck saying, 'Make me feel important.' Never forget this message when working with people.
-Mary Kay Ash

"First the doctor told me the good news: I was going to have a disease named after me."
-Steve Martin

"Never go to a doctor whose office plants have died."
-Erma Bombeck

Either this man is dead or my watch has stopped.
-Groucho Marx

I'm not feeling very well—I need a doctor immediately. Ring the nearest golf course."
-Groucho Marx

Gray hair is God's graffiti.
-Bill Cosby

My doctor said I look like a million dollars—green and wrinkled.
-Red Skelton

Why did God make man before he made woman? Because he didn't want any advice on how to do it.
-Anonymous

We had a very successful trip to Russia we got back.
-Bob Hope

I lived in Miami for a while, in a section with a lot of really old people. The average age in my apartment house was dead.
-Gabe Kaplan

I could dance with you until the cows come home. On second thought I'd rather dance with the cows until you come home.
-Groucho Marx

I sent the club a wire stating, PLEASE ACCEPT MY RESIGNATION. I DON'T WANT TO BELONG TO ANY CLUB THAT WILL ACCEPT ME AS A MEMBER.
-Groucho Marx

I've had a perfectly wonderful evening. But this wasn't it.
-Groucho Marx

Military intelligence is a contradiction in terms.
-Groucho Marx

Time flies like an arrow. Fruit flies like a banana.
-Groucho Marx

My doctor gave me six months to live, but when I couldn't pay the bill, he gave me six months more.
-Walter Matthau

"I am so clever that sometimes I don't understand a single word of what I am saying."
-Oscar Wilde

Before you contradict an old man, my fair friend, you should endeavor to understand him.
-George Santayana

Sanity is a madness put to good use.
-George Santayana

The young man who has not wept is a savage, and the old man who will not laugh is a fool.
-George Santayana

The truth is cruel, but it can be loved, and it makes free those who have loved it.
-George Santayana

Those who cannot remember the past are condemned to repeat it
-George Santayana

In science one tries to tell people, in such a way as to be understood by everyone, something that no one ever knew before. But in poetry, it's the exact opposite.
-Paul Dirac

The point of philosophy is to start with something so simple as not to seem worth stating, and to end with something so paradoxical that no one will believe it.
-Bertrand Russell

Before God we are all equally wise—and equally foolish.
-Albert Einstein

If I had only known, I would have been a locksmith.
-Albert Einstein

If you are out to describe the truth, leave elegance to the tailor.
-Albert Einstein

It is a miracle that curiosity survives formal education.
-Albert Einstein

Only two things are infinite, the universe and human stupidity, and I'm not sure about the former.
-Albert Einstein

The important thing is not to stop questioning.
-Albert Einstein

To punish me for my contempt for authority, fate made me an authority myself.
-Albert Einstein
Try not to become a man of success but rather to become a man of value.
-Albert Einstein

A banker is a fellow who lends you his umbrella when the sun is shining, but wants it back the minute it begins to rain.
-Mark Twain

An Englishman is a person who does things because they have been done before. An American is a person who does things because they haven't been done before.
-Mark Twain

It is better to deserve honors and not have them than to have them and not to deserve them.
-Mark Twain

Don't go around saying the world owes you a living. The world owes you nothing. It was here first.
-Mark Twain

Don't part with your illusions. When they are gone you may still exist, but you have ceased to live.
-Mark Twain

Grief can take care of itself, but to get the full value of a joy you must have somebody to divide it with.
-Mark Twain

Humor is the great thing, the saving thing. The minute it crops up, all our irritations and resentments slip away and a sunny spirit takes their place.
-Mark Twain

I have been through some terrible things in my life, some of which actually happened.
-Mark Twain

The great French Marshall Lyautey once asked his gardener to plant a tree. The gardener objected that the tree was slow growing and would not reach maturity for 100 years. The Marshall replied, 'In that case, there is no time to lose; plant it this afternoon!'
-John F. Kennedy

We need men who can dream of things that never were.
-John F. Kennedy

The Chinese use two brush strokes to write the word 'crisis.' One brush stroke stands for danger; the other for opportunity. In a crisis, be aware of the danger—but recognize the opportunity.
-John F. Kennedy

All human beings should try to learn before they die what they are running from, and to, and why.
-James Thurber

I hate women because they always know where things are.
-James Thurber

There are two kinds of light--the glow that illuminates, and the glare that obscures.
-James Thurber

It is common sense to take a method and try it. If it fails, admit it frankly and try another. But above all, try something.
-Franklin D. Roosevelt

When you get to the end of your rope, tie a knot and hang on.
-Franklin D. Roosevelt

Repetition does not transform a lie into a truth.
-Franklin D. Roosevelt

Do not consider painful what is good for you.
-Euripides
The best and safest thing is to keep a balance in your life, acknowledge the great powers around us and in us. If you can do that, and live that way, you are really a wise man.
-Euripides
Waste not fresh tears over old griefs.
-Euripides

Light be the earth upon you, lightly rest.
-Euripides

Man's best possession is a sympathetic wife.
-Euripides

Leave no stone unturned.
-Euripides

There is one thing alone that stands the brunt of life throughout its course: a quiet conscience
-Euripides, Hippolytus

The government's view of the economy could be summed up in a few short phrases: If it moves, tax it. If it keeps moving, regulate it. And if it stops moving, subsidize it.
-Ronald Reagan

The nine most terrifying words in the English language are, 'I'm from the government and I'm here to help.'
-Ronald Reagan

Every one of us gets through the tough times because somebody is there, standing in the gap to close it for us.
-Oprah Winfrey

I know for sure that what we dwell on is who we become.
-Oprah Winfrey

I trust that everything happens for a reason, even when we're not wise enough to see it.
-Oprah Winfrey

What I know for sure is that what you give comes back to you.
-Oprah Winfrey

Use what you have to run toward your best—that's how I now live my life.
-Oprah Winfrey

To be worn out is to be renewed.
-Lao-tzu

To know that you do not know is the best. To pretend to know when you do not know is a disease.
-Lao-tzu

It takes a great deal of courage to stand up to your enemies, but even more to stand up to your friends.
-J. K. Rowling

Dark and difficult times lie ahead. Soon we must all face the choice between what is right and what is easy.
-J. K. Rowling

It is the unknown we fear when we look upon death and darkness, nothing more.
-J. K. Rowling

Youth cannot know how age thinks and feels. But old men are guilty if they forget what it was to be young.
-J. K. Rowling

Destiny is a name often given in retrospect to choices that had dramatic consequences.
-J. K. Rowling

Once a word has been allowed to escape, it cannot be recalled.
-Horace

Cease to ask what the morrow will bring forth. And set down as gain each day that Fortune grants.
-Horace

Seize the day, put no trust in the morrow! [Carpe diem, quam minimum credula postero.]
-Horace

Failures are steps in the ladder of success.
-James Allen

When mental energy is allowed to follow the line of least resistance and to fall into easy channels, it is called weakness.
-James Allen

You are today where your thoughts have brought you; you will be tomorrow where your thoughts take you.
-James Allen

The truth is that everything that can be accomplished by showing a person when he's wrong, ten times as much can be accomplished by showing him where he is right. The reason we don't do it so often is that it's more fun to throw a rock through a window than to put in a pane of glass.
-Robert T. Allen

A woman is like a tea bag—you never know how strong she is until she gets in hot water.
-Eleanor Roosevelt

Do what you feel in your heart to be right—for you'll be criticized anyway. You'll be damned if you do, and damned if you don't.
-Eleanor Roosevelt

If someone betrays you once, it's their fault; if they betray you twice, it's your fault.
-Eleanor Roosevelt

It is not fair to ask of others what you are unwilling to do yourself.
-Eleanor Roosevelt

Learn from the mistakes of others. You can't live long enough to make them all yourself.
-Eleanor Roosevelt

The purpose of life is to live it, to taste experience to the utmost, to reach out eagerly and without fear for newer and richer experience.
-Eleanor Roosevelt

No one can make you feel inferior without your consent.
-Eleanor Roosevelt

Curiosity killed the cat, but for a while I was a suspect.
-Steven Wright

Last night somebody broke into my apartment and replaced everything with exact duplicates... When I pointed it out to my roommate, he said, 'Do I know you?'
-Steven Wright

Last year I went fishing with Salvador Dali. He was using a dotted line. He caught every other fish.
-Steven Wright

My theory of evolution is that Darwin was adopted.
-Steven Wright

There's a fine line between fishing and just standing on the shore like an idiot.
-Steven Wright

You can't have everything. Where would you put it?
-Steven Wright

Before I met my husband, I'd never fallen in love, though I'd stepped in it a few times.
-Rita Rudner

I love being married. It's so great to find that one special person you want to annoy for the rest of your life.
-Rita Rudner

I was going to have cosmetic surgery until I noticed that the doctor's office was full of portraits by Picasso.
-Rita Rudner

My mother buried three husbands, and two of them were just napping.
-Rita Rudner

Neurotics build castles in the air, psychotics live in them. My mother cleans them.
-Rita Rudner

When I meet a man I ask myself, 'Is this the man I want my children to spend their weekends with?'
-Rita Rudner

Before all else, we seek, upon our common labor as a nation, the blessings of Almighty God.
-Dwight D. Eisenhower

An intellectual is a man who takes more words than necessary to tell more than he knows.
-Dwight D. Eisenhower

What counts is not necessarily the size of the dog in the fight—it's the size of the fight in the dog.
-Dwight D. Eisenhower

We have all a better guide in ourselves, if we would attend to it, than any other person can be.
-Jane Austen

Everything has its beauty, but not everyone sees it.
-Confucius

Forget injuries, never forget kindnesses.
-Confucius

He who will not economize will have to agonize.
-Confucius

Our greatest glory is not in never falling, but in getting up every time we do.
-Confucius

Respect yourself and others will respect you.
-Confucius

Frisbeetarianism is the belief that when you die, your soul goes up on the roof and gets stuck.
-George Carlin

It's never just a game when you're winning.
-George Carlin

They can conquer who believe they can.
-Virgil

That would be a good thing for them to cut on my tombstone: Wherever she went, including here, it was against her better judgment.
-Dorothy Parker

Do not count your chickens before they are hatched.
-Aesop

An economist is an expert who will know tomorrow why the things he predicted yesterday didn't happen today.
-Laurence J. Peter

An intelligence test sometimes shows a man how smart he would have been not to have taken it.
-Laurence J. Peter

Every man serves a useful purpose: A miser, for example, makes a wonderful ancestor.
-Laurence J. Peter

If a cluttered desk is the sign of a cluttered mind, what is the significance of a clean desk?
-Laurence J. Peter

The man who says he is willing to meet you halfway is usually a poor judge of distance.
-Laurence J. Peter

Everyone rises to their level of incompetence.
-Laurence J. Peter, "The Peter Principle"

Competence, like truth, beauty and contact lenses, is in the eye of the beholder.
-Laurence J. Peter, The Peter Principle

Time is an illusion; Lunchtime doubly so.
-Douglas Adams

I believe that freedom is the deepest need of every human soul.
-George W. Bush

An appeaser is one who feeds a crocodile, hoping it will eat him last.
-Sir Winston Churchill

A fanatic is one who can't change his mind and won't change the subject.
-Sir Winston Churchill
Broadly speaking, the short words are the best, and the old words best of all.
-Sir Winston Churchill

History will be kind to me for I intend to write it.
-Sir Winston Churchill

I like pigs. Dogs look up to us. Cats look down on us. Pigs treat us as equals.
-Sir Winston Churchill

It's not enough that we do our best; sometimes we have to do what's required.
-Sir Winston Churchill

Men occasionally stumble over the truth, but most of them pick themselves up and hurry off as if nothing ever happened.
-Sir Winston Churchill

Never hold discussions with the monkey when the organ grinder is in the room.
-Sir Winston Churchill

Success is the ability to go from one failure to another with no loss of enthusiasm.
-Sir Winston Churchill

We make a living by what we get, we make a life by what we give.

-Sir Winston Churchill

RESOURCES—RESOURCES—
RESOURCES—RESOURCES

Unfortunately, these all seem to be in Kentucky, but other states should have similar programs now that you know what to look for.

Check your phone book under headings such as:

- Department of Social Services

- Department of Elder Affairs (Hmmmm, I'm afraid to ask)

- Department of Aging

- Bureau of Aging

- Division of Senior Services

- Commission on Aging

- Department of Economic Security

Sanders Brown Center on Aging
859-323-6040
mc.uky.edu/coa/
This place does a number of different functions not the least of which is to let you donate your tired ol' brain for research when you do the big chill. They also have a number of other resources to assist in your caregiving.
Seriously, this is the premier center to either directly find what you need or at least be pointed in the correct direction.
Tip: Be patient when you call. You may need to place more than one call. Be as articulate as possible as to what kind of info you need.

Coordinator of Aging Services
LFUCG (Lexington-Fayette Urban County Gov.)
859-258-3806
This is the mother lode of service resources that are principally non-UK.

I like this group.

Unless you are a UK alumnus, I would start here because they have it all (plus they are articulate and return phone calls... can U ask for anything more?) They are waiting on your call now... tell em' trader Ben sent ya! (better not, they may send you to the wrong service, ha!) Seriously, they have publications that I never knew existed. Whatever your need... they have got U covered. You will be in good hands.

Bluegrass Area Agency on Aging
859-269-8021

Lexington Senior Citizens Center
1530 Nicholasville RD
Lexington, Ky 40503
859-278-6072
I was never given a clear understanding of what they do here. They have two different programs you could sign up for: one could be crafts and the other program was something to do with old people. I was referred to their website and I still came away with nothing. Anyway I think they must do good work, don't you?

Terri Kanatzar, MSW
Elder Care Coordinator-UK
859-323-4600
www.uky.edu/HR/ElderCare
This is primarily a UK employee service, but they can help refer you even if you are not an employee.
tlk@uky.edu

Alzheimer's Association
Provides local offices, 24 hour support line, and resources for finding home care
800-272-3900
Legal help for Older Kentuckians
1-800-3633
Calls by older Kentuckians and their children or caregivers are welcome
http://www.ajfky.org/lhok.php

Hospice Library
They have a great number of useful publications, books, and other material

Dept. for Aging and Independent Living (State Gov.)
www.chfs.ky.gov/agencies/os/dail

Center for Creative Living
859-277-3855
Can help a caregiver find some relief, open 7:30 am-5 pm, hot lunches, RNs on staff

Faith in Action
859-252-1365
Helps older adults remain independent in their homes with volunteers trained to provide caregiving services such as running errands, respite care, minor home maintenance, telephoning and visiting

Multipurpose Center
859-278-6072
Provides social services, recreation, education, and some health services for older citizens

Senior Outreach Program
859-278-6072
Information clearinghouse for elders and provides assistance with health care, housing, financial planning, and recreational activities.

State Health Insurance Program (SHIP)
859-278-6072
Assists with Medicare, appeals the decision of Medicare, eligibility for Medicaid, QMB or SLMB programs

Nursing Home Ombudsman Program
859-278-6072
Serves 5,000 nursing home and family care home residents and families. Purpose is to protect rights of nursing home residents and help residents make informed choices.

Careers After Sixty
859-278-6072
In home support for seniors, including personal care, meal preparation, running errands, and other services to keep seniors in their homes.

Alzheimer's Association & Best Friends Day Center
859-266-5283
www.alzinky.org

Provides support groups, library, and day care center with sliding fee scale.

Bluegrass Area Agency on Aging Home Care Program
859-269-8021
www.bgadd.org
Provides homemakers, meals, escort services, respite caregiving, and home repair.

Legal Helpline for Older Americans/Access to Justice
1-800-200-3633
Free legal service to seniors age 60 and over. Referrals on non-legal issues and brief legal advice about wills, power of attorney, and help with guardianship.

Book Buddies
859-231-5592

UK Elder Care
859-323-4600
Counseling, seminars, workshops, and support groups and is a free benefit to all UK employees, retirees, and their families

WHAT CAN HOSPICE DO FOR ME? CAN I QUALIFY?

Please understand that Hospice has so many facets to its complex organization that it would be counterproductive to address all of them here. Here is what to expect for a typical acute dementia patient and comes from my experience, others may differ.

SIMPLE ELIGIBILITY REQUIREMENTS FOR HOSPICE

The info below was corroborated by Hospice, not word for word, but rather the message, so if anything is incorrect, it's because of the big plug of earwax I have.

General requirements include that the patient must have less than 6 months to party hearty. (A doctor must certify the patient has less than 6 months to live.) Anybody (you, me, the kid across the street, the mailman, etc.) can refer a patient to Hospice. Yo dawg… it's really that easy… just like callin' yo momma. That just starts the process. There is much more to do & places to see, but if accepted into Hospice, the patient agrees from then on to use their 'stuff', doctors, nurses, and to allow Hospice to review your copies of POA and Living Will documents. This is for your mutual benefit. They want to comply with your legal wishes, but they need to know what they are, right? If you don't understand the legalese (I never do) then they will help you with that. You help them, and they help you.

Q: Do I have to have these documents?

A: This is not a requirement by Hospice and they will encourage, but not make you have these.

Remember, you have full freedom to choose what train wreck you want to be on, but sometimes it is better to leave the train behind and trust someone who has been down that road before.

Q: Will Hospice accept my private insurance?

A: Hospice accepts all types of insurance including Medicare, Medicaid, and ALL types of private insurance. They do not turn anyone away, even if they have no insurance.

Q: Can my patient choose to also see his own doctor and maybe even have an operation of his choice?

A: As long as the patient does not bill this 'out of the Hospice box,' treatment to Medicare or any of the insurance services that they established as a payee to Hospice. Some people may have a military insurance benefit or other private insurance benefit that will allow them to do what they want. Hospice is cool with that.

Of course, if worse comes to worse, you cut through all the insurance questions if ya just dig up that pot of gold in the back yard... Arrrr! Nobody turns down that, matey!

WHAT HAPPENS NEXT

A team of core members will converge on yer bones for a couple of hours. This will include a nurse, chaplain, doctor, social worker, and maybe a couple of aides and onlookers.

Next comes a lot of health equipment that we never needed for him. A machine that concentrates oxygen, an O_2 cylinder, walkers, porta-potties, diapers, pads, wipes and some more I think.

My first patient to go under the Hospice 'wing,' got a young lady to give him a tub bath three times a week. The nurse would visit bi-monthly. The social worker visits less often. Volunteers are assigned to come to his home and just talk with him for a couple of hours just about anything (himself actually ☺). A chaplin will visit from time to time. Homemade gifts (like quilts) are given to him. If the patient likes music they send a woman with a harp to play and sing. All this because he technically only has less than a few months to live.

After my wife and I changed his diet over to 'Kibbles and bits,' he has exceeded everyone's expectation on longevity and he's been with us now for over three years. He mentally mows the grass and does everything but chase the mailman. He was with Hospice over a year. He talked about bequeathing a gift to Hospice from time to time (PS: He's still a little delusional because he keeps thinking he is going to write a novel about his deeds and accomplishment, but that will pass.)

My other patient steadily went downhill and was finally admitted to Hospice and died three days later. I never did quite understand why one patient who was within a few weeks of death still did not qualify for hospice inclusion until three days before her passing.

In summary, I was very impressed with the Hospice presence and intent.

WHAT YOU CAN DO AS A VOLUNTEER CAREGIVER

VOLUNTEER AS A 'FRIENDLY VISITOR'

Not all regions have this program. If your region does not, then consider starting a chapter in your area by calling the Lexington, Kentucky Long Term Care ombudsman. Check information for the current phone number. Whatever your state, there should be similar programs available.

Did you know that in some areas as many as two-thirds of patients in long term care facilities NEVER get a visit from friends or family according to state officials.

You can be a merchant of happiness for these people and it will also have reciprocal benefits for you also. Just getting out and talking to others is a two-way street for happiness.

Friendly visitor's receive professional training before being assigned to visit the nursing homes.

Volunteer because you care. Because soon we too will be seniors in need of care.

RECOMMENDED READING

The Comfort Of Home, 2nd ed., Maria M. Meyer & Paula Derr, RN, Care Trust Publications.

This has got to be one of the most prolifically illustrated books I have come across. The print is easy to read, with plenty of spacing to spare you from eye fatigue. I think the illustrations of equipment, handling techniques, eating utensils are its strongest points. I would buy it for that.

Should Mom Be Left Alone?, Dr. Linda Rhodes, New American Library.

Usually when I see a book authored by Dr. So-and-so, I look the other way because all too often you won't find a PhD who has much hands on experience. This was a pleasant exception. The book is a Q & A about caregiving that is filled with nothing more than Q & A about stuff that is actually relevant. Examples include "What can my mother do about her incontinence?" or "Could my dad be showing signs of diabetes?" The print is small, but still readable because it is laid out well with space, and it's printed on a non-glare off-white paper.

<u>The 36-Hour Day</u>, 4th ed., Nancy L. Mace, M.A. & Peter V. Rabins, M.D., M.P.H., Johns Hopkins Press.

This is "a family guide to caring for people with Alzheimer's disease, other dementias, and memory loss in later life." The book has a lot of descriptive care situations and behaviors that I liked, but the print is tiny and you might become legally blind after reading this, so get out your magnifiers for this one. It does have good usable info such as "when a person can no longer manage money" or "loss of coordination" or "inappropriate sexual behavior."

<u>Caring For The Parents Who Cared For You</u>, Kenneth P. Scileppi, M.D., Carol Publishing Group.

This book outlines some key things to know for the caregiver, some types of behaviors, pitfalls, and some lab interpretations, which I liked. The downside to this book is its tiny print and boring layout, but the info is good.

<u>The Best Friends Approach To Alzheimer's Care</u>, Virginia Bell & David Troxel, Health Professions Press.

This book addresses many nuances of personal care interactions built around the nice concept of the caregiver being a 'best friend.' Discussions range from staff role playing to long-term care facilities. Again, I find the print too small, but the text is laid out well, which makes it very readable.

Bette Midler lyrics—
"THE ROSE"
(Amanda McBroom)

Some say love it is a river
That drowns the tender reed
Some say love it is a razor
That leaves your soul to bleed

Some say love it is a hunger
An endless aching need
I say love it is a flower
And you it's only seed

It's the heart afraid of breaking
That never learns to dance
It's the dream afraid of waking that never takes the chance
It's the one who won't be taken
Who cannot seem to give
And the soul afraid of dying that never learns to live

When the night has been too lonely
And the road has been too long
And you think that love is only
For the lucky and the strong
Just remember in the winter far beneath the bitter snows
Lies the seed
That with the sun's love
In the spring
Becomes the rose

The Hollies lyrics—

HE AIN'T HEAVY, HE'S MY BROTHER

(B. Scott and B. Russell)

The road is long
With many a winding turn
That leads us to who knows where
Who knows when
But I'm strong
Strong enough to carry him
He ain't heavy, he's my brother

So on we go
His welfare is of my concern
No burden is he to bear
We'll get there
For I know
He would not encumber me
He ain't heavy, he's my brother

If I'm laden at all
I'm laden with sadness
That everyone's heart
Isn't filled with the gladness
Of love for one another

It's a long, long road
From which there is no return
While we're on the way to there
Why not share
And the load
Doesn't weigh me down at all
He ain't heavy, he's my brother

He's my brother
He ain't heavy, he's my brother...

NOTES

If you have a caregiving experience for a patient (with any kind of condition) you wish to share for the next book please email to:

qy@insightbb.com

NOTES

NOTES

This book is designed to be grammatically INcorrect. I am a literary genius but I can't let the world know that just now. We are real caregivers taking care of two real parents, one of which passes during the making of this guide. I am in the trenches with U. I purposefully left out the voluminous information on topics that are important but can be acquired later. I get information overload real easy and hate reading fine print so this I spare you. Yo, lighten up and pay attention because this book is really from the big Guy upstairs. I am just the messenger he sent for.